W9-BXO-884

Cry Rape

Terrace Books, a division of the University of Wisconsin Press,
takes its name from the Memorial Union Terrace, located at
the University of Wisconsin-Madison. Since its inception in 1907,
the Wisconsin Union has provided a venue for students, faculty, staff,
and alumni to debate art, music, politics, and the issues of the day.
It is a place where theater, music, drama, dance, outdoor activities, and
major speakers are made available to the campus and the community.
To learn more about the Union, visit www.union.wisc.edu.

Cry Rape

*The True Story of
One Woman's Harrowing
Quest for Justice*

Bill Lueders

TERRACE BOOKS
A TRADE IMPRINT OF THE UNIVERSITY OF WISCONSIN PRESS

Terrace Books
A trade imprint of the University of Wisconsin Press
1930 Monroe Street
Madison, Wisconsin 53711

www.wisc.edu/wisconsinpress/

3 Henrietta Street
London WC2E 8LU, England

3   5   4   2

Printed in the United States of America

A CIP record is available for this title from the Library of Congress
ISBN 0-299-21960-7 (cloth: alk. paper)
LCCN: 2006008062

This book is for
Patty,
and for people everywhere who refuse to let injustice
be the last word.

Contents

Preface

Truth, like beauty, is in the eye of the beholder. Each person's perspective can, in ways subtle and profound, alter his or her perception. Different people making earnest attempts to describe the same events may give dramatically different, even incompatible, accounts.

As a journalist who was involved in some of the events this book describes, I understand that my perspective is limited, and biased. And so, in telling this story, I have sought to include the perspective of others. This book draws on many thousands of pages of primary documents, including detailed police reports and sworn testimony, as well as dozens of interviews.

All representations regarding what any person said or thought come from these sources; no scenes or conversations have been fabricated. Instances where versions are in conflict are noted. All names are real, except two indicated pseudonyms for juveniles, although to protect privacy some characters, including Patty, are referred to by first name only.

While this book is about an injustice perpetrated by the justice system, its purpose is not to vilify the police, prosecutors, or judges who were the agents of this injustice. Indeed, one of the most remarkable aspects of this story is that these individuals did not set out with any ill intent. On the contrary, they were, I believe, committed to doing what they thought was right. That people who possess such tremendous power can be so heedless of their capacity for error should inspire not harsh judgment but humility.

PART ONE

PERFECT VICTIM

1

The Rape

Patty awoke with a sudden jolt of fear. Someone was in her bed, beside her. In the same sickening instant she inhaled the stench of alcohol—overwhelming, just inches from her face—and felt the blade of a knife against her cheek.

"Don't look at me, don't say anything, and no one will get hurt," a male voice said softly, almost a whisper. He was pressed against her left side, between her and the bedroom door, as she lay on her stomach. Patty's heart pounded. She thought of her daughter Misty across the hallway in the next bedroom, eighteen years old and five months pregnant. *No one will get hurt.* Why did he put it that way? Did he know Misty was there?

"Okay," Patty responded. She didn't turn around, didn't try to look. She wouldn't have been able to see much anyway. She was mostly blind—legally blind, they called it—possessing only a small amount of peripheral vision, enough to read with special equipment and get around without bumping into things. When Patty was twenty, around the time Misty was born, she developed Stargardt's disease, an inherited form of macular degeneration. By the time it stabilized five years later, her central vision had become a black hole. More than a decade had passed since then, and Patty, true to form, had learned to adapt. Some people could hardly tell.

The man—Patty sensed he was young, almost a boy—moved quickly. In one swift motion, he pressed a pillow over the back of her head and reached over her to shut off the television, still on from the night before. She was still lying face down, not moving, as he raised

3

himself to kneel beside her. He grabbed the elastic at the top of her pants and pulled them down to her ankles. Patty then understood that he had come to rape her.

Patty thought about fighting back, as she had other times in her life. Once, when she was about sixteen, two guys had picked her up hitchhiking. They made her sit between them and wouldn't let her get out, as they sped down the Interstate. Then, too, it was clear what was going to happen. Patty seized the steering wheel and stamped her foot down on the accelerator. The vehicle plunged over a concrete barrier, ripping off its undercarriage. She fled on foot, flagging down an older couple who took her to where she could call police, who arrested the two youths. Another time, when Patty was in her midtwenties, a stranger walked into the house where she and Misty lived—Patty and Misty's father divorced before their daughter's second birthday—and grabbed her. She mustered her strength and plowed into him, pushing him backward out of her home. The man, who had a history of walking into women's homes and sexually assaulting them, was still on her front porch, furious, pounding on the door, when police arrived. Now someone was in her bed in the middle of the night, with a knife to her throat, her pregnant daughter a few feet away. She thought about fighting back, but didn't dare.

"How old is your daughter?" the intruder asked. Patty was startled. He knew she had a daughter. How did he know this? "She's just a baby," Patty replied. He didn't let the subject drop. "I bet she's a good fuck."

He was drunk. Patty could tell. And she sensed he was high on something, maybe cocaine. He seemed jittery, wired. He crawled up on top of her from behind and tried to insert his penis into her vagina. He had trouble getting it in. She scrunched up her knees to raise her bottom. If she cooperated, she thought, he would be less likely to use his knife. He still couldn't get it in. She felt him move his penis to her anal area. "Can you take it there?" he asked. His voice sounded funny, like he was trying to disguise it. "Yes," she answered.

Patty's head was pressed down on the bed with the pillow shutting out the air around it. Terror gripped her. She imagined him suddenly stabbing her in the back. Half-consciously, she reached around with her left hand and made contact with the knife, which he was holding against her neck; she thought it felt serrated. She didn't even realize that when she brushed the blade it cut into the back of her index finger, by the second knuckle, deep. Blood flowed into her pillow when she brought her hand back. He was trying to force his penis into her rectum. After several tries it slid in, and Patty felt a searing pain.

Suddenly Patty's alarm clock filled the room with an insistent beeping noise, startling both of them. He reached over her to where the alarm clock was resting on the floor and hit the snooze button. Patty had set the alarm for 4 a.m., so she would have time to stop by the gym before work. But she kept the clock twenty minutes fast, so it was really 3:40 a.m. Later this would become a point of contention, one of the reasons that the police turned against her.

"Turn around," he ordered, and Patty did. In the process, the pillow slipped off her face. "I told you not to look at me," he snapped. Patty closed her eyes and began to cry. "I can't even see," she told him.

His reply was so quiet it seemed almost tender. "I know," he said.

Patty's fears were confirmed. This was someone who knew her, or at least knew things about her. This made her more afraid. If she could identify him, he was more likely to kill her.

The man continued to throw commands at her, and she complied. He spoke so softly that, several times, she had to ask him to repeat himself. Maybe he knew Misty was in the apartment and was trying not to wake her. He needn't have bothered: Misty was as sound a sleeper as anyone Patty had ever known. Aerosmith could be giving a concert in their living room and Misty would sleep right though it.

Misty, like many teenagers, was the center of her own universe. She was pretty and vain and made what her mother thought were huge errors of judgment, but they were *her* errors and *her* judgment. During Misty's last years of high school, she had dated a drug dealer named Leonard, whom Patty disliked intensely. A few months earlier, about the same time Misty realized she was pregnant with his child, Leonard, then thirty-two, got into a spat with a young woman who shared his apartment. He dragged her out of bed, accusing her of stealing some of his drugs and a carton of cigarettes. He beat her bare buttocks with various objects, including a curtain rod. Then he shoved a 9-millimeter Beretta pistol up her rectum and threatened to pull the trigger. Leonard eventually calmed down and apologized for his bad behavior, insisting that the woman smoke some crack with him before he left. In the end, this misunderstanding with his roommate drew a twelve-year prison sentence.

Misty's next suitor was a young man named Lonnie, whom Patty had liked. But the relationship didn't last long. Now Misty was dating a twenty-six-year-old man named Dominic; the two of them worked for a cleaning service owned by Dominic's mother, then in jail on a probation violation. Dominic had previously courted Patty's younger sister Brenda. This relationship had ended badly, and when Brenda learned that Dominic was dating her niece, she was furious.

"I want to see your boobies," the intruder announced, as he grabbed Patty's shirt with his right hand, and began pulling it off. She helped him remove it. Now Patty was kneeling on the bed, facing him, eyes closed. His hand seized her long, braided, dark hair, which was pinned up in a bun with barrettes. He yanked hard, pulling her head toward his crotch. "Suck my dick," he demanded, lying back on the bed.

Patty did as she was told. It wasn't as though she didn't know how. The first time she was only five or six years old. The man was her stepfather. This went on until she was in her teens, when she told a friend and authorities intervened. She had revealed only some of what happened, about how he had touched her. She was placed for a brief while in a shelter home. He was never charged. When she returned home, the molestation stopped. No one ever talked about it, even years later, after Patty's mother and stepfather split up. Not a single conversation, ever. It was how her family dealt with problems, by burying them under mountains of denial. Patty even had occasional incidental contact with her former stepfather, without any of this past history coming up.

Having been forced into sex as a child, Patty didn't see much reason to practice abstinence as a teen. She was just thirteen when she got pregnant—the father, her boyfriend, was just a few months older—and fourteen when she gave birth to a daughter. Patty's mother already had ten kids—five from Patty's father, who left when Patty was five years old, and five from her second husband. Patty's daughter made eleven. When the girl became old enough to understand how "Mama Patty" fit into her life, she became resentful. Patty wore the pain of this experience, like others in her life, plainly on her face, in lines and marks that conveyed anxiety and consternation. Her long, flowing hair was like a shield to deflect attention from her obvious hurt.

Patty, at thirty-eight, was solid and strong from years of hard work. Her face, though weathered, was still pretty, especially when she smiled. There was a genuineness about her that other people tended to notice and like. Even though her eyes did not meet theirs, because of her disability, her face was like a porthole to her heart, reflecting what she felt: dread, sadness, sometimes joy. Perhaps because she could no longer see the faces of others, she lost the ability to hide her feelings behind her own face.

"Tell me how big I am," the man instructed. "You're big. You're really big," she replied, though in truth he wasn't. Patty could no longer feel the knife on her neck and wondered if he had set it down. She thought she might have a chance to push him away and make a run for it. But her pants were bunched around her ankles, holding her legs together. Usually, Patty got undressed before going to bed. But the night before she had fallen asleep around 7 p.m., exhausted, still wearing her black stretch-cotton pants and her purple shirt.

Patty had gotten home about two hours earlier from a long meeting with a financial counselor named Connie Kilmark and two representatives from Business Enterprise, a state-run program that provided jobs to the blind. Patty had two business franchises. She ran a coffee shop in the State Department of Agriculture Building, for which she had to hire assistants, meet a payroll, order supplies, pay bills, and wait on customers. She also refilled vending machines at a rest stop on the Interstate, about twenty-five miles from Patty's home in Madison, Wisconsin. Patty had fallen behind in her monthly payments and reporting requirements, so the program tapped Kilmark to help straighten things out. Kilmark had spoken warmly to Patty and expressed confidence in her. But the Business Enterprise reps, Patty perceived, were frustrated with her and mainly concerned about getting the money she owed. When Patty returned home, she said a few words to Misty and retired to her bedroom, opening the locked door. This door was always locked when Patty was not home; she kept money from her businesses in there, and she didn't want Misty or her friends to have access. Patty turned on the TV and slipped into a familiar depression.

Once, when Patty was a teenager, she tried to commit suicide by cutting her wrists; another time she drank rat poison. Twice, in her twenties, she overdosed on pills and ended up in the hospital. One of

Patty's brothers took his own life, and so did his son. But it had been more than a decade since Patty's last suicide attempt. Often, she used alcohol to make herself feel better, as did almost everyone she knew. She had been on Prozac until just recently, when her prescription ran out, and had seen a psychologist until earlier that year. She was doing pretty well, all things considered, but the meeting that afternoon had pushed all of her buttons; she felt humiliated, inadequate. Patty resolved to get up early the next morning and get to the gym, hoping a good workout would improve her spirits. With the TV still on, she got into bed and under the covers. Around 8 p.m., Misty popped in to ask a question about some hair-care product. Patty was already asleep, rousing herself only enough to say she wanted to stay that way. "Bitch," snapped Misty.

And now the stretch-cotton pants Patty had fallen asleep wearing were serving as makeshift shackles. She reached down and pulled the bunched-up material over one foot and then the other. Her assailant had been still, almost as though he were dozing. This brought him back with a jolt: "What are you doing?" He sounded angry. "Nothing," she replied. "My foot was caught." The knife was once again against her neck.

By this time, Patty was starting to think more clearly about what was happening and what she needed to do. The sooner he climaxed, the sooner it would be over. She moved her tongue around the tip of his penis and caressed his testicles. It was a strategic move that would later cause her embarrassment and be used against her, publicly. Worst of all, it didn't work. He moaned appreciatively, but did not finish.

Suddenly, he pulled her up into a sitting position. He was on his knees in front of her. He produced a condom and tore open the wrapper. "Put it on," he commanded. She did, keeping her eyes directed downward and not toward his face. Then she lay back on the bed. He placed a pillow loosely over her face and maneuvered himself to enter her vaginally. She was wet, which surprised her and filled her with shame. And then he was inside her, grunting, his hands at her side. He told her to wrap her legs around him. The snooze alarm sounded at least once more, and he slapped it quiet. After what seemed like a long time, Patty's rapist began groaning—like an animal, she thought. She felt him contract and then relax. He grabbed the base of the condom with one hand and pulled out. A moment later he was on the floor, on the side of the bed. He began pulling off the sheets. He seemed suddenly anxious. There was fear in his voice.

"Where's the rope?" he asked, as though this were a hardware store. Patty was dumbfounded: how could she answer a question like that? She didn't have any rope, but suggested he could use the bedsheets to tie her. He didn't like this idea. She said she could go in the closet. This was okay with him. Patty started to feel a sense of relief. If he was looking to tie or lock her up, he wasn't planning to kill her. All he had come for was sex. And to rob her, as would soon be clear.

"What time do you have to go to work?" he asked. Another strange question, suggesting familiarity with her routine. "Bobby's picking me up at five," Patty replied. Bobby, her brother, wasn't picking her up at all. She had planned to walk to the gym, about a mile away, and from there to take a cab to work. She was trying to increase his sense of urgency.

Patty got up and made her way toward the closet. For a moment, she and her assailant were both standing at the foot of the bed. Light from the neighbor's deck streamed in through the window, and for the first time she got a look at him—not his face, but his body. He was pulling on white sweatpants, and Patty could see his skin in contrast against them. He was a light-skinned black man, or maybe mixed race or Mexican.

Bending down, Patty retrieved her purple shirt from the bare hardwood floor. "See," he told her as she put it on, "that wasn't so bad, was it?" "No, it was pretty good," she said, trying not to make him mad.

"Want some more?" he asked, touching her shoulder.

"No, I can't, I just can't," Patty replied. "I'm too fucking scared."

"I know," he said softly. "I know."

Patty headed to the closet, which was jammed with clothes and boxes. She squeezed into the less-crowded right side, closing the sliding door in front of her. The door bulged outward. From inside the closet, Patty could tell that he turned on the room light and then the TV. She could hear him going to different places in the room, doing something, then rummaging through her backpack, which contained a vinyl bank deposit bag with a small amount of one dollar bills from her vending business. "Where is the rest of it?" he asked. There was no rest of it. Patty had gone to the bank before meeting with Kilmark. But thinking quickly, she said there was more money in the car and that the keys were on her dresser. She heard him fumbling about. At one point, he walked briskly toward the closet and shoved the blade of the knife through the gap between the doors. "I told you not to look at me," he said. "I'm not," she assured him.

He cut the phone cord in Patty's room—she could hear him do it—then asked where the other phones were. She told him about the one in the kitchen, but not the ones in Misty's room and in the living room behind the couch. While he was standing there by the closet door, Patty tried to move a hanger that was jabbing into her head. This seemed to startle him. "You stay in there," he warned. "I mean it." He went into the kitchen. She could hear him doing something to the phone, just on the other side of the closet wall. And then she couldn't hear him anymore.

Patty waited in the closet another minute or two, listening. Slowly, she extricated herself from the cramped space and inched her way to the bedroom door. She reached around to the front and pulled out her keys, still in the lock from the night before. She held the door open slightly, clutching the inside knob of the lock, ready to slam it shut and lock it. After a few seconds, she yelled across the hallway at her daughter's door.

"Misty!"

No answer. Patty was terrified. *Is she dead in there?* She yelled again, this time louder: "Misty!"

Still nothing. Panicked, Patty ran across the hallway and pulled open Misty's bedroom door at the same time as Misty was grabbing onto the opposite handle. Then they were both standing there, in the hallway outside Misty's room, Patty naked from the waist down. "Oh, my God, you're all right!" Patty exclaimed.

"What happened?" Misty shouted, already losing her composure. "What happened?"

"I was raped and robbed." The words hit Misty hard. *Raped and robbed.* Even before she heard any details, Misty knew this was partly her fault. "Oh, my God," she blurted out. "I left the door unlocked." She had thought her boyfriend Dominic might stop by, as he had the previous two nights.

Patty ran to the front door and locked it. Then she and Misty ran to the living room, to the phone behind the couch. Patty picked it up and made the most consequential call of her life. It was a call she assumed would bring help and comfort. Instead, it led to torments that would make being raped in her home by a knife-wielding intruder seem almost insignificant in comparison. She would be drawn into bitter contention with the police, the legal system, and the city where she had lived most of her life. Her self-esteem would be battered, her dignity defiled, her livelihood imperiled, her privacy obliterated. The ordeal would be a crucible in which Patty was melted down and remade—from a woman who learned to retreat in order to survive to one whose survival depended on fighting back. Others, myself included, would be pulled into her drama. The powerful forces aligned against Patty would prevail again and again. Still she persisted, demanding justice, until an amazing thing happened, based on the science of DNA. Even then, her ordeal would drag on, with fresh torments, for years. And it all started with a phone call just three digits long: 9-1-1.

2

Emergency Response

Patty's call came into the emergency dispatch center at 4:13 a.m. on Thursday, September 4, 1997.

"911, can I help you?" answered the dispatcher, a man.

"We were just robbed and I was raped," said Patty, frantic.

"Okay, this just happened or what?"

"Just now, he just left." She was having trouble breathing.

"What was this guy, like, do you know him?"

"No, I didn't know him."

"Did he break in or what?"

A second passed without a response. "Did he break in?" the dispatcher asked again.

"I haven't looked around yet. I think my daughter might have left the door unlocked."

"Okay, so you didn't know the guy. Okay, and it's at 736 Fairmont, right?" said the dispatcher, reading the address off his monitor.

From the background came an odd sound, like a squawk, from Misty.

"Right," confirmed Patty.

"Okay, so can you describe the perpetrator please, the guy?"

Another sound from Misty, this one clearly a sob.

"Not in detail," answered Patty.

"Was he male white or male . . ."

"He was male, I think he was, like, either black or mulatto."

"Okay, you think he was black or mulatto?"

"Right."

"And this just happened, right?"

"It just happened. He's still in the neighborhood."

"Okay. And do you know what direction he went? Did he leave on foot or what?"

"I stayed in my closet. He told me to stay in my closet. My daughter was here. I was afraid he was going to hurt her. I did everything he said."

"Okay. All right. Did he have any weapons?"

"He had a knife, but I believe it was just like one of mine." More loud sobbing from Misty.

"Okay, stay on the phone. I'm going to get them started your way, here. I need a description of the person. How tall do you think he was?"

"He was about five six, five eight."

"Okay. Five eight. Okay. And, ah, was his hair long or short?" The dispatcher was typing information to be relayed to responding officers.

"Very short."

"Short. Okay. How old did he look to be?"

Misty emitted another piercing wail. "He sounded . . . I'm visually impaired and it was dark. He sounded to be about eighteen to twenty."

"Okay. Okay. And then, ah, can you tell about facial hair? Did he have long, a beard or anything?"

"I don't think he had any."

"Okay. How much did he weigh?"

"Ah, not much, maybe um . . ."

"Take your best guess, go 'head."

"Maybe 150."

"Okay, how about clothing? Can you just tell me what kind of clothing?"

"I couldn't. I haven't a clue."

"Okay, do you know what direction he might have fled, or not?" The same question, again.

"No, I was in my closet."

"Okay, so he just kind of surprised you, right?"

"Yeah."

"And then he raped you in the closet then? Is that what happened?"

"No, I was on my bed."

"Okay, but you didn't get a good look at his clothing or anything?"

"No, he made me turn around."

"He made you turn around, okay. Now your daughter didn't get a look at him, did she?"

"No. She did not."

"Is anybody injured at all?"

"No, no."

"Okay, just stay on the phone now. He didn't come in a car. You don't know anything about any vehicle?"

"He asked where my car was. I think he was going to take it."

"Did he take your keys, too?"

"I don't know. He was robbing me while I was in the closet."

"Okay, just stay on the phone, okay?"

"Okay."

From Misty, loud wails. She was falling apart. Patty, protectively, tried to stay calm so as to not make matters worse. This, too, would later be used against her.

The dispatcher asked what kind of vehicle Patty drove. Though she herself could not drive, Patty owned a 1969 Buick Le Sabre, which Misty used to take her around. Patty told the dispatcher about the car, parked on the street. He asked her to check whether her keys had been taken and whether the car was still outside. At this moment Patty's alarm clock began beeping. She called out to Misty to turn it off. The noise stopped.

"I ain't going out there now," answered Patty, with a nervous laugh. "I'll check and see if the keys are gone." Misty continued bawling. The dispatcher relayed to someone on his end, "He had a knife."

After half a minute, Patty returned. "Ah, the keys are not . . . They look like they're gone, I don't know." Actually, the car keys were still in the apartment, just not on the dresser where Patty thought she had left them. The dispatcher asked again about the car, and whether she could check to see if it was gone. She told him she didn't think it was taken.

The dispatcher asked Patty to "just kind of collect your thoughts and tell me anything about clothing you might have noticed. Anything at all, about color, you know, or anything." His persistence on this point paid off: "It seemed like he had on some really white pants," Patty told him. The dispatcher asked whether the man still had the knife when he left. "He took everything. He took my bedsheets"—or so she assumed, having seen him strip them from the bed. "He took . . ."

"Okay, but did he have the knife when he left?"

"I'm sure he did, yeah."

"Okay, well, how big of a knife was it?"

"It was just a big, like, um, like the kind you cut bread with or something."

A female voice came on the line. "Did she check to see if the car was missing yet?"

"Let me go check," Patty answered. "I have to go outside to do it, so I'll be back." At this, Misty screamed an angry stream of words, ending in "goddammit." Said Patty, "They didn't take the car. No, forget it. I'm not going out there. They didn't take it. I would have heard it. It's a loud car." From Misty, loud crying.

"So there wasn't a sexual assault then?" asked the woman.

"Yes, there was," replied Patty. It was a prescient exchange.

The dispatcher asked Patty if she was injured, if she needed an ambulance. "No, I got a little cut from it but he didn't hurt me."

"Okay." The dispatcher said "a bunch of officers" had been dispatched and would soon arrive. Just as he said this, Patty heard the knock. "They're there now," she told him. "Okay, well, go talk to them," he said. "Okay? Thanks." "Okay," replied Patty. "Thanks." That ended the call, six minutes after it began.

Patty went to the door to let in the police: officer Cindy Thiesenhusen and Sergeant Tony Jarona. Thiesenhusen, then in her midtwenties, had been hired just the year before. Jarona was a twenty-six-year veteran with a checkered past. In 1993 he was arrested for punching a seventeen-year-old boy whom his daughter, three years younger, had accused of sexual assault. By odd coincidence, Misty, then in her early teens, had testified at the boy's trial that Jarona's daughter, her schoolmate, had portrayed the sex as consensual. The boy was convicted of seven sex offenses, all involving teenage girls, and sentenced to eighteen years in prison. Jarona was charged with misdemeanor physical abuse of a child, later reduced to a disorderly conduct ordinance violation; he paid a small fine and served a brief suspension. He and several other Madison police officers subsequently toasted their notoriety by getting tattoos on their forearms depicting lightning bolts alongside the initials BBB, for "Bad Boys in Blue." When this came to light—one press account said the lightning bolts were filled in whenever an officer got suspended—Madison Police Chief Richard K. Williams launched a three-week investigation, after which he concluded that the tattoos were "a solidarity thing" and hence no cause for concern.

Patty and Misty lived in a tucked-away working-class neighborhood on Madison's east side. The apartment they shared had pretty hardwood floors and affordable rent. It was, like several other residences on the block, a duplex, a rectangular ranch house split down the middle into two square apartments.

As the officers entered, Patty realized she was still naked from the waist down. She asked to get her pants, and headed for the bedroom. The officers followed, instructing her not to touch anything. Patty found her pants on the floor and put them on. A strong perfume-like odor wafted up from the bed, which was wet in several spots. The rapist had poured out Patty's Flowering Herbs Body Splash, tossing the empty bottle into a laundry basket. Sergeant Jarona, Patty later recalled, surveyed the scene and said, "This guy has definitely done this before." Jarona, whom Misty did not recognize that morning from the earlier matter involving his daughter, would play no further role in Patty's case.

Other officers scoured the neighborhood in search of a fleeing suspect. The police thought he might be on foot, having ascertained that Patty's Le Sabre was still parked on the street. William Kaddatz, a Madison Police Department crime scene investigator, arrived to collect evidence. Thiesenhusen called dispatch to give advance notice to Meriter Hospital that she would soon be bringing in a rape victim for a sexual assault examination. Then she took Patty to the living room to discuss the assault.

Patty was shaking all over. Misty was there, too, crying hysterically, which made it harder for Patty to focus. She was trying to remain calm for Misty's sake, but it seemed as though everything she said set Misty off. "Let's just get through this part, Misty, please," Patty implored at one point. Misty exited the room.

Later, Patty would describe Thiesenhusen as "the most caring and compassionate officer I've ever had the privilege of meeting." Over the years, Patty had had a few police contacts: the two previous rape attempts, the times she tried to kill herself, some trouble for shoplifting when she was a teenager, a few citations for incidents involving alcohol. Nothing had ever happened to make her fear or distrust police.

Thiesenhusen spoke softly and kept asking Patty how she was doing. She was not pushy or impatient, even when Patty was uncertain or confused.

Perhaps because she put Patty at ease, Thiesenhusen managed to gather a great deal of pertinent information in just a few minutes. She learned that Patty was sleeping on her stomach when she awoke to feel a knife at her throat. Patty thought the knife was serrated, possibly a bread knife. The intruder first attempted anal sex, which lasted about a minute; then he made her perform oral sex, which lasted about five minutes; lastly, he had her put a condom on him and penetrated her vaginally, until he seemed to climax. There were signs of familiarity— his saying "I know" when Patty said she couldn't see, his crude inquiries regarding her daughter.

Thiesenhusen asked whether Patty could think of possible suspects, especially anyone who would have known about the unlocked door. Patty came up with a name: Dominic, her daughter's boyfriend. She really didn't believe it could be him, but said "he kind of fit." Patty was thinking about her rapist's skin color—not real dark, as though he were Mexican or biracial—and his white sweatpants, like those she had seen Dominic wearing while visiting Misty.

Misty, when Thiesenhusen spoke to her, also mentioned Dominic— not as a suspect but as the only other person who had recently spent the night at the apartment. She said he had been there twice that week, on Monday and again on Tuesday night. Did Dominic or any of her other friends know the door was frequently unlocked? Yes, said Misty, this was something "everyone" knew.

Patty and Thiesenhusen left the duplex around 5 a.m. On the way to the squad car, Patty remembered that her assailant had touched the TV, as well as the light switch and the snooze button on her alarm clock. Patty stayed in the squad car while Thiesenhusen conveyed this information to Kaddatz. Suddenly the squad door opened and there was Patty's mother, whom Misty had called. Patty and her mom hugged and cried. "I was so scared," Patty told her. "I thought he was going to kill me."

Thiesenhusen drove Patty to Meriter Hospital. In the waiting room, she obtained the "statement of nonconsent" required for all crime victims. This entailed asking Patty whether she had given her permission to be raped, cut, and robbed by a knife-wielding intruder. Thiesenhusen apologized ahead of time for asking.

Back at the apartment, Kaddatz continued his investigation. The bed had been stripped mostly bare, except for two bloodstained pillows toward the top and a bunched-up bedsheet toward the bottom. Kaddatz confirmed that the smell from the wet spots on the bed matched that of the empty bottle of Flowering Herbs Body Splash. He took photos of the room and close-ups of all evidence. If he noticed the small bag of marijuana on Patty's dresser—she didn't smoke herself but had some on hand for friends—he decided to overlook it. When Patty returned later, she found it was still there, surrounded by fingerprint dust.

Kaddatz made a field sketch of the room and the apartment. He and another investigator searched inside and out for the knife, condom, and condom wrapper, without success. They dusted the television, the kitchen phone (which had not been disabled, as Patty believed), the area around the bedroom light switch, and the vinyl pouch that had contained Patty's money. No latent fingerprints were found.

Starting at 6:11 a.m., Kaddatz began collecting items: Patty's discarded bra, the pillowcases, the perfume bottle, the phone and the cord that went from it to an answering machine, the alarm clock (which he unplugged without checking what time it showed, or when the alarm was set for), a pink and white bedspread, and a blue queen-sized flat bedsheet. The items were bagged and tagged, along with the plastic gloves used to collect them.

Kaddatz's investigation was completed by 8 a.m., and the collected items were taken to the police property room. One of these items contained the key to solving the crime.

3

Under Examination

Jill Poarch was at home sleeping when the call came in. A woman had been sexually assaulted and Poarch needed to perform an examination. She was the nurse on call for Meriter Hospital's SANE program, which stands for Sexual Assault Nurse Examiner. She also worked full time in the hospital's emergency room. Like other SANE nurses, Poarch had received extensive classroom and clinical instruction, followed by a period in which she was paired with a more experienced nurse. But she had been doing these exams for four and a half years now, usually working solo. Poarch arrived at the hospital around 5:20 a.m., the same time as Patty.

Hospitals across the country have set up SANE programs because sexual assault examinations require special skills. Besides giving aid and comfort to victims of terrible crimes, SANE nurses are trained to collect evidence. They work closely with police and are often called on to testify in court. In a sexual assault, the victim's body becomes the crime scene, possibly containing wounds, excretions, hair, or other evidence. It must be probed, combed, photographed, and documented. For some victims, the examination is nearly as traumatic as the assault itself. Poarch, a good nurse, tried to make it no more traumatic than it had to be.

She began by introducing herself and asking Patty what happened. She needed to know details—whether and where there was penetration, for instance—so she'd know how to conduct her investigation. So, with Thiesenhusen present, Poarch asked a lot of questions. Did Patty know who raped her? No. Can she describe him? About twenty years old, Hispanic or mixed race. What happened? He had a knife. He told her not to look at him. Patty was worried about her eighteen-year-old daughter, in the next room. She was assaulted in her rectum and vagina, and forced to perform oral sex. Did he ejaculate in her rectum? No. Did he ejaculate in her vagina? She thought so, but he was wearing a condom. Did he kiss her, lick her, use any kind of lubricant? No, no, no. Had she taken a shower, douched, brushed her teeth, or changed clothing since the assault? None of the above. Then came questions about Patty's medical history, through which it emerged that she'd had a hysterectomy and could not get pregnant. Had she ever been treated for a sexually transmitted disease? No.

Poarch explained to Patty what the sexual assault examination would entail, that it was invasive and unpleasant, and that she needed to sign releases allowing portions to be videotaped and information made available to the police. Poarch saw that there were cuts on Patty's face, neck, and hand. No one mentioned to her that Patty was visually impaired, but she noticed that Patty didn't seem to look at her directly and held the consent forms very close to her face to see where to sign. So she asked whether there was some problem with her eyesight.

"I'm legally blind," Patty replied, explaining that she had macular degeneration. Poarch wasn't sure how to spell this, so she just put down "legally blind." She asked Patty whether she wanted an advocate from the Rape Crisis Center, which would delay the examination. Patty declined. "I just want to get out of here," she said. Most victims, in Poarch's experience, declined an advocate, for precisely this reason. (Later, the hospital began calling the local Rape Crisis Center at the same time as the SANE nurse, so an advocate was on hand right away. Subsequently, most victims wanted the advocate present.)

Patty's mother arrived, and for a while the two were in the room alone. Perhaps it was the intensity of Misty's reaction, or the fear that came from not knowing, but Patty's suspicions began to center on Dominic. "I think I know who did this," she said. Her mother had some preternaturally apt advice: "If you don't know for sure, don't say anything."

The sexual assault exam began at 6:30 a.m. Thiesenhusen remained in the room throughout. Two clean sheets were spread on the floor, one on top of the other. Patty stood on these and removed her clothes. Her clothes and the top sheet were bagged and tagged; the bottom sheet, which collects mainly dust from the floor, was discarded. Patty provided a urine sample, not wiping afterward so as not to remove evidence. Then she was asked to lie naked on a table for a head-to-toe examination. Her knees were up high, her legs spread apart, her feet in stirrups. Hair samples were taken as well as saliva and vaginal swabs. Blood was drawn—separate vials for the evidence kit and tests for syphilis and HIV. These were baseline samples only, since any infection from the assault could not yet be detected. Patty's pubic area was combed, and pubic hair samples collected.

Poarch examined Patty's vagina with a Wood's lamp, which casts ultraviolet light to detect body fluids like semen. None were found. She also did a "wet mount exam," which involved taking a swab from Patty's vagina and examining it under a microscope in search of sperm; again, nothing. Poarch inserted a medium speculum into Patty's vagina to look for evidence of internal injury. Lastly, she used a colposcope—a kind of sophisticated magnifying glass attached to a video camera—to probe Patty's vagina and rectal areas. With this, she documented a bruise to Patty's inner left thigh and an abrasion on her anus Poarch described it as a small scratch. This surprised Patty, because it hurt like an open wound—a searing pain.

Patty's various injuries were measured and recorded. There were two lacerations, both superficial, on her left cheek; one was seven centimeters long, the other four centimeters. On the left side of her neck was another laceration that measured five centimeters. It was hooked, like a check mark. The cut on the back of Patty's left forefinger was only one centimeter long, but it was deep enough that Poarch summoned a doctor, who put in two sutures of 5.09 nylon. The apparently fresh bruise on Patty's thigh measured one-by-two centimeters. The abrasion on her anus—at a position recorded as "ten o'clock"—was round and measured one centimeter in diameter.

Poarch gave Patty a tetanus shot and two antibiotics: 500 milligrams of Cipro to prevent gonorrhea and a gram of erythromycin to prevent chlamydia. She did not do a pregnancy test or offer "morning after" birth control pills, due to Patty's hysterectomy. Patty was given a printed list of aftercare instructions, which advised her to be on the lookout for swelling and infection, and to arrange a follow-up visit with her primary physician to remove the sutures from her finger and test for hepatitis and HIV. This form, which Patty had to sign, included an admonition to "buckle up" on the way home. Poarch told Patty to call her if there was anything she needed. Patty would indeed call, a few weeks later; it would be a conversation that made this sexual assault different from any other in Poarch's experience.

The exam ended at 7:55 a.m. Officer Thiesenhusen gathered the "evidence from the victim"—blood, hair, saliva swabs, pubic combings, vaginal swabs, urine, clothing, and the sheet over which she undressed. A form documenting the chain of evidence was completed and signed by Poarch at 8:10 a.m. Thiesenhusen would return to the hospital the next day to collect thirteen pages of records produced by Poarch, including an anatomical sketch showing the location of Patty's injuries.

Patty's mother had left, but Patty's longtime friend Mark was waiting for her outside the examination room. Patty and Mark hugged, and both began crying. Patty had known Mark, then forty-three, for several years; the two of them had dated off and on for the last year and a half. It was a tempestuous relationship, oriented largely around their mutual fondness for alcohol. Patty was at this point mainly a weekend drinker; her job required her to get up too early for her to drink during the week. But on weekends she would stay at Mark's place, and they would indulge their passion—for inebriation.

Mark, a short, scrawny man with long, dark hair tied back into a ponytail, owned a large two-flat house on Madison's east side; he lived downstairs with a male roommate and rented out the upstairs. Recently divorced, Mark was wary about getting into a serious relationship with Patty and had pulled back. Patty suspected that Mark was seeing other women (he denied it), and she was prone to jealousy. In May, Patty had dated another man, Doug, but this ended after two months. Patty's romantic relationship with Mark never really got back on track, although they did have sexual relations one more time in mid-August, during a weekend getaway to Sheboygan, a small city along the Lake Michigan coast.

It was Misty who called Mark to let him know what had happened. The night before, Mark had been out drinking with his ex-wife's sister. They visited three Madison watering holes and were completely sloshed when they got back to his house after the bars closed. Around 4 a.m. they both passed out—he on his bed, she on the floor. That's where Mark left her several hours later when he got Misty's call.

on the clean clothes that Misty had brought along. Then into Mark's van to drive downtown to Madison police headquarters in the City-County Building, the hub of local government. The building, which also contained the courtrooms of Dane County; the offices of the mayor, county executive, and district attorney; and the county jail, is about a block from Lake Monona, the smaller of two lakes that form Madison's geographic heart. On the isthmus between these two lakes reside the city's two main attractions, the Capitol and the University of Wisconsin, positioned, like weights on a barbell, on opposite ends of an eight-block artery called State Street.

The police photographer took pictures of the wounds on Patty's face, neck, and finger. Like everyone else Patty met that day, he was kind and sympathetic. He expressed his hope that her assailant would be caught. Patty cried, as she had all morning when someone connected with her emotionally.

Afterward, Mark drove Patty and Misty back to the east side. The plan was for Patty to stay at Mark's house. But first she had to stop by her place to pick up some clothes and other belongings, and she asked Mark to come along, since she was afraid. Mark, however, said he needed to take care of some things at his place. He didn't specify that the thing he most needed to take care of was the woman passed out on his floor. He said Misty and Patty should come over later in the van that Patty owned for her vending machine business. But the van was in the auto shop, having just been repaired. So Mark dropped Patty and Misty off at the shop, paid the $415 bill, and hightailed it back to his house.

Mark roused his guest and told her it was time to get going. Just then a neighbor knocked on Mark's door, telling him that the engine of his van was smoking. Like the motorist who drives faster to avoid running out of gas, Mark decided he'd better get his drinking companion home before his smoldering van got any worse. He made it only a few blocks before the vehicle broke down. Mark left the woman at a nearby tavern and walked back to his house. Sadly, all of his scheming was for naught: on their way over, Patty and Misty spotted his van on the street and made inquiries of a bystander, who reported seeing the driver and a tall female companion leave on foot.

Patty's long, dark hair was down now, and as she stood outside of Mark's house she combed through it with a brush. To her horror, several large clumps fell out. She remembered then how her rapist had grabbed her hair and pulled her head toward his crotch, a detail she hadn't mentioned to Thiesenhusen or the Meriter nurse. Other details would come back to her in similar ways, in the days and weeks ahead.

Within minutes, Patty's brother Bobby called her from work. Lean and sinewy with hair that fell to the small of his back, Bobby was as volatile as an active volcano, his rage over his own painful past ready to erupt at the slightest provocation. "I'm fine," Patty hastened to assure him, afraid of his reaction, but as she said this she began to sob, the first time that day she had really let herself go. They talked, and afterward she felt better.

The antibiotics Patty was given at the hospital caused diarrhea, which made the pain in her anal area more severe. It felt like the blade of a knife was stabbing her. She filled the bathtub with warm water; Mark put in some bubbles and lit a candle. Patty popped open a beer and slid into the tub. It felt good—both the warm water and the alcohol, her pain reliever of choice.

Throughout the day, support for Patty flowed into Mark's house. Her sister Betsy, who worked nearby at a local charity, was the first to arrive. She sat with Patty on the deck in the back of the house. Next came Patty's sister-in-law, Peggy, who worked for the Dane County Sheriff's Department; they hugged and cried. Bobby came by later, as did Brenda. Everyone was drinking. It was hardly a festive occasion, but as the afternoon stretched into evening there was laughter and some joking around. Misty was annoyed by this. She hated it when her mother drank, even though most of her own friends abused alcohol and drugs. Patty, for her part, was glad for the numbness, the familiar refuge of intoxication. Later, she and Mark argued about the woman he had been seen with that morning. He told her it was someone from the neighborhood who needed a ride; she didn't believe him.

That evening Misty's boyfriend Dominic stopped by. This infuriated Brenda, whose own relationship with Dominic had ended in acrimony. At one point she called him a "spic." He left soon after, without speaking to Patty except for a brief greeting. Patty pondered her suspicions. Was Dominic's showing up a sign that he was not the man who raped her? Or was he just so confident that he could get away with it? It was past midnight when Patty went to bed.

The next morning Patty sat on the back deck, alone, letting the events of the previous day sink in. It was already arranged that she would miss work; her employees would fill in for her, as they had the day before. She cried some more, feeling helpless. After several hours she called the police department to see if there was any news. She assumed that the police had found evidence. The man who raped her had touched the TV, the alarm clock, the light switch. He must have left fingerprints, maybe even hair or semen. Everyone Patty had spoken with the day before had seemed so optimistic. The police would get this guy, family members assured her. There was no doubt about it.

At a minimum, Patty expected her case would be handled by caring professionals, like the ones she had already encountered. None of the people she spoke to—the 911 dispatcher, officer Thiesenhusen, nurse Poarch, the police photographer—had expressed skepticism regarding Patty's account. They believed her, and it never occurred to her that anyone wouldn't.

This was, after all, Madison, Wisconsin, a community that exudes confidence in its superiority: its schools are better, its politics cleaner, its institutions of justice more just, its response to crime victims more compassionate. The Madison Police Department has long regarded itself as among the most progressive in the nation, oriented toward community policing and responsive to the citizenry. For more than two decades, the department had been led by David Couper, a reformer who adorned his office wall with portraits of Mahatma Gandhi and Dr. Martin Luther King Jr. Couper squeezed out the department's old guard, whose approach to policing was immortalized in scene after scene of protesters being clubbed and teargassed in *The War at Home*, the acclaimed documentary of Madison's anti–Vietnam War movement. He hired women and minorities and raised the expectation of professionalism to where, by the time he left in 1993, the vast majority of Madison police officers had undergraduate degrees, and many had advanced degrees. The department worked with citizen advocates to ensure that victims of sensitive crimes were treated with sensitivity.

Madison's swollen sense of pride owes to decades of accolades and good fortune. In 1948, *Life* magazine extolled the city's can-do civic spirit, bountiful parks, and exemplary planning in a cover story called "The Good Life in Madison, Wisconsin." In 1996, *Money* magazine named Madison the best place to live in the United States. In 1997, *American Health for Women* deemed it number one, and *Parenting* magazine ranked it the nation's third best place to raise a family. That year, the unemployment rate for Madison, population two hundred thousand, and surrounding Dane County, with six other cities, several dozen towns and villages, and another two hundred thousand people, stood at 1.6 percent, the lowest in the nation. Major new brick-and-mortar projects—a huge World Dairy Center, including the State Department of Agriculture Building where Patty ran her coffee shop; a convention center based on a design by Frank Lloyd Wright; and a campus sports arena—added luster to the city's image. Soon a local businessman would donate $205 million, more than twice the annual budget of the National Endowment for the Arts, to build a cultural arts center. Madison was on a roll.

The Madison Police and Fire Commission picked Richard Williams, an African American, to succeed Couper as chief of police, and Debra Amesqua, a Native American, Hispanic, and lesbian all in one, as fire chief. In April 1997, Madison elected its first female mayor, Sue Bauman, and Dane County its first female county executive, prompting *The Capital Times* daily newspaper to proclaim the area "Dame County," predictably affronting some readers' sensibilities. That year, the isthmus area was represented in the state Assembly by Tammy Baldwin, who would go on to become the first "out" lesbian in Congress. Dane County ranked among the top ten counties in the nation in its percentage of same-sex couples, and the national magazine *Lesbian Connection* reported more subscribers in Madison's 53704 zip code than in any other.

But Madison's liberalism, then as now, owes largely to its isolation from realities, economic and social, that the rest of the nation confronts. The jobs are more secure, the pay is higher, the crime rate lower, and the community less diverse. (The 2000 census found the city to be 84 percent white and less than 6 percent African American.) And, in terms of how it operates, there is little that marks Madison as enlightened. Money and power enjoy the same intimate relationship within the city's limits as anywhere else. Madison's proudly progressive spirit is manifest mainly in proclamations of tolerance amid a dearth of actual diversity, punctuated by occasional bleats of political correctness.

The first indication that things would go horribly wrong was when Patty called the police department on that Friday morning, the day after the rape. No, she was told, no suspect had been found, and none of the evidence had been analyzed. What's more, no one would even be working on her case until the following Monday, three days away. There was only one detective assigned to handle sexual assault cases on this side of town, she was told, and he was off until then.

Patty was so surprised by this news that she called the local Rape Crisis Center, asking whether it was normal for four days to pass before police even begin to look into a sexual assault. The person she spoke to didn't know, and the center's legal expert wasn't available. Patty put down the phone and cried some more. She was afraid to go back to her own place, to sleep in her bed, thinking that the man who raped her might return.

She didn't know it yet, but Patty had more reason to be afraid of the detective the Madison Police Department assigned to help her. She had been given his name and wrote it down: "Tom Woodmansee."

4

Detective Woodmansee

For Tom Woodmansee, being a cop was not just a job; it was a calling. "I can think of no other field of worth that I could be a member of than that of law enforcement," he wrote on his application to the Madison Police Department in 1990, when he was twenty-seven. Already, he seemed persuaded of his own moral rectitude. "I believe I have done a good job in keeping my sense of values and integrity and that I will continue to do so throughout my life," he assured his employer-to-be. Yes, he had smoked marijuana and there were a few times, especially in college, when he had had too much to drink. And now and then he had a cigarette, a bad habit to be sure. But for the most part Tom Woodmansee was, in his own estimation and that of his fellow officers, upright and honest, sensitive and caring. He was tall, trim, and in excellent shape. He had played baseball in college, transferring from the University of Wisconsin at Eau Claire to the UW–Whitewater, a big baseball school, where he graduated in 1985 with a major in speech and a minor in Professional Business Retailer Distribution. For a while he studied martial arts. He still played baseball, softball, basketball, and golf. He was married, enjoyed chess, and sometimes rode a motorcycle. He was a well-rounded guy.

In his seven years as a Madison police officer, Woodmansee had shown competence and courage. Just a few months earlier he played a pivotal role in nabbing two armed robbery suspects, both nineteen, who had commandeered a man's car and forced him to drive to ATM machines. When the man escaped and called police, Woodmansee chased one suspect down on foot and "directed [his] body into the brick wall," as he put it in his report. Woodmansee later identified the other suspect from mug shots and handled the interrogation, getting the young man to admit his involvement and implicate his partner. Both were convicted.

Woodmansee had a gentle, confident manner and a knack for winning other people's trust. Early in his police career he worked undercover, from January 1992 to December 1993, primarily making drug arrests. He had no qualms about arresting people for marijuana, a drug he himself had used and possessed. As he later rationalized it, "I was not a police officer at the time." In March 1996, Woodmansee got permission to conduct an alcohol-impact study. At his direction, thirty central-city officers and supervisors kept incident logs for scattered night watch shifts during a six-month period. The study found that alcohol was a known factor in more than half of all nighttime police calls, including 67 percent of sexual assaults, 80 percent of domestic disturbances, 82 percent of batteries, and all five of the most serious calls—two involving suicide and one each involving sexual assault of children, reckless endangerment, and weapons violations. Woodmansee expressed his frustration in his report.

"I am concerned that our department and community have become almost immune and apathetic to the problems stemming from alcohol abuse," he wrote. "There is no current system in place to proactively combat the problems stemming from alcohol abuse and its detriment upon our community and our department." His suggestion: impose an "alcohol abuse enhancer" fee of twenty-five dollars on offenders in cases where alcohol is a direct factor, possibly using this to provide alcohol treatment to the indigent.

Nothing ever came of this idea, but in January 1997, just as the results of his study were made public, Woodmansee was promoted to detective, which had the incidental benefit of bumping his pay from $44,668 to $46,774 a year. He was assigned, as new detectives often are, to sensitive crimes: child abuse, domestic violence, and sexual assault. It was an area where his ability to elicit the trust of those he encountered would prove invaluable, given the special challenges for investigators that these cases pose. Often there are complicated histories between perpetrators and victims, and sometimes people's perceptions are so skewed by all this past history that getting to the truth is like peeling away layers of an onion; you get deeper and deeper without ever reaching a solid core.

Woodmansee's approach was to be thorough—much more thorough than the officers who initially responded and filed the preliminary reports. He would spend hours, if that's what it took, going over the same events, peeling away layers until he found what he was looking for: the truth.

Sadly, in some sexual assault cases, the truth is that people file false reports, for a variety of reasons: to cover up consensual relations, to obtain sympathy and attention, or to get revenge. The same thing that makes sexual assaults so hard to prove—the fact that they occur in private, involving conduct that is not inherently illegal—also makes them easy to lie about. And being called a rapist is a hard accusation to live down, even if it isn't true. As Sir Matthew Hale, a seventeenth-century English jurist known for his zealous prosecution of witches, expressed it, rape "is an accusation easy to be made and hard to be proved, and harder to be defended by the party accused tho' never so innocent." (Until the 1970s, some version of Hale's caution was routinely delivered to juries in rape trials in the United States.)

On this difficult issue of false reports, American society remains divided. On the one hand, people are aware that for decades the sexual abuse of women was minimized and dismissed. It doesn't take a lot of familiarity with popular culture to summon up the image of a tobacco-spitting southern sheriff, circa 1960, telling a bruised and bleeding woman there isn't any law against a man having sex with his wife. On the other hand, there are signs that society thinks that the pendulum has swung too far in the opposite direction, that rape crisis advocates and touchy-feely police have created a situation where women, in particular, can use false accusations of sexual assault to punish or manipulate. After all this clamoring for equality, critics say, women want special treatment in the form of police intervention every time they give in to some red-blooded young stallion, only to wake up with a hangover and a bad case of regret.

Just how often do people make false accusations of sexual assault? Rape crisis advocates say the incidence of false reporting is about 2 percent, the same as for other crimes. But some law enforcement officials estimate that 10 percent of all sex-crime allegations are false, and studies have come up with numbers as high as 50 percent, which seems incredible. One factor driving these higher-end estimates is the intellectually dishonest proposition that any complaint that doesn't lead to a successful prosecution is false. If a clever defense attorney wins an acquittal in court, is it correct to conclude there was no assault? If a victim drops a complaint due to pressure from the perpetrator or skepticism from the police, does that always mean she was making it up? If a woman says a man had sex with her after she passed out from having too much to drink, but prosecutors decline to press charges because he swears it was consensual, should that be counted as a false report?

Even if false reporting were occurring at epidemic levels, it seems clear that many more people are getting away with sexual assault than being wrongly accused of it. National studies consistently estimate that fewer than one in five sexual assaults are brought to the attention of police. One reason for this is the fear of victims that the police won't be able to help or, worse, will not believe them. That's why women who file what are deemed to be false reports of sexual assault are rarely prosecuted—the justice system does not want to compound the anxiety of actual victims. It's also why police departments across the country have set up special units devoted to sensitive crimes, to ensure that the cops who deal with victims have special training and skills. Ironically, however, that doesn't mean they are more empathetic. A study done in New York City in 2001 found that Special Victims Squad detectives were more than twice as likely as regular detectives or uniformed officers to get negative reviews from sexual assault victims. In fact, about 20 percent of the victims surveyed decided against filing complaints as a direct result of their experiences with these specially trained detectives.

Tom Woodmansee had received basic training in sexual assault investigations at the police academy and advanced training at a sexual assault investigating school in Illinois. He participated in a state-run program that helped train other officers on the handling of sensitive crimes, especially domestic abuse. And he worked with representatives of battered women's shelters and the local Rape Crisis Center to develop state training protocols.

In his eight months as a detective before he was assigned to Patty's case, Woodmansee was involved in numerous child abuse and sexual assault cases, sometimes as the primary investigator, sometimes helping out other detectives. As an especially enlightened representative of an unusually well-trained department, he was aware of the need to treat victims of sensitive crimes with courtesy, compassion, and respect. He also knew they were sometimes lying, and that part of his job was to catch them at it.

In early 1996 the Madison Police Department experienced a rash of "false" sexual assault reports—four separate cases over a three-month period. In the first three cases, the complainant eventually admitted having lied. In the fourth, the twenty-one-year-old alleged victim stuck to her story about being abducted by a man in a dirty red van with sliding doors. But police determined she was lying, in part because she had the wrong kind of cuts. "She should have a stab wound, instead of a slash wound," said the department's spokesperson, lamenting the waste of "time and energy" spent investigating her report. None of these four cases led to criminal charges.

Woodmansee, in his own brief experience, had investigated three false reports of sexual assault. The first case involved a woman who said her neighbor sexually assaulted her. After making the initial report, she recanted to Woodmansee, saying the sex was consensual but her husband compelled her to claim otherwise. In the second, an apparently mentally ill man reported to police that another man forced him to perform oral sex in a parking lot. The patrol officer brought the man to see Woodmansee, who questioned him about inconsistencies and got him to recant. And finally, there was a woman who reported being assaulted at a hotel by a friend with whom she had been drinking. When Woodmansee pointed out problems he perceived with her account, the alleged victim admitted the sex was consensual. She filed a false report, the detective later explained, "out of revenge and spite" because the man had left the hotel "to return to his girlfriend or wife."

Remarkably, in all three of these cases, Tom Woodmansee was able to get to the truth of the matter, after other officers had been confounded. It was his special gift to get people to open up, to spill their secrets, to alleviate their terrible weight of guilt. Indeed, less than two weeks before Patty's alleged rape, Woodmansee had expertly secured a confession in a child abuse case. He was brought into the investigation on the second day and solved it, almost single-handedly, by the end of his shift.

The case concerned a thirteen-month-old girl, "Alicia," whose right leg had been fractured in two places. The injuries were discovered after

Alicia's longtime child-care provider, twenty-seven-year-old Susan Pankow, called the girl's mother to report that she had been fussy all day and had a temperature of 105. The first doctor who examined the girl missed the injury to her leg, but the next morning her pediatrician, Dr. Edward McCabe, ordered the X rays that showed both lower bones, the tibia and fibula, of the right leg were broken.

Madison police were contacted and the case was assigned to Lauri Schwartz, a young detective who also worked on sensitive crimes. Schwartz met with the girl's mother, who seemed to implicate Pankow. The detective asked Woodmansee and a social worker to join her when she interviewed Pankow the following afternoon.

The interview, in the basement of Pankow's home day-care center, lasted two and a half hours. Woodmansee asked Pankow to describe the events of the day she had called Alicia's mother, which she did for about a half hour before realizing that she was describing the wrong day. Pankow had to start all over. About two hours into the interview, Woodmansee turned up the heat. He noted that Pankow had not inquired as to the nature of the injury being investigated, and said he suspected she knew more than she was letting on.

Pankow admitted it. That morning, when Pankow was changing Alicia's diaper, she had lifted her leg upward suddenly and the girl had cried out in pain. The detectives had Pankow demonstrate this abrupt upward motion using a rag doll that happened to be present. Woodmansee then asked Pankow whether she thought she may have caused Alicia's injuries. Pankow said she hadn't meant to but maybe she had, because of how sudden the motion had been. "Oh, God, if I did this . . . ," she exclaimed.

"I was in such a hurry," said Pankow, explaining that because Alicia was fussy she felt she was neglecting the other children. Woodmansee asked if Pankow was frustrated and she replied, "a little bit," explaining that she was under a lot of stress. "I was frustrated. I guess you could say I was on the verge of being angry." Woodmansee asked if Pankow had heard a cracking noise and she said "possibly a crack."

Soon after, Woodmansee spoke with Dr. McCabe, who told him that what happened to Alicia's leg was not consistent with accidental injury but was indicative of child abuse. To break the girl's leg in two places, he said, required the application of a great deal of force. In essence, the doctor said the injuries could not have resulted from the event—a sudden upward movement during a diaper change—that Pankow related.

But rather than doubt that Pankow was responsible, Woodmansee, in his report, concluded that she must have broken the little girl's bones deliberately and then concocted this story to make it seem like an accident. Nor was he shaken from his theory by the reaction of Alicia's parents when told that Pankow had confessed to breaking their little girl's leg in a fit of anger and frustration. According to his report, "They did not wish to pursue a complaint against Sue because they felt that she was a good day-care worker and they did not believe she had done this intentionally."

Woodmansee's report and other evidence were forwarded to the Dane County District Attorney's Office for review and probable charges. In the meantime, Pankow, who had no criminal record, was forced to surrender her state day-care license and shut down her business. Woodmansee moved on to other cases, including the one waiting for him when he came to work on Monday, September 8. It was an alleged sexual assault of a thirty-eight-year-old woman on Fairmont Avenue in Madison.

Patty had spent the day at Mark's house, replaying the details of the assault in anticipation of having to go over them with the detective assigned to her case. The police had said he would be back that Monday, and that his shift began at 2 p.m. Patty waited, but he didn't call. It was unbearable. At 4:30 p.m. she called him at the Madison Police Department's detective bureau. They spoke for a few minutes.

Woodmansee, it turned out, was not prepared to meet with her that day. He had other things to do, including background work on her case, and so he arranged to interview Patty the following afternoon at her duplex. But he took this opportunity to get a few details. Officer Thiesenhusen's four-page report, which he reviewed, noted that Patty named her daughter's boyfriend as a possible suspect. Did she still feel it might be him? Yes, Patty said, it might be. She told Woodmansee where Dominic lived and that he worked for his jailbird mother's cleaning service, as did Misty. But Patty said she did not want her daughter to know of her suspicions unless there was substantiating evidence. Woodmansee asked her to prepare a list of possible suspects.

Patty reiterated that the man who raped her seemed to know she had a daughter and kept money from her business in the apartment. And she said something that aroused Woodmansee's suspicion: "He didn't want to hurt me. He was somewhat sensitive, even when we were having sex." What kind of rape victim refers to what happened as "having sex"? And why would Patty give her assailant credit for being sensitive? In fact, while Patty's rapist *did* hurt and injure her, he did not seem to go out of his way to do so. Patty's comment may have also reflected her history of childhood sexual abuse, and her resulting tendency to internalize and minimize.

That evening, Woodmansee ran a criminal background check on Patty, pulling in reports of every police contact on file with Madison police and the Dane County Sheriff's Department. These records showed that Patty had a juvenile theft charge and adult noncriminal citations for trespassing and disorderly conduct. There was also a record regarding a past suicide attempt, in 1986. Detective Woodmansee's investigation was underway.

5

One on One

It's common knowledge that visually impaired people tend to have more highly developed other senses. Because they can't rely on sight, they're often better at processing other input—sounds, smells, sensations. In Patty's case it wasn't so much that her other senses were sharper as that she was more attuned to nonvisual cues, like the inflection of a person's voice. For instance, on the day before the rape she had known, more clearly than a sighted person may have, that the Business Enterprise representatives with whom she met were frustrated and annoyed. Ostensibly they had the same goal—helping Patty straighten out her business woes—as Connie Kilmark, the financial counselor brought in for this meeting. But in terms of attitude, they were coming from different places, and Patty picked up on it.

Likewise it didn't take Patty long to realize that Detective Woodmansee was coming from a different place than the officer, sexual assault nurse, and police photographer she had met five days before. He arrived at her apartment as promised at 3 p.m. on September 9. Patty had gotten a cab ride home from her job at the coffee shop, after putting in a full day's work. Misty and Patty's brother Bobby were also present. Woodmansee introduced himself, asking Patty to call him "Tom." She was struck by how tall he was, a towering presence compared with her five-feet-four-inch frame, and how young, although at age thirty-four he was only four years younger than herself.

Woodmansee asked to talk with Patty in private, one on one. As her guests exited, the detective explained that he was going to ask some of the same questions as the other officer, only he would do it "better." She perceived him as arrogant, an impression that would not change over time.

The detective asked Patty to escort him through the residence and identify the bedroom where the rape occurred. He said it wasn't necessary that she come into the room—he understood this might be difficult—but she said it was okay, and followed him in. Right away Woodmansee noticed something strange. The closet Patty had allegedly been forced into was extremely full, with items protruding. He asked if the closet was in this condition the night of the assault and she said it was. Woodmansee saw the bloodied pillow, still on the bed. He peeked into Misty's bedroom, a few feet across the hall from Patty's. Then they returned to the front room to talk.

Woodmansee ascertained that Patty and Misty had been living at the Fairmont Avenue duplex for three years. Patty and her boyfriend Mark had been dating off and on for a year and a half. The detective asked about Dominic. Patty had known him since that spring, when he dated her sister Brenda. They broke up after about three months, not amicably, and Misty and Dominic hooked up a month after that, in July. Brenda was "very bitter" that Dominic was now seeing her niece. Patty was also not thrilled with this relationship, because she knew that Dominic had genital herpes.

Patty estimated that Dominic had been to her apartment five to ten times and had stayed overnight on several occasions. They had spoken only a handful of times, and Patty had never gotten close enough to discern his facial features, although he seemed about the same size and had the same color skin as her assailant. She knew he drank a lot of beer, because he sometimes left it in her refrigerator. She also told Woodmansee, "He gets jealous of Misty talking to men. He hates black men."

As Woodmansee requested, Patty had drawn up a list of suspects, with Misty's help. It named a half dozen of Misty's friends and acquaintances, including Dominic; his roommate David W., who went by the nickname "Slim"; and "Lonnie Alvord, eighteen years old." While Patty had been careful not to share her suspicions with Misty, it was obvious that Dominic fit the physical description and had to be included. Even Dominic, in a conversation with Misty, agreed this should be done, to rule him out.

Before discussing the alleged assault, Woodmansee asked Patty for a detailed account of the week leading up to it, an area of inquiry she had not expected. She described the previous week in terms of her normal routine: going to bed Monday around 8 p.m., getting up Tuesday at 4:30 a.m. and arriving to her coffee shop by 6 a.m., returning home around 3:30 p.m. and promptly heading to her second job, stocking and retrieving money from vending machines. That would take until 7 p.m. and she'd be in bed an hour later, usually falling asleep with the television on and waking up around 2 or 3 a.m., when she'd watch a little "Nick at Nite." She was starting to describe Wednesday when she realized the previous Monday, September 1, had been Labor Day, and her recollection was out of whack. "I'm screwing everything up," she said apologetically. "I was thinking of the week before." Curiously it was the same mistake Susan Pankow had made.

Actually, Patty now recalled, she had stayed at Mark's that Monday night. The Green Bay Packers were on *Monday Night Football* and he had some people over to watch the game. That evening, after Patty had gone to bed but before she fell asleep, Misty and Dominic stopped by. Misty popped into the bedroom to give Patty some cigarettes, and Dominic had a beer. The next day Patty took the day off from her job at the coffee shop but still made her vending machine run.

At this point in the interview—Woodmansee recorded the time as "approximately 3:50 p.m."—Misty returned briefly to the apartment before heading out to fill in for her mom on that day's vending run. She mentioned Dominic, in connection with her cleaning job, and Woodmansee intuited that Misty did not consider him a suspect in her mother's rape.

Patty continued her chronology. On Wednesday, the day before the assault, she left for work in the early morning. She did not notice that Dominic was there, but learned later he had been. Patty got home about 5 p.m., watched a little TV, and fell asleep between 7 and 8 p.m. She had not had any alcohol, drugs, or medication. The television was on ABC, the volume at a "normal" level. Patty was still wearing her knit pants and purple shirt when she fell asleep, which was unusual: "I'm such a routine person, but this is different, I fell asleep with my clothes on." This also struck Woodmansee as strange, as did the fact that Patty did not on this night wake up at 2 or 3 a.m., which, he later put in his report, "she stated she always does."

Patty recounted the events of the rape, beginning with hearing a male voice warn her to do as he said so no one would get hurt. He spoke into her left ear as she lay on her stomach. He had a knife. "I felt the knife and saw a knife," she told him. "It seems like I'd seen it but maybe not at that point." Woodmansee wanted her to be more precise. Patty said she felt the blade against her left cheek and thought she saw that it was a knife but wasn't sure. "I felt something sharp-edged laying on me. I knew it was serrated."

Woodmansee pressed on. Wasn't the man very close to her? Yes. Wasn't his face within six inches of her own? Yes. Didn't she notice anything prior to hearing his voice? No: "The second I woke up, he was already in bed." Weren't they nose-to-nose, just six inches apart? "He was a little higher," she corrected. "I smelled alcohol on his breath, a strong smell." What kind of alcohol was it? She wasn't sure. Was the door to her room open or closed when the suspect was lying next to her? She wasn't sure. Did he have facial hair? She didn't think so, but wasn't sure.

The detective asked what, if anything, Patty had been able to see. "I could see there was a guy there, but not what he looked like," she answered. The room was dark when he entered, except for light from the TV, which he turned off right away. And she was lying face down on the bed, her face pressed into a pillow. Patty had already explained that she was legally blind. Woodmansee would later state in his report that he "did not note anything distinctive about her vision being impaired." In fact, he never determined the nature of her visual disability or what it meant. People with macular degeneration are often adept at discerning larger objects. It's much harder for them to distinguish detail, especially in poor lighting, because peripheral vision is nowhere near as good as central vision. A common complaint among people with macular degeneration is that they cannot recognize faces.

At what point, asked Woodmansee, did Patty suspect Dominic was her assailant? "I know it was early on when I thought it was him." What aroused her suspicions? That was hard to say. "I think it was the short hair." When did she notice the intruder had short hair? "It was later," she admitted.

Things got worse as the questions grew increasingly explicit. Patty told Woodmansee her assailant reached up and pulled her pants down to her knees. How had he done this? "Quickly," she replied. Was he still lying next to her? Patty thought so. Were her legs together or apart? Together. Was she still lying on her stomach? Yes. Woodmansee was perplexed. "When you're lying on your stomach, and he's pulling your pants down, did you stay on your stomach or did you scrunch up with your butt?" Patty thought for a moment, then replied, "I guess I scrunched up to help him get the pants down, then I was back flat again." So her claim about being on her stomach when he removed her pants wasn't true after all.

The pattern was set: Woodmansee got frustrated and Patty got frazzled. She had been so sure she would be able to recall what happened, having gone over it in her head during the last five days. But in short order, Woodmansee's barrage of questions had her befuddled, unsure of what had happened. She sensed his irritation and impatience, heard his sighs when she was unable to provide details. She felt that she was under suspicion—not of lying but of being a bad rape victim, one who made the cops' job more difficult by being unable to answer the simplest questions. At one point, Patty later recalled, Woodmansee was so displeased with her answers he pointed to the bedroom where the assault occurred and said, "If we have to go in there and role-play this thing, we will."

Patty described how the intruder had difficulty entering her vaginally from behind and asked whether she could "take it here," meaning her anus. Woodmansee noted that Patty had not yet said anything about the man taking off his own pants. She couldn't remember him doing this but agreed it must have happened. Then he was behind her, pushing himself inside. "The way I was laying, he couldn't get it in that far," she said. "He must have been short." She said this with a little laugh, a reaction Woodmansee would flag in his report and later include on his list of reasons for believing she was lying about being raped.

Woodmansee asked whether the intruder penetrated her completely, whether he used a condom or lubricant, whether Patty had ever before had anal sex. He was struck that she described the man's voice as "almost sympathetic" when she said she couldn't see and he answered, "I know." He thought it strange that she referred to the fellatio as "giving him oral sex."

Was the suspect's penis fully erect? Yes. Could she describe it? "It seemed fatter than it was long." How long was it? "Maybe five inches." This would later emerge as one of Woodmansee's key reasons for doubting Patty. That saying the penis seemed "fatter than it was long" was an exaggeration, like saying the assault "seemed to last forever," did not occur to him. Instead, he took it to be a literal description of an improbable penis, one he eventually concluded did not exist.

Other details flowed forth, like how the man had pulled off her shirt so that she was completely naked. How he was startled and accusatory when she tried removing her bunched-up pants. How after five or six minutes of oral gratification he produced a rubber and instructed her to put it on. How there was a moment, between the oral and vaginal part of the assault, where she could have looked up and maybe gotten a good look but didn't. "I really should have looked at him," she said, with another laugh.

Woodmansee asked whether or not she was naturally lubricated in her vaginal area. No, Patty answered, she was dry. This was the only knowingly untrue statement she made to Woodmansee during his investigation. There were other things she guessed at, because the detective wanted precise answers and seemed irritated when she wasn't sure. But when asked this question, Patty didn't want to admit, and then explain, that her body had lubricated itself. And so she said she was dry. Ironically, this one actual lie was never among the things that caused Woodmansee to doubt her account. She did tell him, truthfully, that the man used a lubricated condom and that when he entered her it was not painful.

Patty described the rest of the assault, which ended when the man seemed to climax. "I could feel the rubber almost coming loose," she said. "I could feel it filling." This, too, aroused Woodmansee's suspicions. Later, he purportedly asked "several women" of his acquaintance whether it was possible to feel a condom fill when a man ejaculated. They said it was not.

Afterward the pillow slipped off Patty's face and she saw the man use his right hand to hold the condom at its base as he withdrew. Woodmansee asked if she managed to get a better look at the suspect. "I remember seeing his shape," Patty replied. "He was small for a man." She said he was only about 150 pounds and not much taller than she was. Patty laughed again.

Suddenly Patty remembered something she neglected to mention earlier, despite Woodmansee's efforts to obtain a thorough account. Her alarm clock, set for 4 a.m., had gone off several times during the assault, and each time her assailant hit the snooze button. Woodmansee wanted to know when was the first time it went off. "I can't remember if we were having anal sex then or, I mean, if he was having anal sex on me." This odd nomenclature—"having anal sex"—would also make his list.

Patty, prodded by Woodmansee, provided the remaining details. How her assailant asked about rope and she suggested he use the bedsheets to tie her up or have her go in the closet. How when the two of them were standing near each other at the foot of the bed, she saw, in the light from the neighbor's yard, his white sweatpants and the color of his skin. How the closet was so full that when she got inside the doors were bulging outward. How he stuck the knife into the crack and warned her not to look. How he cut the cord of the phone in her room and asked about the other phones. Patty laughed and said an interesting thing—that maybe it wasn't Dominic because he knew where all the phones were.

The time was now 6:15 p.m., more than three hours after the interview began. Woodmansee decided this would be a good time for a break, but said he would need more information and tentatively set up another interview for the following evening. He also advised Patty that he would be contacting her daughter. She said this would be okay. He gave her his card.

Patty took a cab back to Mark's house. That evening, Misty and Dominic stopped by. Patty noticed that the cologne he was wearing smelled like that of the man who assaulted her. She called Woodmansee the next afternoon to tell him about it. Patty also asked if the two of them might be able to meet that evening a bit earlier than planned. She remembered that she and Mark had tickets, purchased well in advance, for a concert that night at a local music club by a blues performer, Clarence "Gatemouth" Brown. Patty stressed that she didn't have to see the show. Woodmansee, she would later recall, said it was fine to reschedule and urged her to have a good time.

Later, this would also make his "she's lying" list: "Canceled next day appointment to go to a tavern. Did not seem to matter to her that I get all the information promptly."

6

Misty and Dominic

Nobody ever accused Patty of being a perfect parent. Certainly her own past—getting pregnant at age thirteen, dropping out of high school—hardly put her on firm footing to impart life lessons to her daughter. And her instinct to back down when challenged, acquired over a lifetime of hurt, made her a poor match for Misty, headstrong and insouciant. Patty's sister Brenda would later say Misty went through "the same old rebellious crap that every other teenager goes through." But it was worse. Misty was reckless and immature, Patty irresolute and self-effacing. Her ability to influence Misty's often bad choices was somewhere between nominal and nonexistent.

Yet Patty loved her daughter and did her best to provide, despite being a single parent with a serious disability. The two had always lived together, except for one summer when Misty stayed with her father in a small town outside Madison and another summer she spent with her half sister, Patty's older daughter, out of state. When Misty was younger, she and her mother lived for a year and a half in Waukesha, a suburb of Milwaukee, and for four years in Sheboygan, an area best known for bratwurst and plumbing fixtures. They moved back to Madison around the time that Misty started high school; she later transferred to an alternative public school, named after Malcolm X, for students who feel as though they don't fit in. Misty ended up getting a high school equivalency diploma. Her ambition—highly ironic given that many of her closest associates, including the imprisoned father of her unborn child, were drug dealers and thugs—was to become a law enforcement officer. She was short and thin, with stringy blond hair and cool blue eyes. Like her mom she smoked cigarettes, and her default facial expression was a pout.

It was just after 5 p.m. on September 10 when Detective Woodmansee arrived at the Fairmont Avenue duplex to interview Misty. He got there before she did and had to wait, since Misty was coming from her job at the cleaning service. Misty arrived, driving Dominic's car.

Misty said that on the night of the assault her mother had gone to bed early and was already asleep, with the TV on, when she tried asking a question around 8 p.m. Misty herself went to bed around 11 and left the door to her room partly open, although the next morning it was shut. She described herself as a heavy sleeper, saying that on this night as usual she slept with the radio tuned to a local station at a low volume.

The following morning Misty remembered hearing a male voice on the radio say, "It's a few minutes to five," shortly before her mom woke her to break the news about the assault. Given that the 911 call was made at 4:13 a.m., this may have been seen as a sign that Misty's recollection was less than reliable. Instead, Woodmansee would view each discrepancy between Misty's account and that of her mother as evidence of Patty's duplicity.

There were not a lot of discrepancies. Misty said her mother was wearing a shirt and pants when she woke her up. Patty had said she was naked from the waist down until after police arrived. Woodmansee would add this to his list of reasons without even asking the responding officers, Thiesenhusen and Jarona, what they observed. There was also confusion over whether the front door was closed or partially open following the rape, and which of the two women locked it.

Woodmansee was especially interested in Patty's demeanor just after the alleged rape. "She was more rational than I was," said Misty. "She was shaking but she was more calm than I was. She was trying to calm me down." Misty said her mother was upset but not crying when she called 911. In fact, the only time she saw her cry was at the hospital when Mark arrived and later, when her Aunt Peggy stopped by. Woodmansee asked Misty if she was surprised by her mother's reaction. "Yes, I am," she replied. "I think she's taking this better than expected."

Misty told Woodmansee she went into her mother's room and saw blood on the pillow and wet spots on the mattress. The alarm clock was beeping and she turned it off—which substantiated what Patty said about the snooze alarm. Asked who she thought may have assaulted her mother, Misty replied, "I'm almost positive that it's someone who knows us." She had upward of twenty male friends who knew where she lived, possibly five of whom would know the front door was left unlocked. But the only one who spent the night there, or used the unlocked door to enter unannounced, was her boyfriend Dominic.

The two had started dating that July 4, about a month after Dominic and her Aunt Brenda broke up. Misty thought she and Dominic had a good relationship, although he drank too much and got jealous. Woodmansee asked when Dominic last stayed over, before the rape. Misty said it was the previous night. Two of his roommates, including Slim, had dropped Dominic off at her place around 3 a.m. "He was completely out of it," Misty recalled with a laugh. "He was dazed, like he had drank six bottles of tequila." Dominic slept until about 10 a.m., long after Patty had left for work. He and Misty did a cleaning job late that morning and knocked off by early afternoon, because he was so hung over. Dominic planned to come over again that night but never did. The next morning, from the hospital, Misty called Dominic at his mother's place. His sister woke him up.

"Was the door unlocked?" Dominic had asked. Misty said it was, and he got angry, saying "I'm sick of this shit." This, she explained, was his way of expressing concern for her well-being. "He's always told me to lock it since we've been dating. He knows the door is unlocked and it bothers him."

Misty called Dominic on his cell phone later that day to give him an update, and he stopped by Mark's house that evening. He did not speak to Patty except to say, "How you doing?" Misty was upset that people at Mark's place were "drinking and laughing and having fun," given that her mother had just been raped. "I was pissed off," she said.

Woodmansee proceeded to ask intimate questions about Misty's relationship with Dominic. When was the last time they had sex? It was the night before this interview, at his house. Did he have herpes? Yes, and currently had open sores. What type of contraceptives did they use? "Class Act" condoms, which come in a blue wrapper. Did they ever have anal sex? No. Woodmansee asked Misty to describe Dominic's penis when erect. It was normal size, perhaps a bit smaller, and not unusually thick or thin.

Misty would later say she was offended by these questions. It was a reaction Patty anticipated, having herself endured a marathon encounter with Woodmansee's inquiring mind. In fact she had told him, when they spoke that afternoon, that Misty didn't like to be asked a lot of questions. But Woodmansee didn't perceive any umbrage on Misty's part, and later put Patty's warning on his list of reasons, saying, "She did not want me to ask detailed questions."

During Misty's interview, Dominic called twice. Woodmansee asked to speak to him and set up a meeting at police headquarters. He left Misty and headed downtown for a face-to-face with Dominic. He arranged to have a more experienced detective, Linda Draeger, sit in on this interview.

Draeger, then forty-four, was a twenty-year department veteran with sharp instincts and a no-nonsense approach. She had a reputation for being abrasive; other members of the department, she once boasted, considered her a "bitch." But she was also seen as one of the department's best detectives. During the past decade she had worked on a dozen murder cases, a third of Madison's total. Her triumphs included helping nail a young Madison woman named Penny Brummer for the 1994 murder of her gay lover's best friend. There was no physical evidence connecting Brummer to the crime; her conviction was based on circumstantial evidence, including an alleged nod of her head when detectives accused her of involvement. Draeger also played a key role in sending away seventeen-year-old Darnell Hines for a drug-related killing in 1995. Again, there was no physical evidence tying Hines to the crime, but Draeger persuaded a woman who earlier said she hadn't seen a thing to admit, and later testify, that she watched Hines shoot the man at close range. Draeger was so pleased when the verdict came back as guilty that she wept and hugged the prosecutor in court. "There was never a doubt in my mind" that Hines was the killer, she said at the time. Others—including the Wisconsin Innocence Project, which investigates possible wrongful convictions—would later flag both cases as ones where the local police and Dane County District Attorney's Office may have put innocent people behind bars.

Dominic arrived at the police department's detective bureau around 8:20 p.m. Woodmansee greeted him and introduced Detective Draeger. They went into an interrogation room. Draeger didn't ask many questions or write a report. Her role was to provide support and be a witness. (Ironically, when asked about this interview later, under oath, she remembered almost nothing about it.) Woodmansee, by this time, had already run a criminal history check on Dominic, finding evidence of impulsive and violent behavior.

In 1992, Dominic had been arrested in Racine and charged with vandalism and battery for drunkenly smashing his own head into the dashboard of his sister's car before punching another sister twice in the face with a closed fist. The next year, back in Madison, the mother of one of his two young sons obtained a domestic abuse restraining order against him. She described repeated threats and abuse, including one incident where he allegedly held a gun to her head, threatened to kill her, and then choked her until she collapsed to the pavement.

Dominic, the detective would note, was mixed race and light skinned, five feet five, 135 pounds, with short black hair, an acne-scarred complexion, and hoop earrings in his left ear. He said he sometimes slept at Misty's place, mostly on weekends, when Patty was away. He had never been in Patty's room, which he said was always locked. The last time he stayed overnight before the rape was Monday, September 1, Labor Day. The next night, he was out drinking with friends and took some Percocet—which, he told the detectives, "mellow you out"—before returning to his apartment to sleep around 3 or 4 a.m.

This contradicted Misty's account, which was that Dominic ended up in her bedroom that night. But Woodmansee either did not notice or decided not to challenge him on it. Dominic went on to explain that he was feeling ill that Wednesday and had left work early, as Misty had said. He went to his mother's place, where his sister was staying with her new baby. He planned to see Misty again that evening but fell asleep on his mother's sofa. The next morning Misty called and told him what had happened. He later stopped by Mark's place but left after Brenda called him names. Asked if he could think of anyone who might be responsible, Dominic named his roommate Slim, who besides fitting the physical description of the alleged rapist had commented more than once that he found Patty attractive.

Next, Woodmansee asked Dominic to describe his sexual relationship with Misty—everything from how often to which positions to what he did during a herpes outbreak. Dominic said he often used condoms but did not know which kind, other than that they came in a pink wrapper (contrary to what Misty had said). Woodmansee asked whether Patty had ever been flirtatious toward him or expressed any sexual interest. Negative. Dominic also said there was currently no animosity between himself and Patty. He described her as outgoing and friendly, although it was his impression that she drank too much. The same, he added, could be said about himself.

When was the last time Dominic was intoxicated? He said it was just after Labor Day, and that he had ended up at Misty's place. Dominic paused for several moments, then stated that he may have been mistaken about the last time he had been at Misty's prior to the rape. He now believed it was that Tuesday night, after his booze-and-pill bender with his roommates.

The detectives took a break and got Dominic a soda. When they resumed questioning at 9:50 p.m., they took a tougher tack. Would Dominic be willing to take a lie detector test with regard to these events? He said he would. Did he have any involvement in Patty's sexual assault? None. Was there any reason his fingerprints or pubic hair would be found in Patty's bedroom? Not unless someone moved them there from someplace else, he insisted. "I've never been in her room."

Seeing that Dominic was upset, Woodmansee escalated. He announced that Patty believed he was the person who sexually assaulted her. "You're kidding!" he responded. Woodmansee explained that Dominic was facing serious potential charges; he continued to deny involvement. The detective said he had reason to believe Dominic knew more about the incident than he was letting on. Dominic reacted with alarm. "If you want samples or whatever you want, you can have them. Right here, right now, tonight," he sputtered. "I was not in that goddamn room!"

Dominic then came up with a theory for why Patty would accuse him: "Sir, I swear, she's overreacting because Misty and I started dating." This came a moment after saying that, as far as he knew, Patty bore him no ill will. He also speculated that Patty was biased against him because of Brenda and because he was involved with drugs.

The detectives may have figured, with some justification, that anyone dumb enough to make an admission like this to the police was probably not smart enough to lie about a sexual assault. Dominic continued to protest his innocence, making what Woodmansee would describe as "severe body movements" in his chair. "There's no way I would ever do that," he insisted. "If I'm going to have sex, I want it to be intimate." He reiterated his willingness to submit to tests.

But Woodmansee and Draeger didn't ask him for samples. They told Dominic he was still a suspect and escorted him from the building, a little more than two hours after the interview began. Woodmansee never made any attempt to check out Dominic's alibi or investigate other individuals whose names were provided as possible suspects.

By this time, Woodmansee's focus had shifted. He was no longer investigating an alleged sexual assault. He was investigating the alleged victim.

7

Another Suspect

It didn't take long for Patty to find out what Woodmansee had done. Misty heard from Dominic, who was livid, and confronted her mother. Patty promptly backed down, saying she didn't think it was Dominic and hadn't meant to accuse him.

A number of things, thought Patty, made Dominic the most likely suspect. These she had discussed with Brenda, who wrote out a list. Dominic knew the door would be unlocked and how to find his way around the apartment. He sometimes came in late, after filling up on booze and drugs. The cologne seemed to match. He had the same skin color. He liked to have Brenda wrap her legs around him during sex, just as the rapist had done, and expressed interest in anal sex.

Still, Patty was never sure it was Dominic and was distressed that Woodmansee had confronted him. She had expected police to examine the evidence and make an arrest based on what it revealed. Telling Dominic that she had named him as her assailant and then letting him go was not what she had in mind. As soon as she found out, that Thursday, September 11, she left Woodmansee a voice-mail message expressing her concern.

Woodmansee didn't get Patty's message right away because he was at Meriter Hospital, talking to the SANE nurse, Jill Poarch. He had her provide a synopsis of her exam, and he viewed the tape of the colposcope that documented Patty's injuries. The anal abrasion, she noted, looked more like a fingernail scratch than something caused by penile penetration. Woodmansee asked if it could have been self-inflicted.

Poarch said this was possible but felt it was consistent with a rapist trying to "gain penetration."

The detective was working on a different theory—that the rape never happened. As Poarch later recalled their conversation, "He felt that there should have been more injury, that he had had some discussion with some other police officers and that they all felt that someone who had been sodomized should be kind of ripped apart, should have more injury. And I kind of laughed and I said, you know, 'How many SANE exams have they done?'" Poarch held firm, saying Patty's exam "was consistent with her having been sexually assaulted. A lot of times in a sexual assault you don't find that people are ripped apart and have a great deal of injury."

Woodmansee asked whether Patty's other injuries—the bruise to her inner thigh and cuts to her hand, neck, and face—could have all been self-inflicted. "That could have happened," Poarch replied. "I can't say that that absolutely did not happen." But she had no reason to suspect this and felt the injuries squared with what she would expect to find based on the events Patty described. At the end of their talk, Poarch would later say, "I'm not sure we came to a mutual conclusion." Indeed, they hadn't.

When he returned to his office, Woodmansee received Patty's voice-mail message and called her back. He said he found it unusual that she did not expect him to interview the man she identified as the most likely suspect. She said she was disappointed he had moved so quickly in talking to Dominic. He asked whether she still thought he was the one, and she said yes, especially after talking things over with Brenda. She wasn't able to identify his voice because "the guy did not use his voice. It was like it was forced, like he tried not to sound like himself."

While Woodmansee had Patty on the phone, he asked her some more questions. When was the last time she had voluntary sex? Patty said it was with Mark about three weeks earlier, during a trip to Sheboygan. When was the last time she changed her bedsheets? About two weeks before the assault. Had anyone besides herself and the man who assaulted her been in the bed since? No. Woodmansee asked about Patty's injuries. How did she get the cuts on her face? Probably early in the assault, when the intruder held the knife against her. What about the cut to her forefinger? "He didn't cut me, I did it," replied Patty, explaining that this must have happened when she reached around and touched the blade.

Some of Woodmansee's questions—for instance, whether Patty was sure she was wearing only a shirt when police arrived—were clearly geared toward investigating her story, not the assault. And almost all of Patty's answers fed into Woodmansee's theory of the case. She said that after a certain point she didn't feel her life was in danger and now thought, looking back, "I could have kicked his butt. It wasn't that threatening a knife." Very suspicious. The description she now gave of the knife seemed more detailed than two days before. Very suspicious. Patty also remembered that when she and the rapist were standing at the foot of the bed, he said to her, "That wasn't so bad, was it?" and touched her shoulder. Woodmansee was stunned, asking why she had not recalled this before, during their initial three-hour session. She didn't have a good explanation. Very suspicious.

On Monday, September 15, Woodmansee picked up the sexual assault kit from the police property room and delivered it to the Wisconsin State Crime Laboratory for processing. Two days later, he stopped by Mark's place at around 7:30 p.m., hoping to talk to him. That he wanted to interview Mark—someone who knew Patty but had no first-hand knowledge of the assault—was another sign as to which way his investigation was heading. Mark was working, but Patty was there. Patty asked Woodmansee if they could talk, and they went out to the back porch. Mark's dog knocked over a small grill and Woodmansee watched with interest as Patty cleaned it up. She seemed to have no trouble seeing this, even though it was dark.

Patty said she understood why Woodmansee had confronted Dominic but was upset because of the position it put her in. He asked whether she still thought it was Dominic, and she said she was more and more sure. He asked if she was positive, and she said she was not. He asked if there was anyone else she could think of, and she mentioned Misty's friend Lonnie. Why, Woodmansee wondered, hadn't she mentioned this person before? "Well," replied Patty, "Misty told me that he was out of town."

Actually, Misty's list of names did include "Lonnie Alvord," her former boyfriend. It was not the correct spelling, as Woodmansee might have realized from that afternoon's editions of *The Capital Times*. The main page of the local section carried an article about the arrest of eighteen-year-old Alonzo Elvord Jr. and twenty-one-year-old Joseph Bong in connection with an armed robbery/abduction. Early in the morning on the previous Saturday, the two used a sawed-off shotgun to rob a hotel just outside Madison; they abducted two employees, who managed to escape. The newspaper reported that, besides armed robbery and false imprisonment, Elvord was charged with obstruction and Bong with fourth-degree sexual assault. The two men were cousins, and Misty had known them both.

But tracking down possible rapists was apparently no longer on Woodmansee's agenda. The only suspect in his sights was the one he was talking to at Mark's house. He asked about Patty's alarm clock, which had a nine-minute snooze delay. How many times did it go off? Earlier Patty had said five or six, but now thought it may have been as few as three. She said the alarm was set for 4 a.m., but the clock was set fast. Woodmansee asked why she had not said this earlier; she thought that she had. He would include this on his list of reasons for believing that the rape did not occur: "Changes clock time when I ask detailed questions about alarm and time frame."

Woodmansee asked what Patty thought should happen to Dominic, if he was the one. "He should be put in prison for a long time," she answered. And, Woodmansee continued, "If [Dominic] is telling me he had nothing to do with this, is he lying to my face?" As usual when challenged, Patty said what she thought would give the least offense, in this case a wary "yeah." Woodmansee's tone made her again feel like she was wasting his time. She told him, "It wasn't the rape so much as it was waking up to a knife at my throat that upsets me." This, too, would make his list.

After this interview with Patty, Woodmansee drove to her old apartment. He spoke to the next-door neighbor, who was home the night of the alleged assault but did not see or hear anything until the lights of the police squad cars woke him up. Misty was at the apartment, and Woodmansee stopped in. She expressed confidence that Dominic was not to blame, saying her mother had admitted as much: "She said she would know if it was him." Woodmansee told Misty this wasn't true, that her mother had in fact named Dominic.

The detective asked about Mark. Misty said he and Patty argued a lot. She wasn't sure if they were still romantically involved: "I don't know what the situation is with those two. Mom tells me they are just friends, but then there is this jealousy thing." Overall, she found their relationship "confusing."

Woodmansee asked Misty if he could look around in Patty's bedroom. The door was locked, but after the rape Patty had hidden a key, expressly in case police needed to get back in. Somehow or other, Misty knew where to find it. Woodmansee turned the lights off and TV on, and, according to his report, "noticed that the TV illuminated the room well." It was an odd observation, since Patty had said the set was on for only the first minute of the assault, when her face was pressed into a pillow. The detective then thrust his six-foot-two, 195-pound frame into the closet and found it was difficult to do so, because it was so full. He checked the floor of the bedroom and closet for dried blood and did not find any. But he did locate "two small amounts of dried blood" on the right side of the kitchen phone, which he believed to be the one Patty used to dial 911.

This was, in Woodmansee's mind, a major piece of evidence. If Patty was bleeding when she was on the bed and again when she called 911, why was there no blood in the places where she was in-between? In fact, Patty had not used the kitchen phone, which she thought the rapist had disabled, but the one behind the couch. And if these spots were in fact dried blood from Patty's cut, as he assumed, they had somehow not been noticed by the crime scene investigator, who had examined the phone and dusted it for prints thirteen days earlier.

The following evening, as arranged, Mark arrived at the Madison Police Department's detective bureau. During this interview, Woodmansee asked almost nothing about the alleged assault or possible suspects. His sole purpose, it seemed, was to obtain his case's crucial missing element: motive. Why would Patty make up something like this?

Woodmansee quizzed Mark about their relationship. Mark said he had known Patty as a friend and drinking companion for more than twenty years, but it was only a little more than a year ago that they started going out. In recent months, he had "been somewhat trying to get out of the relationship" because she wanted "a real marriage-type commitment" and he didn't. "I have even quit making love to her," he said, explaining that the last time they were intimate was during the trip to Sheboygan, just as Patty had said. "I like her, but I'll be honest with you: I'm looking to settle down with someone, but not with Patty." She was too jealous; once she "became unglued with me at a bar" when he began talking to a female acquaintance.

Mark was a fount of information pertinent to Woodmansee's case. He told the detective Patty was overly concerned about her weight and that "her doctor has her on Prozac." She "gets real emotional about things" and has a lot of stress from her two jobs. Like him, she tended to drink too much. "At times," he said, "Patty seems like she might have what someone calls a mental chemical depreciation." Woodmansee put this nonsense term in his report, and later on his list, as though it were some actual diagnosis.

Was Patty suicidal? Mark, noting that Patty's brother and nephew had taken their own lives, replied, "I have a fear that she will commit suicide, but she's never really laid that on me heavy." He said Patty had confided to him that she was sexually molested as a child, by her step-father. Mark found it strange that Patty maintained a cordial relationship with this man. But he also was convinced, based on his talks with Patty, that the abuse did occur.

What about Patty's visual impairment? "I don't know how blind she is," replied Mark. "If we're driving down the street and I look at a woman she's right on it and gets upset."

Could he describe Patty's demeanor on the day of the assault? "She seems pretty tough over this," said Mark, noting that people react differently to being sexually assaulted. "She wasn't overly emotional." He added that Patty had mentioned the anal assault and complained about pain in this area.

How did Mark feel about Patty staying at his house? Conflicted. On one hand, it seemed almost as though Patty were moving in, and he was uncomfortable with that. He did not wish to pursue a relationship, and she understood that. Although the two shared a bed, they were not intimate. Mark wanted it to stay that way. On the other hand, "I'm not going to make her go home. I'm taking it day by day."

Did Mark have any concerns about Patty? Yes, he told Woodmansee, according to the detective's report; he was worried about "her scorn" if he did extricate himself from the relationship. "Obviously a sexual assault must have occurred," he said, since Patty told him "there was all this evidence." Woodmansee explained that while items were collected, no one had yet determined if there was evidence of an assault.

"Do you think she would make this up?" Woodmansee asked. Mark wasn't sure. "I think in some instances, Patty . . ." He paused, fumbling for words. "I guess her temper takes over her rational mind. I would hope she wouldn't do something like that but there is something that makes me think she could make this up to get me to stay with her, but I hope not."

Woodmansee had what he was looking for. He thanked Mark for his time and escorted him from the building. The next day Woodmansee contacted Kaddatz, the crime scene investigator, and asked him to process Patty's alarm clock, to see if he could determine what time it had been set for. Kaddatz said this information had been lost when the clock was unplugged. He checked it for fingerprints, finding none.

During the next week and a half, while he waited for the sexual assault kit results, Woodmansee took no further action on Patty's case, other than to discuss his suspicions with other detectives. He also had Detective Draeger listen to the tape of Patty's 911 call; she agreed that Patty sounded too calm. One of Woodmansee's supervisors, Captain Jeffrey LaMar, said he had heard from residents of the Fairmont Avenue area who were worried about a possible rapist on the loose. If Woodmansee's suspicions proved correct, and Patty was making it up, LaMar advised, the department should issue a press release to put such concerns to rest.

On September 29, a Monday, Woodmansee got a call from the state crime lab. Its examination of the sexual assault kit turned up no semen or other evidence. Woodmansee also had Kaddatz run tests on items collected from the crime scene. The Flowering Herbs Body Splash bottle was checked for fingerprints; none were found. Patty's pants and shirt were examined for traces of blood; again, the result was negative. The other items—Patty's bedding, bra, and bedroom phone—remained unexamined.

Tom Woodmansee had all of the evidence he needed. He called Patty to set up a meeting at the detective bureau. His intention was to confront her, but he didn't tell her that. Instead he lied, saying he needed some additional hair samples. They arranged to meet at 6 p.m. on Thursday, October 2. Patty came away from the call believing there had been a break in the case. Finally, she thought, some good news.

8

The Confession

Patty arrived at police headquarters in an upbeat mood. Misty had dropped her off, and she arrived carrying a wrapped birthday present for Brenda, whom she planned to see later. Woodmansee met Patty inside the building and led her down a hallway to a room with a small table and large windows. After a few minutes he took her to a tiny room in the building's basement. It was a former jail cell, with cement block walls and no windows. It contained a table and chairs, a sink against one wall, and a toilet. Woodmansee introduced Patty to another detective, Linda Draeger, who would be sitting in. Patty was glad to have a woman present. Discussing a sexual assault with a male detective was difficult, and she assumed a woman would be more sympathetic. She was in for quite a surprise.

Woodmansee got coffee for everyone and closed the door behind him. Draeger asked about the wrapped package on the table, and Patty explained that it was a birthday present for her sister. It was just a T-shirt, she said jokingly: "Cheap, but a gift nonetheless." No one laughed.

The detectives got right to the point. "I know who did this," Woodmansee announced. Patty was heartened, thinking this was the good news she was hoping for. Then he lowered the boom: "You did." Patty laughed. She thought he was joking. He wasn't. Woodmansee said he believed Patty made a false allegation, that there had been no sexual assault. "I know you made this up."

Patty was thunderstruck. She had no idea this was coming. She began breathing heavily. "I can't believe this," she said. "I'm scared to sleep in my room." How could the police not believe her? "There was someone in there," she insisted. "He was in there a long time."

Woodmansee had had enough. He told Patty he had worked many hours on her case and produced many pages of reports, all of which led him to the same conclusion: it didn't happen. Meanwhile, he had put off investigating several other cases—child abuse cases, she remembered him saying. This made her feel guilty. "I know, I know it was for nothing," she said, according to his report. Woodmansee said he knew Patty suffered from depression and had seen a counselor in the past. He mentioned her past suicide attempts and the fact that her brother and nephew had taken their own lives. He brought up her past history of sexual abuse as a child. She and Mark were not getting along, and she had problems with Misty. She had lied to her daughter about having named Dominic as a suspect. And Mark had given him reason to believe she was capable of making up the whole thing.

Patty asked that her case be assigned to another detective and was told this would not happen because the rape did not occur. She offered to take a lie detector test or undergo hypnosis to prove she was telling the truth. Draeger said Patty could hire a polygraph examiner if she wanted, but police had no need for this information because they knew she was lying.

Woodmansee proceeded to cite the inconsistencies and lack of evidence that led him to conclude the rape did not occur. Blood was not found where he thought it should be. The alarm clock times did not add up. The closet she claimed to have stood in was full of stuff. She could not see the suspect, yet seemed to have no trouble picking up the knocked-over grill. Her vision, said Woodmansee, did not appear to be noticeably bad. Patty, typically, agreed with this attempt to minimize her disability: "I don't think it is that bad."

The state crime lab, Woodmansee told Patty, found no evidence of sexual assault. All of the other detectives he talked to thought she was lying. He said the sexual assault nurse at Meriter found no sign of trauma. All of Patty's injuries were consistent with self-infliction. There was no sperm on the cotton swabs, no stray pubic hairs, nothing to prove she was raped. "There wasn't even any rubber residue," Woodmansee told her, explaining that a test for latex residue from the condom she claimed her assailant used had come back negative. This was a complete fabrication, a "ruse" he concocted to increase the pressure on Patty to confess. These are all things Woodmansee admitted, either in his report or later, under oath.

By Patty's account, he also told her, "You don't act like a rape victim." He later denied saying this; Draeger said she couldn't remember. Patty said he warned that, unless she confessed, the consequences would be more severe. She would be charged with the crime of obstruction, the media would be notified, and everyone—Mark, Misty, and Dominic—would be told she lied. "If you thought I was good working for you," she remembered Woodmansee saying, "you should see me working against you." But if she admitted to lying, the matter could be resolved quietly. The police would help her cut a deal with the district attorney's office, perhaps to get into a first offenders program. Woodmansee later denied making these statements; Draeger couldn't remember.

Patty also maintained that she asked to come back the next day with a counselor or an attorney, but Woodmansee refused, saying, "You'll just change your story." Woodmansee and Draeger later denied this. Patty asked to leave to smoke a cigarette but was not allowed, even though she offered to leave her purse and package to ensure she would return. Draeger said she let Patty smoke in the room, in violation of the building's no-smoking rule, to spare her from inclement weather. It was one of the few things about the events of October 2 that the veteran detective was later able to recall, and it was a critical point, since the only way police could legally question Patty without giving her Miranda warnings was if she was free to leave at any time. Draeger said it three times, three ways, all under oath: it was "cold and crummy," "cold and raining," and "cold and rainy." Actually, according to the National Climatic Data Center, Madison's weather that night was unseasonably warm—sixty-six degrees at 6 p.m.—with scattered clouds and no measurable precipitation.

At some point, Draeger asked Patty if she knew the story about "The Boy Who Cried Wolf." Draeger would later testify that she wanted Patty to "understand the importance of clearing up what had happened because I wouldn't want to see her in a situation where later down the road she may file another report and because there's one sitting out here that's questionable, this one might . . . bring questions to people's minds." The message, as Patty received it, was more blunt: if she didn't admit to making this up, she could never again expect police to believe her or to come to her assistance in a time of need.

At any rate, Patty's "confession," as recorded in Woodmansee's report, was couched in the language of fear. "What do you want to hear?" she told the detectives. "I'll say whatever you want." Woodmansee said he wanted the truth, to which she replied, "If you're going to drop this, I'll say whatever you want."

The first thing Draeger wanted to hear was contrition. "I think you owe Tom an apology," she said, citing the time and energy he had spent on her case. "You're right," Patty said, "I'm sorry." As she said this, Woodmansee noted in his report, "she looked directly at me"—which, given her visual disability, meant she couldn't see him at all.

"Do you believe that I know this is a lie?" Woodmansee asked Patty. "Yeah," she responded, her will overwhelmed. "Okay, I'm lying."

Next the detectives wanted to know why Patty had lied. She could not come up with a reason. "I don't really know why," she said. "I'm sorry, I'm very sorry. I didn't mean for this to happen." Had she told anyone else she lied about the incident? No. Did she ever consider telling Woodmansee she was lying? No.

This was not good enough. The detectives wanted details. When had the idea of fabricating a rape come to her? She said it was that same morning. Did she cut herself with the knife? Yes. Where did she get it? From the kitchen. Did she cut her finger and then place it against the pillow? Sure. Did she cause the cuts on her neck by pushing the knife or dragging it? Dragging it. Where was the knife now? "I don't know what I did with it."

The detectives continued to press Patty as to her motivation, and she continued to draw a blank. At one point, she muttered, "I wish I were dead." Woodmansee asked if she was suicidal on the day of the alleged assault and she said she was not. Draeger asked if there was a connection between Patty taking Prozac and her decision to fabricate a rape. No, Patty assured them, this wasn't it either. Woodmansee said he wanted something to put in his report so it would not look as though she were doing this for no real reason. "I'm sorry," she replied. "I just can't." She even asked the detectives why any woman would say that she was raped if it didn't occur. Patty was shocked by Draeger's response: "Women do it all the time." Draeger later admitted saying "something similar to that."

After a while of not being able to come up with the reasons they sought, Patty told the detectives her confession was phony: "I'm just saying this to get out of here." Whereupon, she recalled, Woodmansee angrily threw down his notebook and said it was time for a break. He later denied this, saying "I may have dropped it." Draeger couldn't remember.

Woodmansee left the interview room several times. He brought Patty another cup of coffee. By her account, during one of these return visits, he said his supervisor was "really pissed" to learn of her confession since he had fielded "a ton of calls" from concerned residents in the Fairmont Avenue area. Woodmansee later admitted telling Patty that his supervisor had gotten calls from people in the community concerned for their safety, but denied using the word pissed. Draeger couldn't remember.

The interrogation resumed at 7:10 p.m. From this point on, Patty didn't say anything to contradict the detectives. Had she lied about hiding in the closet? Yes, she had lied about that. Had she dumped perfume on the bed? "I dumped the perfume on the bed." Did she know she was going to lie about this whole matter when she woke up that morning? "Yeah." Was it her alarm clock that woke her? "I think so." What did she do then? "Probably got up and smoked a cigarette, 'cause I usually do."

Draeger kept at it: "Did you absolutely lie about this and plan to lie to the police about this?" "Yeah," answered Patty. Then why was it so difficult for her to come up with a reason? "I can't," was all she could say. Draeger asked Patty if she "just wanted the attention." "Apparently," answered Patty. Was she seeking attention from Brenda? "No." From Mark? "No." From Misty? "No." Did she feel closer to her daughter on the morning of the assault? "Yeah." In terms of a motive, this was as close as she came.

The detectives asked Patty how she was feeling. "Pretty bad and sad," she said. They expressed concern that she might hurt herself and she assured them she was not suicidal. She gave them the name of a psychologist, Linda Moston, whom she had seen in the past. Woodmansee left the room to call Moston but was unable to get through. He told Patty the police might hold her in jail overnight on "suicide watch." She took this as a threat. Her thought: *I have to work tomorrow!* She was given another option: go to the Dane County Mental Health Center for an evaluation. She agreed.

At about 8 p.m. Woodmansee drove Patty to the center, a nonprofit agency. On the way, he again asked why she fabricated the rape, and again she couldn't come up with anything. On arrival he told the two female crisis counselors that Patty had just confessed to making a false report. He noted that she had attempted suicide in the past and had a history of suicide in her family. He also said she had falsely accused her daughter's boyfriend, who was "in emotional turmoil" as the result of these accusations.

Patty still considered herself to be in police custody, and it was her sense that Woodmansee wanted the center to detain her. In his presence, she agreed that she lied about being raped to keep her boyfriend from leaving her and to jeopardize her daughter's relationship with the man she accused. But Patty insisted she had no intention of harming herself. The counselors let her go home on condition that she call in at two prearranged times, once before she went to bed and again in the morning.

Woodmansee gave Patty a ride back to her place on Fairmont Avenue. On the way, he asked again how she was feeling. "Embarrassed," she said. "I don't know what I'm going to say to my family and friends." He asked if she would like his help breaking the news to Mark, and she said that would be fine. He asked if there would be a problem with Misty. Patty didn't think so. As they arrived at their destination, Woodmansee asked Patty to call him the following day after she had spoken with her therapist. He asked one more time if she was feeling like hurting herself, and she said no. As Patty stepped from his police car, she said to him, "Thank you, Tom, thank you." He put it in his report.

9

Fighting Back

In some respects, the events of October 2, 1997, were more emotionally devastating to Patty than the rape itself. The man who came into her home and forced her to have sex caused terror and left lingering fear, but at least she knew that she was not to blame. The detectives who came into her life and forced her to deny this experience left deeper scars, because afterward she was filled with humiliation and remorse. If only she had stood up for herself. But, of course, Patty was never very good at that.

When Patty got back inside after Woodmansee dropped her off, Misty wanted to know what police had found, given her mother's earlier optimism. Did they have a suspect? No, said Patty, they didn't know anything. She couldn't bring herself to tell Misty what happened. She was quiet, fighting back tears. When Misty left to run an errand, there was no reason to hold back. Patty began sobbing, overcome with guilt and pain. She called the Rape Crisis Center's emergency hotline.

Later, Patty would remember little about this call, except that she cried throughout. She didn't get the name of the person she spoke to, and the person she spoke to—a volunteer named Annie—did not get hers. But Annie did log a call at 9:21 p.m. from a woman who said she was raped the month before and had just been forced to recant under pressure from police. She said police wouldn't let her go until she admitted that she made up the whole thing. Now she was afraid the perpetrator would come back, having gotten away with it the first time. Annie provided some comfort and suggested that Patty contact a lawyer with regard to her experience.

Misty returned and found her mother in tears, but Patty didn't want to discuss it. She called Mark to ask about the remarks Woodmansee had attributed to him. Mark denied ever doubting that she was raped and suggested she come over. Misty drove Patty to his place, but they saw from the car parked outside that one of his male friends was visiting. Patty was in no mood for this; Misty drove her back home.

Patty didn't sleep at all that night. As promised, she called the mental health center twice to confirm that she was still alive. She made the second call at 4 a.m., before she left for work. She didn't say a thing about having made a forced confession. Woodmansee had taken her to the center in what she perceived to be an attempt to have her locked up, and while his concern that she might harm herself was probably sincere, she didn't feel as though these were people she could trust.

That morning, at work, Patty went into her tiny coffee shop office, closed the door, and called the lawyer whose name she had gotten from the Rape Crisis Center the night before. The lawyer, a woman, said there was nothing that Patty could do, unless or until charges were filed against her. Patty asked about taking a lie detector test; the lawyer strongly discouraged this. Feeling helpless, she called the Rape Crisis Center and set up an appointment to see a counselor. She also talked to her friend Cheryll, who worked in the agriculture building where Patty ran her coffee shop, telling her the whole story.

Patty's assistant drove her home early, before noon. That afternoon, she called the Wisconsin Coalition Against Sexual Assault, as Cheryll had suggested. The woman she spoke to was stunned: "This was a *Madison* detective?" Patty also called Linda Moston, the psychologist. She had counseled three of Patty's siblings and had seen Patty regularly for several years. Moston, then fifty, with a thin face and long blonde hair, considered herself a "spiritual counselor" who served as a "teacher" to her clients, whom she sometimes called students. She didn't believe in medication; her approach was to confront painful problems head on. Patty and her family presented an almost inexhaustible supply of painful problems.

Moston was on the porch at her home in Waunakee, a Madison suburb that trumpets its distinction as "the only Waunakee in the world," when Patty called. She said the police had accused her of making up a rape, even though the rape was real. From the start, Moston believed Patty. She knew Patty's past history and secrets, her weaknesses and insecurities. She knew that while Patty might be compelled to deny she was a victim, she would never make false accusations to this effect. Patty's major issue was her sense of powerlessness, owing to her childhood sexual abuse and the loss of her eyesight as a young woman. She had low self-esteem and trouble setting boundaries with others, especially men. She felt immense grief over how people had treated her and how relationships had turned out. She didn't need to manufacture new reasons to feel bad.

Indeed, while Moston was at first surprised that Patty hadn't called her about the rape itself, later this made perfect sense. Patty had plenty of experience being a victim; it was something she could handle without outside help. But the shame of having failed to stand up for herself, an issue on which Patty and Moston had worked, was too much to bear. Moston set up a time for Patty to come in.

That evening, Woodmansee called Patty at home, asking why she had not called as he had asked. According to his report, Patty "stated to me that she was now denying that she had made up the story and that she felt pressured into telling me that she had lied about it." He told her that she would be prosecuted for obstructing an officer.

Over the next several days, Woodmansee wrapped up his work on the case. He called Mark to say Patty had admitted fabricating the rape, then recanted her confession. He called Dominic to say he was no longer a suspect; Dominic had already heard the news and said he was considering suing Patty. Woodmansee also finally got through to Moston and "arranged to meet with her at a later date." No such meeting ever took place, for reasons that would prove illuminating.

Woodmansee, according to his undated report, contacted the district attorney's office on October 10 to say he would be forwarding the case for prosecution. He claimed that the police department had gotten "repeated calls" from "throughout the community" regarding "our inability to apprehend the suspect" and thus would be releasing information to the media, to allay public fears. Woodmansee's report spilled out more than twenty-five thousand words over forty-eight single-spaced pages but neglected to mention that he got Patty to come in for an interrogation under false pretenses and concocted a ruse regarding the alleged rubber residue. This was especially ironic given the report's final sentence: "Case status: Referred to DA's office for charges of obstructing."

He was asking that Patty be prosecuted for lying to police, without disclosing the lies he told to trip her up.

Meanwhile, Patty was trying to deal with the twin traumas of being raped and then disbelieved. She met with a counselor from the Rape Crisis Center and with Moston, both for about an hour. The Rape Crisis counselor, a young woman, was so upset by Patty's story that she began to cry. She suggested that Patty find a new apartment. Patty was no longer staying at Mark's house but never again spent the night in her bedroom on Fairmont Avenue. She slept on the couch and lived in fear, made worse by her belief, implanted by Draeger's speech about "The Boy Who Cried Wolf," that she could no longer turn to police for help.

One night in early October, Patty got a cab ride back to her duplex; she expected the driver would wait until she got inside, as usual. But the cab drove off, and Patty found herself hurrying to the door, keys in hand, heart pounding. She got the door open and slipped inside, in such a panic that she left her keys in the lock. She pressed her back against the door and slid to the ground. She sat there, on the floor, her body a wedge against the man she imagined would presently be trying to force his way inside. A moment passed, and Patty began to cry, thinking to herself, *If this is the way I'm going to live the rest of my life . . .*

Patty bought some pepper spray to carry in her purse. Just having it made her nervous; she could imagine reaching for it in an emergency and spraying herself in the face. So she practiced in her backyard. She sprayed a very small amount on her finger and sniffed; that made her start choking. Later, when she went to the bathroom and wiped herself, the pepper spray somehow seeped through the tissue paper. She stood there, yowling in pain and self-recrimination, as the bathtub filled slowly with warm water.

As suggested, Patty found a new apartment, a few miles away. She and Misty, then six-and-a-half months pregnant, began moving in mid-October, although the transition took until the end of the month to complete. Patty started staying at the new apartment right away, even before she moved her bed and other furniture. Her lease on Fairmont Avenue ran through June, and she was obligated to pay the rent in full until her landlord found a new tenant. The apartment remained empty until January, so Patty had to pay two rents through the end of the year—$600 a month for the old place on top of $850 a month for the new one—and even then her obligations to her former landlord would not be satisfied.

At her new apartment, another duplex, Patty set a rule: none of Misty's male friends were allowed inside, ever. One day, while they were still moving in, Patty came home to find Dominic helping Misty fix a borrowed rug cleaner. She made him leave.

Throughout this time, Patty never gave any thought to the possibility that she might be charged with a crime, as Woodmansee had announced. She considered it an idle threat and, as the days passed without charges being filed, it seemed more and more remote. She saw Moston for several more sessions. According to Moston's detailed notes and later recollection, the issue never came up. Compared with Patty's fear for her safety and anger over what police had done, it didn't even register as a concern. Patty thought about how the detectives had surprised her, accused her, threatened her, and broken her will. It offended her sense of right and wrong and made her worry about how other rape victims were treated. Still, she was prepared to swallow the humiliation and sublimate her rage, to let herself be the victim and not make a fuss.

All that changed on the morning of Wednesday, October 22, just shy of three weeks after her recantation. Patty was talking with her friend Cheryll at the coffee shop. "See the news last night?" Cheryll asked. Patty hadn't. One of the local TV stations had reported that a woman on Fairmont Avenue had admitted making a false report about having been raped the month before. Patty got a copy of that morning's *Wisconsin State Journal*, one of two local dailies, and a story was there too:

Police Say Woman Was Not Raped

MADISON—Police say a rape and home invasion reported by a Madison woman last month never happened.

A 38-year-old resident of the 700 block of Fairmount [*sic*] Avenue falsely told police a knife-wielding man came through an unlocked front door on Sept. 4 while she slept, officer Tom Snyder said Tuesday. She claimed he raped her in her bedroom.

Detectives got suspicious when they couldn't find physical evidence and when the woman's statements were inconsistent. Snyder said they confronted her . . . and she admitted fabricating the story.

The Dane County District Attorney's Office is reviewing the case for possible charges against the woman, police said. Calls to the office were not returned.

The other daily newspaper, *The Capital Times*, had run an article the day before under the headline, "Woman Admits Lying about Rape." It quoted Snyder saying such cases have repercussions for the entire community: "It affects the real, legitimate victims, the officers who spend hours investigating the case, the citizens who pay for their overtime and the neighborhood residents who were upset by the idea of a stranger assaulting this woman." Both stories were prompted by a police department press release issued October 21.

Patty did not see the *Capital Times* article until much later. The one in the *State Journal* was enough. Being publicly branded a liar with such specificity as to identify her to anyone who knew she had reported being raped—all her friends and family members—trumped Patty's concerns about taking actions that might call attention to herself. And so she adopted her posture of last resort: fighting back.

The first thing she did was contact Jill Poarch, the SANE nurse at Meriter, something she had wanted to do since October 2. Patty asked about the representations Woodmansee had attributed to her. That there was no evidence of sexual assault. That Patty's injuries were all consistent with self-infliction. That even the test for rubber residue had come back negative. Poarch told Patty she had never said any of these things and that, so far as she knew, there wasn't such a thing as a test for rubber residue. Poarch also related that Woodmansee's approach had caused her discomfort. "She said she felt interrogated," Patty later recalled. "She told him there was nothing unusual about my case but he was arguing with everything she said."

Later that day, Patty wrote a letter to the *State Journal*. At the time, the printer for Patty's primitive computer was not working, so she wrote it out by hand in large letters in her distinctive script, in which every line tilts downward, and had Misty type it up. The letter, addressed to "Editorials Department," was angry and crude.

"I cannot believe you would release such a story," it began, "without hearing from the victim. Have you asked the detectives in this case why I suddenly changed my mind and said I made it up? For one thing, the detective has met me only twice and claims to know my entire psychological make-up. I was interrogated for two hours in a closed room, without any possibility of leaving unless I said it did not happen."

The letter, without mentioning the detectives' names, listed some of what Patty described as the "many threats" made against her, including the comment, "If you think I was good working for you, you should see me working against you." She said she was told the matter would "go away quietly" if she admitted to making it up.

"What would you do?" Patty wrote. "The only answer is to say what they want to hear and get out of there so I could start trying to prove what happened. I am trying to do this with no help from the police department. The detective made the statement [that] 'women do this all the time.' Now, we have to wonder if this is true or if most women drop their case even though there is physical evidence because of the brutal treatment from the police and the court system."

The letter concluded, "The investigating detective on my case was not only unprofessional, but he may have put myself as well as other women in danger by not taking my complaint seriously. He is sending out the message that we are not to be believed." The letter was dated "10-22-97" and signed, "Sexual Assault and Police Brutality Victim."

Patty also penned another letter, this one to Woodmansee's boss. As with the first letter, she wrote it out by hand across several sheets of lined notebook paper. Misty was no longer around, but Patty's brother Bobby stopped by, and he rewrote her missive in smaller though still urgent block letters that filled two pages. It read,

Dear Supervisor:

Enclosed is a copy of the response [Patty's letter to the *State Journal*] to the irresponsible article that your detectives released to the press.

I'm sure that you've asked your detectives what led to my confession and *if* they were honest with you, they would have told you that I had no choice but to do so. It was completely obvious to me that they were not going to let me leave until they heard what they wanted to hear. When I told him 1½ hours into interrogating me, after trying to answer questions I couldn't possibly answer, that I was just saying these things to get out of there, he threw a fit, said it was break time and periodically left the room. When I offered to leave my purse and package in the room and step out for a cigarette, I wasn't even allowed to do that. I was allowed to smoke in the "non-smoking" interrogation room.

It has been proven that just about every thing these people said in that room was a lie.

I am very concerned about how your people treat victims of sexual assault. Before this happened to me I would have strongly recommended to any assaulted woman that she report it. Now I would strongly recommend that she settle down immediately afterwards, gather her thoughts, think about her next step, and prepare to be victimized again, especially if, heaven forbid, she has any history at all with depression or any minor mental illness that WILL BE used against her.

I'll tell you right now you can use this as you wish, but Tom has caused me more harm to my mental health than the entire rest of my life has.

Patty signed the letter, and wrote down her phone number. The next morning she called the Madison Police Department and got the name of Woodmansee's supervisor, Lieutenant Dennis George Riley. She missed his first name, addressing the envelope to "Lt. George Riley," adding "Please open immediately" in the upper right corner. She enclosed her letter to him, as well as a copy of her typed letter to the *State Journal,* and had it delivered to police headquarters by cab. She sent the letter to the paper via regular mail. It was never published.

Riley received and reviewed Patty's letters on the day they arrived, October 23. Madison Police Department rules require that all complaints about the conduct of police officers be forwarded to what was then called the Professional Standards Unit. Instead, Riley left the letters for his rookie charge, after affixing a Post-it note that said, "Det. Woodmansee, see me on this." That afternoon, they met to discuss the letters and what should be done with them. Riley would later say he intended that the letters be forwarded to the district attorney's office. The department was probably obligated to do so, since Patty's accusations that her confession was coerced arguably fell into the category of exculpatory evidence. Woodmansee later said that if this was Riley's intent, he misunderstood it; he put the letters in his case file and left it at that. This oversight was all the more glaring considering *when* Woodmansee referred the case to the DA's office for prosecution. But this information would remain hidden for years, known only to a handful of people with a vested interest in keeping it secret.

After sending her letter, Patty waited anxiously for a call from Woodmansee's supervisor. The number she had given was the one at her Fairmont Avenue address, where she still had her answering machine set up. She checked it every day. But he never called.

Patty continued to see Moston, going over the details of the assault and her experience at the hands of Madison police. Worried that her rapist was on the loose, she wracked her brain for details that might aid her effort "to prove what happened." Moston suggested hypnosis. Patty subsequently had two sessions with a Madison psychologist named Elizabeth Lindner, but never went under. Lindner's office was in downtown Madison, and Patty was distracted by the sound of traffic from the street outside.

On November 17, Patty visited Charlene Ackerman, a hypnotist in Janesville, a city about thirty miles from Madison. This time it worked. Patty felt as though she were in a dream state. She tearfully remembered the assault from the first moment to the last. Toward the end, as Patty was describing how she stood at the foot of her bed, alongside her assailant, Ackerman asked her to look at him. Patty tried but still couldn't tell who it was. Ackerman recorded the session and gave Patty the tape. She couldn't bear to listen and gave it to Moston, who did, taking copious notes. Moston was struck by how various bits of recollection—the cologne, the white sweatpants, the color of the assailant's skin—pointed to Dominic. In her mind, it seemed obvious that he was the one.

Patty felt pressured from all quarters to resolve her doubts about Dominic. From Brenda, from Bobby, from her other siblings, and now from Moston. Even her deteriorating relationship with Misty pushed her in this direction. Whereas throughout Woodmansee's investigation she was always less than certain, and even in her letter to the *State Journal* referred to Dominic as "one of the suspects," Patty now reached a kind of certainty.

Around this time Patty wrote some thoughts in a notebook, framed as though it were a letter to Dominic. It began: "You and I both know what happened that morning, I don't have the slightest doubt anymore." It said that although "the system is letting you off," Patty was not. "If you harm 1 hair on my daughter's head you will know power as well as what it's like to live in hell. Beware." She never sent this note to Dominic or anyone else. But, due to her daughter's greatest act of betrayal, it would be delivered nonetheless.

One night toward the end of the year, Patty got home past midnight with her friend Xavier. She thought she heard sounds coming from Misty's bedroom and reacted angrily. "Who's in there?" she demanded.

"No one," insisted Misty. But Misty's door was uncharacteristically locked and she refused to open it. Patty began pounding on the door and yelling. Xavier, in the spirit of chivalry, offered to kick the door down. Misty finally opened it, and Patty searched the closets and under the bed. No one was there.

Patty was disintegrating—mentally, physically, financially. She was drinking more than ever. She was gaining weight. She was angry with the police, with Misty, with Mark. She was paying rent on two apartments, which was at least one more than she could afford. Misty's ability to help out with household costs was about to end; her baby was due in early January. And Patty's businesses were still struggling. One bright spot: the Business Enterprise Program where Patty worked had finally authorized payment for five sessions with Connie Kilmark, the financial counselor she had met the day before the rape.

Kilmark, a frequently quoted financial expert and regular guest on Wisconsin Public Radio, had taught classes on the psychology of money for the University of Wisconsin Extension and supervised graduate students from the UW School of Social Work. Her approach in helping people with financial problems went beyond teaching traditional money-management skills to addressing underlying psychological forces. She was part financial counselor and part counselor. Kilmark and Patty got together, this time without the program reps, on January 7. At the start of the interview, Kilmark remarked that it had been quite a while since their initial meeting, wondering rhetorically when that had been.

"It was September 3," said Patty. Kilmark was taken aback. How on earth did Patty remember that? At first Patty was quiet. But, after further prodding, she revealed what had happened that night and later, during the interrogation by police. Kilmark was shocked—the forced recantation struck her as the kind of thing that could never happen in Madison—but she got a strong sense that Patty was telling the truth. Kilmark also felt it was important, not just for Patty but in the interest of justice, that the truth come out. Patty mentioned that she had written a letter to the detective's supervisor, complaining about how she was treated, but had never heard back. That gave Kilmark an idea.

The duplex on Fairmont Avenue, in a crime-scene photo taken September 4, 1997.

Patty's stripped-down bed and bloody pillows.

Above: The cut phone cord along right side of bed.

Left: The bottle of Body Splash in the clothes hamper as police found it, covered with a sock.

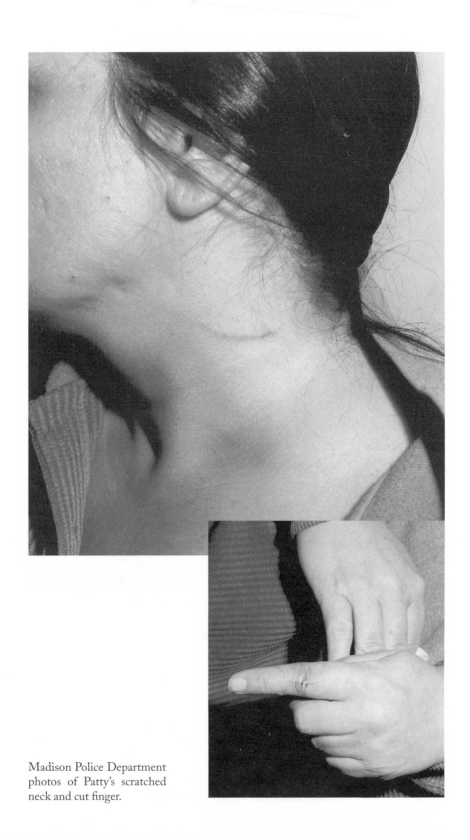

Madison Police Department photos of Patty's scratched neck and cut finger.

Left: Detective
Tom Woodmansee.

Below left: Detective
Linda Draeger.

Below right: Detective
Lauri Schwartz.

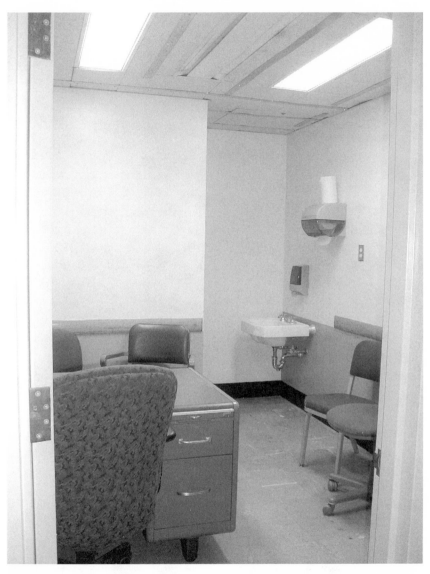

The police interrogation room where Patty's "confession" was obtained. (2005 photo by Linda Falkenstein.)

Left: Attorney
Hal Harlowe.

Below left: Judge
Jack Aulik.

Below center: Police Chief
Richard Williams.

Below right: Mayor
Sue Bauman.

PART TWO

THE NEED
TO BE BELIEVED

10

A Story to Tell

At first, Connie Kilmark wouldn't even tell me the woman's name, only that she was a client. "She's had a hard life," Kilmark related in a phone call on January 8, 1998. "Lots of family trauma, very low self-esteem. She's legally blind. Works for a state blind industries program." The day before, this client had told Kilmark that she had been raped by a knife-wielding intruder, and then badgered by police into recanting. The detective had said no one believed she was telling the truth, including the nurse who examined her. But this nurse later told the woman she had no reason to disbelieve her. Neither did Kilmark: "After twenty-two years in practice, I have a pretty good crap detector. The idea that she could be making this up flies completely in the face of my instincts about her. She has enough trouble in her life."

From what Kilmark knew of this client—and she knew a good deal, including her history of childhood sexual abuse—it made perfect sense that, when confronted by the police, she would back down.

I was acquainted with Kilmark from her appearances on Wisconsin Public Radio and because she'd been a source on stories about personal finance and consumer debt for *Isthmus*, the weekly newspaper at which I had worked for more than a decade. Kilmark decided to contact me because this woman, she understood, had tried to complain about the detective in a letter to his supervisor. This was, for *Isthmus*, a familiar subject.

It began in 1994, when I learned about a complaint filed the previous year by Madison Police Sergeant Mark Bradley against another officer,

Detective Linda Draeger. A federal prosecutor had reported that Draeger had expressed her disgust with the methods used by Bradley and a federal drug agent during the 1991 arrest of a small-time marijuana dealer. She said the pair had questioned the dealer, John Steele, with guns drawn and even held to his head, warning that he would never see his wife and children again unless he cooperated, which he did. Steele, a bit player in a large marijuana supply ring, had accused the police of this conduct at trial and ended up getting at least an extra year in prison for "lying." Indeed, Steele's eighty-seven-month sentence was far harsher than that given the ring's major players, despite undisputed testimony that he didn't use drugs himself and actually lost money in his bungled efforts to sell pot. This he did to pay medical bills for his infant son, who was born with spina bifida, hydrocephalus, and bilateral clubfeet.

When the prosecutor revealed Draeger's remarks, Steele's attorney filed a motion seeking a new trial, and Bradley lodged his complaint against Draeger. As a result, she was under investigation by the Madison Police Department and facing possible disciplinary action when an evidentiary hearing on the matter was held in December 1993. Draeger testified that Bradley had in fact held a gun to Steele's head but denied saying other things the prosecutor reported. Bradley's complaint against Draeger was "not sustained."

Madison Police Chief Richard Williams, who had overseen the department's internal investigation, told me that Draeger had merely accused Bradley of *pointing* his weapon. This was not true. Draeger, at the hearing, testified that what upset her was Bradley "putting a gun to somebody's head," not merely pointing it, adding, "there is a difference." I was struck by two things: first, that Williams apparently fudged facts to cover for an underling who allegedly held a loaded gun to a suspect's head, and second, that the department's complaint apparatus may have been used to make Draeger repudiate the statements the prosecutor reported.

Isthmus sought, under the state's open records law, copies of all complaints against Madison police officers during an eighteen-month period, as well as records showing what action was taken. Concurrently, the *Wisconsin State Journal* requested complaints against police made by members of the public—that is, not including internal complaints like the one Bradley filed against Draeger. Williams denied both requests, expressing his concern that "highly trained police officers and qualified applicants for such positions would choose other employment or make fewer arrests in order to avoid the potential invasion of privacy if they knew the contents of complaints and resolutions might be made public." Both papers sued, charging the department with violating the records law. When the cases were consolidated, the focus was narrowed to just citizen-initiated complaints.

People began contacting me with related stories. One example: A local man named Thomas Frutiger said drug task force members executing a search warrant on his apartment broke into his bathroom, threw him down, and kicked him, including one kick to the back of his head that resulted in a broken nose. No drugs were found. Frutiger lodged a complaint, which Williams ultimately deemed baseless. "I do not believe they kicked you," he wrote. "I believe your sunburned nose was bruised when you were initially placed on the floor." Williams even denied that Frutiger's nose was broken. But two physicians who treated him confirmed to me that his cartilage was fractured and he had "multiple body abrasions and contusions." In a photo taken at the time, Frutiger's face looked as though he had been pelted with rocks.

In November 1995 a Dane County judge strongly affirmed the newspapers' right to obtain citizen complaints: "Usually police officers behave in appropriate ways. But without a doubt there are officers who exceed their powers and take advantage of individuals. In order to minimize abuses of police power, society needs to have a great deal of scrutiny and oversight into any allegations of police misconduct. The alternative is to risk that police agencies go, in effect, unpoliced, and become the masters rather than the servants of society." The judge ordered the complaints released and the papers reimbursed for the $37,000 in legal costs they incurred due to the department's failure to obey the open records law.

The released records—several years' worth in one batch—showed that complaints by citizens against police were almost always resolved in favor of police. There were signs that police investigators were inclined to discount complainants' versions of events while giving accused officers the benefit of every doubt. On the other hand, some complaints were apparent attempts by citizens to shift culpability for their own bad behavior to the officers who were called on to respond.

According to the police department, the complaints most likely to be "sustained" were those filed by other officers. This became the next legal battleground. *Isthmus*, the *State Journal*, and *The Capital Times* made requests for these "internal" complaints, which would include the one from Bradley against Draeger. Chief Williams again refused, and all three papers filed another lawsuit. The police were outspoken in their opposition, and the resulting political pressure forced then Mayor Paul Soglin to retreat from statements he had made in favor of openness. His successor, Sue Bauman, promised during the campaign that she would seek to settle the lawsuit. But after the election she sided with police in their determination to keep these records secret.

The papers ultimately won this second lawsuit, although the judge ruled that the names of officers could in most cases be blacked out. Again, the city was ordered to reimburse the papers for their legal costs, which this time totaled more than $59,000. Bradley's complaint against Draeger proved threadbare and vague, and the judge's ruling did not apply to other documents, like transcripts of interviews from the police department's internal probe. The records Steele hoped would substantiate the claims for which he received an enhanced sentence were never released. His infant son would be seven by the time he got out of prison.

Sure, I told Kilmark, I would be glad to meet with this client of hers. But privately, I considered it unlikely that her story would check out. It wasn't the sort of thing I thought could possibly happen in Madison.

Several days later, Kilmark called to say the client was receptive: "She's very pleased that somebody's going to listen." Kilmark told me the woman's first name, Patty, and the detective's last one, Woodmansee, which I recognized from his study on alcohol-related police calls. We left it up to Patty to make the contact.

It was nearly the end of the month—January 27, the day newspapers across the country reported President Bill Clinton's unequivocal denial of a sexual relationship with a White House intern—before Patty called. She had deliberated for days whether this was something she wanted to do. She was still angry about what had happened, and Kilmark had impressed on her the importance of her story being told, for the sake of other women. But she was worried, with good reason, that I wouldn't believe her.

Our initial phone conversation lasted only a few minutes. Patty mentioned the letter she had sent to Woodmansee's supervisor, and I asked for copies. I had just reviewed the first of two batches of citizen complaints released by the department in response to my request for all such records from the previous year, and hadn't seen anything that resembled it. We arranged to talk more that afternoon, at the office of *Isthmus,* across the street from the Capitol.

Patty took a cab from her workplace to mine. We used the glass conference room in the front of the office. I noticed she had no trouble getting into the room or finding the chair. This didn't surprise me, since I knew from experience—including having a legally blind brother—that people with even small amounts of eyesight can often get around well. Patty said she could see peripherally, and I noticed that she looked off to the side as we spoke. She was nervous—this was clearly something she was making herself do—but she struck me as guileless. Now and then she let out a rat-a-tat nervous laugh. While we were talking, a Madison police car pulled up on the street directly in front of the office—a coincidence, no doubt. Patty didn't see it, and I didn't point it out.

The version of events that Patty provided that day was my first exposure to the facts of the case, other than Kilmark's brief synopsis. But everything she said, I would later realize, was consistent with every other account she had given up to that time, or would give, in the months and years ahead. She described how she had given in to the intruder's demands, in fear for her life and that of her then-pregnant daughter, now the nineteen-year-old mother of a newborn baby boy. How she called 911, talked to the responding officers, and went to the hospital for an exam: "I did everything I was supposed to do." How the investigating detective, Tom Woodmansee, seemed frustrated and impatient, but she never suspected he doubted her. How he and Detective Draeger had confronted her and applied all kinds of pressure to get her to recant. How she found out later that there wasn't even such a thing as a test for rubber residue.

"He just made that shit up," Patty told me. "I just fell for it." She said that as horrifying as the rape had been, the events of October 2 were worse: "Nothing could compare to what Tom did to me." She produced copies of the letters she sent to the *State Journal* and

Woodmansee's supervisor, whose name she could not remember and had not written down, except on the envelope she had used to send it.

As Patty discussed the assault and its aftermath, she would pause to remember, adding details she forgot to mention earlier. I knew from years of reporting that people who are applying spin or trying to deceive often come across as slick and practiced, while people who are trying to stick to the truth are more likely to correct themselves as they go along. But I also knew that even if Patty was telling the truth, as she saw it, her version of events might not hold up under scrutiny. At the end of our interview, I looked at her, indirectly in the eye, and asked a very important question: "Is everything you've told me true?"

"Yes," she answered. I decided to check it out.

11

Checking It Out

As I began looking into Patty's story, my first and most crucial interview was with her therapist, Linda Moston. I believed that if Patty were delusional, or prone to making false accusations, or had a tendency to exaggerate, these things would have likely been noticed by a trained psychologist who had known her for years.

Patty gave Moston permission to talk with me. We met in Moston's tiny office in a labyrinthine complex on the city's east side. She had worked with other members of Patty's family and knew well her "long history of sexual abuse as a kid growing up." She recalled that when Patty contacted her the day after her meeting with police, she was "more hysterical about that than the rape." Several days later Moston spoke briefly to Detective Woodmansee, who had left messages for her. Moston said Woodmansee told her straight off he didn't believe Patty was raped and was eager to close the case. His attitude gave her the creeps. "I didn't trust him," she told me. "I just intuitively got the sense about this guy that it was dangerous for me to talk to him." And so she didn't.

Moston produced pads of yellow legal paper filled with detailed notes of her sessions with Patty. She had also listened to and taken notes on Patty's taped session with hypnotist Charlene Ackerman. These notes conveyed intimate details of the assault, including a reference to the passing of gas. Moston even told me the one thing about which Patty, in talking with Woodmansee, had been untruthful—saying she was dry in the vaginal area. "She did this out of fear that if she told Tom she was wet this would indicate a willingness to participate in the assault," she said, reading from her yellow pads. The lubrication was her body's attempt "to diminish the amount of pain involved in the rape."

Patty, explained Moston, assented to the intruder's demands "out of survival and fear for her life and the safety of her daughter." Being "the type of person who doesn't like to risk conflict," she did not want her daughter to know she suspected Dominic, who Moston seemed convinced—perhaps more so than Patty—was the rapist. "She was terrified of the repercussions with her daughter and her boyfriend," said Moston, who felt Woodmansee used "psychological terror" to manipulate Patty's conflict-avoidance instincts. Besides, "Here's a person who's basically ignorant of her rights. He totally took advantage of that ignorance and went for the kill." Moston called Patty "the perfect victim" because "she doesn't stand up to anybody."

Several times, Moston said there was "no doubt in my mind" that Patty was telling the truth, about both the assault and her experience with police: "This woman does not have the personality nor the desire to make up something like this." And Moston supported Patty's decisions to write Woodmansee's supervisor and tell her story to the press. "Patty," she told me, "is the type of person who would bury this. She has to grieve this and learn from this experience, give other women the courage to come forward."

I also spoke with Ackerman, the hypnotist in Janesville. She told me it was possible for a person to fake being hypnotized or to lie under hypnosis, but she was pretty sure that didn't happen here: "My educated guess from all my experience is, yes, she was hypnotized, and she was recalling the experience correctly."

Patty's encounters with Moston and Ackerman occurred *after* the police had determined that she lied about being raped and succeeded in getting her to recant. Why would Patty scrape together money for sessions with a therapist and hypnotist and then lie all the way through them? It didn't make any sense.

My next calls were to experts in the field of sexual assault, regarding false claims. Erin Thornley, then head of the Wisconsin Coalition Against Sexual Assault, said, "Women rarely lie about being sexually assaulted," and noted that not all unsubstantiated reports are false. Sometimes, a case might not be pursued because the rapist "goes bowling with the chief of police or hunts with other police officers in town." Sometimes charges are not filed because prosecutors don't think there is enough evidence. Sometimes victims "change their minds because of fear."

Michael Morrill, education director of the local Rape Crisis Center, agreed false reporting was rare but said recanting was not. "Victims do recant, and they do it for a variety of reasons," including pressure from their families, social groups, and rapists. He even knew of cases where victims said that "the police haven't believed their story and have pressured them to say they lied." But he didn't think this happened in Madison, where the police took an especially "progressive" approach to these crimes. Morrill singled out one detective in particular, a fellow who no longer handled sexual assaults but still took part in a Violence Against Women training group that went around the state teaching other officers to be more sensitive. The detective's name was Tom Woodmansee.

"He's outstanding," said Morrill, who at the time knew nothing about Patty's case. "He's absolutely first-rate. If we could have everyone like Tom, we'd be in great shape."

I looked into how often the legal system sees cases of false reporting, and how it responds. Patti Seger, who worked in the district attorney's Domestic Violence Unit, seemed to think there were already too many disincentives to reporting assaults, like being subjected to "intensely personal" questions and getting "ripped to shreds" by defense lawyers. Indeed, she told me, "If I were a sexual assault victim, I don't know if I'd report it." Seger could think of "at least one case" where a false report led to prosecution and directed me to Judy Schwaemle, one of the office's three deputy district attorneys, for more information.

Schwaemle was a veteran prosecutor—tall, imposing, dedicated, tough as a jailhouse wall. Technically, she was the first female district attorney in Dane County history, since she headed the office for about a week the previous fall before the newly named Republican appointee, Diane Nicks, took over. Schwaemle was well liked and respected, but her reputation had one notable blemish: In 1991, she secured a sexual assault conviction against a man named Anthony Hicks, who was freed after serving nearly five years in prison when DNA tests excluded him as the source of a pubic hair found at the scene. Schwaemle, saying the new tests only introduced an element of "reasonable doubt," never admitted error or apologized, drawing an editorial rebuke from the conservative *Wisconsin State Journal.*

Most of the sources I spoke to indicated the justice system was wary about prosecuting "false" sexual assault reports, for fear of discouraging others from coming forward. But Schwaemle, when I interviewed her on February 2, said "sexual assault is no different than any other crime when it comes to false reporting." The charge of obstruction was a Class A misdemeanor punishable by up to nine months in jail and a $10,000 fine. But the only specific case she could think of where her office had charged someone for making false allegations of sexual assault was "not a matter of public record" because charges had not yet been filed. It started to dawn on me what case she was talking about. Schwaemle confirmed it: Patty, whom she identified by last name, was going to be formally charged with obstruction later that week. She should have already received a summons to appear.

Patty, it turned out, had not gotten the summons because it had been sent to her old address, on Fairmont Avenue. She didn't know about the charges until I told her, the following day. She reacted with great surprise. "I wasn't even scared of that," she told me. "I didn't think they'd have the audacity." And in fact, not once in our conversations had she mentioned any concern about criminal charges. Four months had passed since Woodmansee made this threat, and nothing had happened.

Patty hoped police would "admit what went on in that room" on October 2, but tempered any optimism with a fateful prediction about Woodmansee: "He's not ever going to admit he's wrong." She knew she needed a lawyer, and I suggested David Knoll, the son of Erwin Knoll, the late editor of *The Progressive* magazine. Knoll, a thin, wiry reed of a man with a predilection for using big words, had graduated from law school a few years earlier to begin a career "keeping ne'er-do-wells out of prison," as his father proudly put it. He agreed to represent Patty, at least for her initial court appearance.

In the meantime, I asked police spokesperson Tom Snyder about the case. "We get lied to all the time, of course," Snyder told me, after checking in with Woodmansee. "In most cases no one is charged. In this case, it was because of the significant amount of time he put into the case. He put in forty-plus hours of investigation before she admitted she made up the story."

Snyder presumably did not know, nor would I until much later, that nearly all this time was spent investigating the alleged victim and not the alleged crime. "I know it was troubling for Tom," Snyder continued. "He told me he wanted to believe this woman, he wanted to believe the story was true, and he wanted to arrest the bad guy. But nothing added up." Later, Snyder related something else Woodmansee had told him— that he came to doubt Patty's story because she "didn't act like a rape victim."

Woodmansee, who recently had transferred to the Dane County Narcotics and Gang Task Force, a multijurisdiction unit that primarily investigates drug activity, declined my interview request. He left me a voice-mail message: "My supervisor won't allow me to discuss the case while it's in the DA's office, which I'm sure you're probably aware of and understand. I just wanted to return the call because I heard you were trying to reach me."

Becky Westerfelt, executive director of the local Rape Crisis Center, confirmed that Patty had spoken to one of the group's volunteers on the evening of October 2 and later came in for counseling, maintaining that her recantation was coerced. "We don't have any reason to think she's not credible," said Westerfelt, who couldn't fathom why criminal charges were being filed. "What makes this case so egregious?" She thought this undercut her group's goal of removing barriers that keep victims from reporting.

Jill Poarch, the nurse at Meriter, was reluctant to discuss the particulars of Patty's case and worried about any story that might call attention to a woman not being believed. I asked about rubber residue. Poarch, after checking with the Wisconsin State Crime Laboratory, reiterated her original belief: "There is no such test, so they would never tell anyone there was no rubber residue found."

Poarch's supervisor, Colleen O'Brien, contacted Woodmansee's supervisor, Lieutenant Dennis Riley. Afterward, she told me that Riley had provided "all this information" about the case that set her mind at ease as to the conduct of police. As a result, O'Brien advised me it would be unwise to regard Patty's account as reliable. I spoke again with Poarch, who acknowledged feeling that Woodmansee approached his investigation with some "preconceived ideas" that aroused her concern. She also admitted being upset by the things Woodmansee reputedly said—that she found no evidence of sexual assault and did not believe Patty was raped. But since my initial contact, Poarch had talked with Woodmansee, who denied saying these things. "Now that I've spoken to him and his boss, Dennis Riley," Poarch told me, "I don't know what to believe anymore."

Patty still could not remember the name of the supervisor to whom she had sent her letter of complaint. She thought it was an old name, maybe "Frank" or "Fred." I called Riley directly, to see what he knew. Riley was evasive, saying his policy was not to talk to the media: "I don't trust them." Was Riley the person to whom Patty sent her letter? "Not to my knowledge," he told me. I read portions of Patty's "Dear Supervisor" letter aloud to him and he drew a complete blank: "I do not remember the letter. I do not have a copy of the letter."

Well, then, who did? On February 5 I called Lieutenant Patrick Malloy, then head of the Madison Police Department's Professional Standards Unit. By now I had reviewed what the department said were *all* the complaints received from citizens in 1997, and Patty's was not among them. Malloy knew of no such complaint, but promised to look into it. Early the next morning Malloy told me what he found: "What was delivered up here was to Lieutenant Riley and Riley basically gave this to Woodmansee to put in his file and that's where I retrieved it yesterday afternoon."

Malloy said this should not have happened—the letters should have been forwarded to his unit for review. Even so, Malloy planned no action against Riley nor any investigation into Patty's complaint, which he interpreted as being primarily a response to the fact that she was facing criminal charges: "I would assume that what she said in these letters is basically what her defense will be in court."

Patty came to court on the day she was supposed to, accompanied by Knoll, her friend Cheryll, and a legal advocate from the Rape Crisis Center. But Patty's case was never called; the summons, sent January 21, had come back as undelivered and was in the process of being refiled. In the hallway, Knoll sternly admonished Patty not to talk to me. Not then, not ever. It was not surprising: defense attorneys typically discourage their clients from talking to the press. But my research was mostly complete, and there was no turning back on my plan to write about the case.

Patty's initial appearance was rescheduled for February 9. She met Knoll at the courthouse, missing another morning of work. Knoll stood mute as the charges were read, and the court commissioner entered a not guilty plea on Patty's behalf. She was released on a $500 signature bond, a pretrial conference was set for April 2, and the criminal complaint became public. Curiously it contained nothing that contradicted Patty's account. It said she had reported being raped and later, when confronted by Detectives Woodmansee and Draeger, admitted, "Okay, I'm lying." Okay to what? Why had the detectives doubted her account? What did they tell her before she confessed? The complaint, signed by Deputy District Attorney Jill Karofsky, shed no light on these things.

The issue of *Isthmus* containing my forty-four-hundred-word story on Patty's case hit the street three days later, on February 12, 1998. It was one of the few times in my career that I expected a piece of writing to have a dramatic impact. Police and prosecutors would see what I had found — the testimony of Moston, Misty, Kilmark, Ackerman, and Patty herself — and reverse course. They would realize there was a chance, if not a likelihood, that an actual rape victim was being charged with a crime. They would take a new look at the case and make sure Patty's original report was more fully investigated. I was very naive.

12

Up against the System

There persists, in some quarters, a belief that the criminal justice system is fundamentally about justice. But most people with real-world familiarity with how courts and law enforcement work harbor no such illusion. Sooner or later, they come to see that the key word in the phrase "criminal justice system" is not "justice" or even "criminal" but "system."

In the week after my article was published, I tried to talk to Police Chief Williams, but he did not return my calls. Neither did Mayor Bauman, the only local official with statutory authority to give orders to the police. Patty's prosecutor, Deputy District Attorney Jill Karofsky, a petite thirty-one-year-old with a squelched, Kermit-the-frog voice, stood by her charging decision: "I read the article. I also saw the police reports. I can see there are a lot of differences." She wouldn't elaborate.

What about Patty's recently unearthed letters alleging police coercion? Karofsky had received them but felt they contained "no new facts." What about Moston's therapy notes or the hypnotist's tape recording, in which Patty provides a detailed account of a rape the cops say never occurred? Wouldn't these be of interest? Not in the least.

Karofsky's boss, District Attorney Diane Nicks, was equally tight-lipped and defensive. A thin, fidgety former assistant attorney general who nearly knocked herself out trying, with only limited success, to win the confidence of people in her office, Nicks said she was ethically obligated not to say anything that might interfere with Patty's pending prosecution. Didn't she also have an ethical obligation to intervene if a person was being wrongfully prosecuted? Nicks called this area of the law "extremely complicated."

Becky Westerfelt said several women had called the Rape Crisis Center wondering whether it was safe to report a sexual assault to the Madison police. She suggested two alternatives: asking one of the center's advocates to be present during questioning or reporting the assault to the state Justice Department, rather than the Madison police.

I wrote a short follow-up article that incorporated these reactions under the headline, "Can Rape Victims Trust the System?" Like the first, it generated no media interest and only a few, mostly negative responses. Several men praised the police for taking a skeptical view toward women who cry rape, citing studies showing epidemic levels of false reporting.

Being charged with a crime placed a huge additional burden on Patty's already fragile psyche. She and Mark had resumed a platonic relationship, but it was even more strained than before. He denied saying the things Woodmansee attributed to him, but Patty remained resentful. One night she got drunk and took it out on his car, which he had left in her garage. She flung chairs at it, cracking the windshield and putting large scratches and dents in the exterior. Misty came down and made her stop. Despite this, Patty and Mark remained friends and he continued to help her with her vending business.

Another time, when Patty had been out drinking, she came home to find that Misty had allowed Dominic's nephew to sleep on the couch. She flew into a rage, and she and Misty got into a physical fight. Misty, already in her bed, heard Patty yelling things like "it runs in the family" and "you're all assholes" at her houseguest. The nephew sought refuge in Misty's room, and Patty followed. Misty got up and pushed her mother to the wall in the hallway. Patty grabbed her daughter around her neck. Misty, swearing up a storm, kicked her mother in the stomach to free herself, then locked herself in her room. She even called the police but, as the altercation subsided, declined their offer to send assistance.

Knoll thought my coverage of Patty's case "substantially complicated the process of trying to do something for this woman. You've raised the stakes on this." His job, as he saw it, was "not to tilt at windmills or try to change the police department." No good could come from that or from shining a spotlight on injustice. That would only make people in the system dig in their heels.

At the time, I considered Knoll's perspective offensively cynical. If the system was making a mistake, then the media's job was to point it out. Keeping quiet about injustices as a strategy for correcting them cut against my instincts. Surely the system wasn't so sinister that it would rather be wrong than admit its own capacity for error. Or was it?

I tried getting a tape of Patty's 911 call. The director of Dane County Public Safety Communications, coincidentally named Jimmy Patty, declined my oral request, saying Madison police opposed its release. I filed a written request reminding Patty that he was the official custodian, and the cops were not. Patty listened to the call and applied what under Wisconsin's open records law is known as a balancing test—weighing the public's right to know against any possible harm from disclosure. On the basis of this review, he decided to release the tape; he notified the district attorney's office and police of his intent. This triggered a visit from Madison Police Detective Lauri Schwartz, who physically removed the tape from the 911 center. I then tried getting it from the police department, whose records custodian turned me down, saying Karofsky felt its release "may seriously jeopardize prosecution."

On another front, I looked into the conduct of Lieutenant Dennis Riley, who had received Patty's letters of complaint only to hand them over to Woodmansee. The department's official rules on "Complaint Acceptance and Investigation" set forth: "Every employee of the department has the responsibility to insure that a citizen complaint, on being expressed, is received and referred to the appropriate unit or supervisor." Unless the complaint was considered minor—defined as alleging conduct that, if confirmed, would result in discipline less than a letter of reprimand—Riley was required to pass it on to the Professional Standards Unit.

It was hard to see how Patty's complaint could be considered minor. The allegations it leveled—that police detectives used lies and threats to coerce a rape victim into recanting—were significantly more serious than any of the thirty citizen complaints the department acknowledged receiving in 1997. (Among these bona fide complaints: a handwritten letter to "Police Chief Willie Williams" from a jail inmate alleging the officer who arrested him was racially biased, and a grievance from a man seeking "the names and addresses and phone numbers of the young ladies who falsely accused me of following them.") Even for a minor complaint, Riley was rule-bound to investigate and inform the complainant of various options, which he didn't do. Plus he apparently lied to me in denying any knowledge of Patty's letters. I informed Marc Eisen, my editor at *Isthmus,* that I wanted to file charges against Riley with the Madison Police and Fire Commission.

State law charged the PFC with hiring police and fire chiefs and imposing major discipline on officers. While the law gave the commission explicit authority to initiate disciplinary proceedings on its own, in practice the only complaints it heard were those brought by chiefs and, on occasion, by citizens. The process was hardly user-friendly—the complaining party had to marshal evidence and present a case—but by law it was open to anyone. "In fact," PFC attorney Scott Herrick boasted, "when chiefs use it for discipline purposes they are using exactly the same process that a citizen can use." There was even a precedent for its use by media, as the founding editor of *The Capital Times* had once filed charges against the chief of police. Eisen said he'd think it over.

In mid-February I was contacted by a local physician who reported that her teenage daughter's best friend, on seeing my article, exclaimed that this was "the same detective," Tom Woodmansee, with whom she had a bad experience. The girl wanted to tell her story and her parents gave me permission to talk to her, provided that I use a pseudonym. "Cathy" and a friend came to the *Isthmus* office on a Sunday and we spoke in the glass conference room. She was eager to talk: "This guy is obviously not working for people but against people and that's scary."

The previous September, during a sleepover at another friend's house, Cathy woke to find her friend's brother, also a juvenile, in bed with her, touching her breast and moving his hand down to the buttons of her pants. Cathy reported this to her mother, who contacted a counselor at East High School, which both Cathy and the perpetrator attended. The counselor, Kim Gary, called the police. The case was initially investigated by officer James Witalison, who the year before got a sixty-day suspension and $326 fine for urinating into an unsuspecting homeless man's whiskey bottle and then watching him drink from it before arresting him for open intoxicants. Witalison spoke to the boy, who admitted getting into bed with Cathy but denied touching her. The case was then assigned to Woodmansee, who met with Cathy in her home on September 25. The interview lasted three hours. Cathy felt that Woodmansee doubted her account. "He came across a lot different than the other officer [Witalison]," she told me. "He came off as a jerk." Later I spoke to Cathy's father, who also thought Woodmansee was cocky, especially regarding his plans to interview the boy: "He said he had a way of making people talk."

On October 3, the day after securing Patty's "confession," Woodmansee interviewed the boy at his home. He now admitted touching Cathy's breast and lying about it to Witalison. The boy's mother told me that Woodmansee had promised the boy his earlier denials would not be held against him. The Dane County District Attorney's Office initially decided against prosecuting. Cathy and her mother protested this decision, and the office reversed itself. The boy was charged with fourth-degree sexual assault and obstructing an officer for lying to Witalison. (He was eventually convicted on the assault charge and sentenced to six months' probation.)

In mid-November, four days after this charging-decision reversal, Woodmansee showed up at East High, where he saw Cathy in the school office. He asked to speak with her in private, escorted her to an empty room, and closed the door. There, according to Cathy, he demanded to know why she had changed her mind about wanting the boy charged. (Earlier, she had just wanted him to admit what he had done and for no one at school to find out about it.) Woodmansee, she related, dug into her: "What do you want me to do, put him in prison and throw away the key?" Cathy said she wanted the boy punished because he was continuing to harass other girls at school. To which Woodmansee allegedly replied, "I can't put him in jail for being an asshole. He has to break the law. If he runs a stop light, then I can get him." At one point, Cathy remembered, Woodmansee pulled back his coat so she could see his badge and gun. He asked her what she wanted done. Cathy's response: "I want to leave. Right now." She bolted from the room.

Woodmansee left and counselor Gary was summoned to the scene. "I remember it well," Gary told me. "She was very upset and crying." Cathy called her mother from school. "Oh, Mom, he was so mean to me," she said, according to her mother's contemporaneous notes. Cathy's mother tried contacting Woodmansee's supervisor, Riley, to complain, but never got through. When she told me this, I mentioned that the police department had a complaint unit and even forms. Cathy subsequently filed a five-page handwritten complaint.

Woodmansee again refused to talk to me. Assistant Principal Lee Thomas said Woodmansee was at the school on another matter and just happened to run into Cathy. But then Thomas learned that the meeting took place behind closed doors, a clear violation of school district rules that required police to get permission before interviewing students on school grounds. "You can't just come in here and talk to somebody," Thomas said. "Not if you're a detective. Not if you're a parent, or a friend. Not if you're the mayor." The longtime principal, Milt McPike, a former professional football player, forcefully agreed: "A detective does not come into this building unless he comes to me."

Madison school officials ended up winking at this flagrant violation, on grounds that Woodmansee was purportedly in the building for another purpose. John Olsen, then the district's safety coordinator, put it like this: "The police concluded it was inadvertent. We're certainly sorry she felt traumatized by this event. But we don't think he intentionally broke the rules."

The police department dismissed Cathy's complaint with similar dispatch. Woodmansee was exonerated of any and all wrongdoing. I wasn't. Cathy, in speaking to Malloy, the complaint investigator, mentioned something I had said—that her coming forward might be helpful to Patty, about whom she had expressed concern. Malloy relayed this to others in the department. One officer later breathlessly notified the mayor's office that I "SOLICITED another citizen, a juvenile, to file a complaint against Woodmansee." The cops were digging in their heels.

13

The People's Lawyer

Hal Harlowe understood as well as anyone that while the criminal justice system could be, in a word, "ugly," it could also be ennobling. He had seen the system at its best and worst, from both sides. Early in his career, he had prosecuted criminal cases as an assistant district attorney in Wisconsin's Rock County and for the state Justice Department. He also had worked as a criminal defense attorney in Milwaukee and Madison. Over the years, Harlowe had seen dangerous criminals avoid punishment and good people who made mistakes involving drugs or anger get railroaded by prosecutors who seemed to have anger-management issues of their own. "What would really invigorate the system," he often said, "would be having DAs and public defenders switch jobs every few years."

In 1973, when Harlowe was a state prosecutor, he handled a horrific case involving a young Chippewa man who allegedly beat two elderly women to death on an Indian reservation. The man had a long history of violence and told a friend he committed the crime. But the evidence against him was slim, due in part to shoddy police work. (Harlowe himself found the murder weapon, a tire iron tossed into a hamper that local authorities managed to overlook.) A self-described "hotshot," Harlowe thought he put on a good case and was confident in a conviction; instead, the all-white jury returned a not guilty verdict. The Native Americans in the room began wailing. "It was like the unrestrained moaning you hear at a funeral," he later recalled. "It came straight from their souls. It went back in time and bespoke ages of suffering." That sound—of justice denied—was forever etched in his mind.

Nine years later, Harlowe, then with a public interest law center that advocated on behalf of juveniles and the disabled, ran for Dane County district attorney and won. During the campaign, he characterized the position as "the people's lawyer." After a few months in office, he was less sanguine, calling the job "the ultimate test of someone's optimism. The inclination to appeal to people's meaner and baser instincts can be pretty strong."

As district attorney, Harlowe reorganized the office, creating a separate unit for misdemeanor and traffic cases, which Jill Karofsky later came to head. During his tenure, the number of local prosecutions for domestic violence rose from about a dozen to six hundred a year. Like most district attorneys with large staffs, Harlowe personally prosecuted only a handful of cases. One of these was a double murder that for him evoked memories of the killings on the reservation.

In 1984, an imprisoned white supremacist, Joseph Paul Franklin, confessed to murdering an interracial couple in Madison seven years earlier. Franklin had been convicted of slaying two black men in Salt Lake City who offended him by jogging with a white woman. (He was acquitted of the 1980 shooting of civil rights leader Vernon Jordan and suspected of other crimes, including the 1978 shooting that paralyzed porn publisher Larry Flynt.) Franklin, angling for a transfer from a predominantly black federal prison, said he had come to Madison to kill a local white judge who made national news by ascribing blame to a white teenage girl who was sexually assaulted by three black men. At the shopping mall, Franklin decided on the spur of the moment to "send this nigger and white bitch to hell."

Harlowe noted that despite four life sentences, two each under state and federal law, Franklin might someday get out of prison. Moreover, he felt the families of his Madison victims deserved justice. And so he had Franklin brought back to Dane County for a week-long trial. Just prior to the verdict, in the library of Harlowe's office, there was another spontaneous eruption of emotion: family members clasped hands and prayed for justice. The jury found Franklin guilty; the judge added two more life sentences and sent him back to the same federal prison.

After three terms as district attorney, Harlowe in 1989 returned to private practice, doing criminal defense and professional licensing. He remained remarkably charitable in his view of human nature, even resisting the temptation to demonize Joseph Paul Franklin, an easy target. "People like Franklin are convenient to use as foils in the struggle against evil in the world and against the evil that may lurk in each of us," he reflected several years after the trial. "And you can pretty comfortably align yourself against a man like that in an effort to place yourself on the side of good. But I think once you go beyond that and try to judge an individual, you should do it with humility and compassion."

Harlowe became one of the Madison area's most successful defense attorneys. His forte was not flashy, high-profile cases, but situations where people exercised bad judgment and ended up in the system's tentacles. One of his clients was Dominic's mother, whose arrest on drug charges triggered parole revocation proceedings in Wisconsin and Texas. Harlowe ultimately prevailed, but only after she spent nearly a year in jail. Like other defense attorneys, Harlowe usually represented people who were more-or-less guilty as charged; his job was to minimize the consequences. But in late 1997 Harlowe landed a client whose innocence he believed in absolutely. Her name was Susan Pankow.

Pankow was accused of deliberately breaking the leg of thirteen-month-old "Alicia" at her home child-care center. She was charged with intentional physical abuse of a child, a felony that carried a maximum ten-year prison sentence, as well as misdemeanor child neglect. She had already lost her child-care license and with it her livelihood. The major evidence against Pankow was the confession obtained by Detectives Tom Woodmansee and Lauri Schwartz. At a probable cause hearing in December, Harlowe had gotten Woodmansee to describe, without conceding the possibility of error, how he had planted the suggestions for Pankow's distraught admissions. How he had asked Pankow if she was "frustrated" while changing Alicia, before she used this word herself. How he asked if she heard a cracking noise and she answered, "possibly a crack." How even her confession was speculative: "Oh, God, if I did this . . ."

On February 20, 1998, Harlowe filed a motion seeking to suppress Pankow's statements. No Miranda warnings were given "although such warnings were required by the circumstances of the interrogation." The interrogation lasted more than two hours, "during which time the defendant was isolated and subjected to intimidating and coercive techniques. The resulting statements were involuntary." Harlowe knew it was unlikely that Pankow's statements would be thrown out; contrary to the impression given on television shows, criminal suspects are rarely read their rights and judges seldom exclude incriminating evidence. But he thought it was worth a try, and he wanted to signal his displeasure with Woodmansee's approach.

The detective, Harlowe felt, had used a well-known but risky style of interrogation that involved planting suggestions, inviting speculation, and then misinterpreting answers in ways that ratcheted up culpability. He skillfully used these methods to get Pankow to make admissions that could be used against her. Then, whether due to inexperience, arrogance, or a lack of supervision, he came to believe that he had solved the crime. Harlowe considered Woodmansee "dangerous."

And so Harlowe was intrigued when his friend Connie Kilmark asked him to consider taking over as Patty's attorney. David Knoll had advised Patty to plead guilty to the obstruction charge in exchange for getting into a deferred prosecution program for first offenders. Patty didn't want to do this, since it meant publicly admitting that the police were right and she had lied about being raped. She asked Kilmark, who was still counseling her on financial matters, if she knew an attorney who would be willing to fight.

In mid-March Harlowe met with Patty and Kilmark at his law office, a gorgeous historic landmark in downtown Madison, a stone's throw from Lake Mendota. They went into Harlowe's spacious chamber and sat around the conference table. Patty got a good feeling from Harlowe, who was soft-spoken and patient. Harlowe liked Patty and considered her credible but left open the possibility that, as was often the case with criminal defense clients, the story she told initially was not the whole truth.

Harlowe required a $5,000 retainer, a sum beyond Patty's means. She scraped together $2,000 and borrowed $3,000 from her sister Sue, who lived in La Crosse, in western Wisconsin, and was married to a police officer. Patty sent Knoll a thank you card saying she had decided to "finish this case with another attorney" and asking him to send a bill. Knoll, in an equally thoughtful gesture, never did.

On March 26 Deputy District Attorney Karofsky offered a settlement, the same that Knoll thought he could obtain: if Patty pled guilty to the obstruction charge, her office would refer her to a first offenders program. This meant there would be no jail time and, if Patty kept out of trouble for a prescribed period, her conviction would be dismissed. Harlowe brought the offer to Patty, calling it hard to pass up. If she went to trial and lost, she would probably get probation, at least, and be publicly humiliated.

Patty didn't blink. She emphatically rejected any deal that would require her to admit guilt. Harlowe was gradually persuaded that, in Patty, he had another of his profession's most elusive finds: an innocent defendant. He had given her plenty of room to amend her original story, but she had no need to. She was credible, consistent, and, above all, courageous. "I was struck by her bravery," Harlowe said later. "It really was courage in the purest sense of the word. She was terribly frightened and yet she was determined to go right into the jaws of what she feared most."

Karofsky's settlement offer was accompanied by the police reports, including Woodmansee's forty-eight-page tome, which provided the basis for the prosecution's case. When Harlowe read through this material, he was shocked that Woodmansee had included so much information that raised doubts about his investigation and the reliability of Patty's "confession," right down to noting that she had prefaced it by stating, "If you're going to drop this, I'll say whatever you want." Harlowe also took note of references to Patty's vision, which Woodmansee concluded was not "noticeably bad." He contacted Dr. Thomas Stevens, an ophthalmologist who had examined Patty in the past. Stevens confirmed that she had a severe visual impairment and most likely could not distinguish a person's features in a dimly lit room.

Beyond that, Harlowe thought the case against Patty was woefully weak. The only "evidence" that she had lied, aside from her recantation, was Mark's comment, in response to Woodmansee's leading questions, that "there is something that makes me think she could make this up to get me to stay with her, but I hope not." Reading this portion of the report, Harlowe scrawled in the margin, derisively, "The truth revealed! The boyfriend breaks the case!" Harlowe, in reviewing the reports, also noticed that much of the evidence collected at the crime scene, including Patty's bedding, was never sent to the state crime lab for analysis. This was not done until several weeks after he took on the case, apparently as the result of his inquiries.

After additional discussions with Marc Eisen, my editor at *Isthmus,* I got the go-ahead to bring a Police and Fire Commission (PFC) complaint against Lieutenant Riley. At Eisen's urging, I called Riley in late March to tell him of my intent. I acknowledged the possibility that my understanding of the situation was incomplete and invited him to provide any information that might clear things up. Riley chose not to and hung up.

The following Monday morning, Detective Lauri Schwartz called me at *Isthmus.* She said she had something very important to discuss and asked to meet. I had some prior contact with Schwartz, regarding her concerns over media access to citizen complaints against police, after which I had praised her in print as "a good cop, one of many in Madison." The only thing I knew about Schwartz's involvement in Patty's case was that she had seized the 911 tape to keep it from being released to me. We went to the coffee shop across the street.

Schwartz had just had a profound experience in the form of a three-day seminar called the Landmark Forum. This somewhat controversial program, an outgrowth of Werner Erhard's "est," helps people achieve personal breakthroughs, after which they are expected to bring in prospective recruits to hear testimonials. Schwartz, glassy-eyed and galvanized, decided to pick me, saying she realized the good that could come to the community from our connecting on a personal level. She even offered to pay the seminar's $350 cost. As a final incentive, she said she was now the lead detective on Patty's case, and would be willing to discuss it with me once we had, thanks to Landmark Forum, "a common vocabulary."

I ended up going to Chicago—a three-hour trip each way—to hear Schwartz and others deliver testimonials to the program, followed by a high-pressure pitch to sign up for the experience, which I resisted. The next day, April 1, 1998, I filed a formal complaint against Riley with the PFC. It charged that he had violated department policy regarding complaint acceptance and investigation, then lied to me in denying knowledge of Patty's letters.

Schwartz and I remained in contact. She assured me she had no doubt Patty was correctly charged, saying the officers involved were "believable" and "trustworthy." She said there was evidence, including phone calls, that she could not share with me. And, she insisted, if an error had been made, there would be no reluctance to admit it: "We are committed to owning our mistakes."

On the evening of April 14 Schwartz called me at home, saying Karofsky had asked her to get a "witnessed statement" regarding the case. While another detective listened in, Schwartz asked if I had any relevant information. I said there was plenty of information in my articles, such as the corroborating testimony of therapist Moston, hypnotist Ackerman, and counselor Kilmark. Schwartz said she had not read these articles.

Harlowe, when I spoke to him the next day, scoffed at this: *Of course* she read the articles. What detective wouldn't want as much information as possible? But Schwartz, it turned out, was apparently as clueless as she claimed. In her police report on this contact, she got details wrong—such as rendering Moston's name as Linda M. Auston—that were stated correctly in my articles. Schwartz never contacted these other individuals. Her only interest, as Harlowe surmised, was to shore up the prosecution's case. "Don't trust her," he warned me. "She's potentially ruthless. She's trying to manipulate you."

As for Karofsky, Harlowe felt she was "trying to salvage a bad case." He knew that, when challenged, the first instinct of prosecutors and police is always to circle their wagons. And so he endeavored to appeal to their better instincts, to not put them on the defensive or make them feel that they would "lose face" by acting in his clients' interest. It was through this sort of backdoor diplomacy, not by expressing the indignation he felt, that Harlowe managed to get the charges against Pankow dismissed.

A Philadelphia-based expert who examined X rays at Harlowe's request found evidence of two previous breaks to Alicia's leg. Medical records showed her parents had some months back sought treatment for a leg injury they claimed was due to a swing accident. The expert, who had previously worked only as a prosecution witness, was prepared to testify that these breaks were consistent with systematic abuse.

Harlowe met with District Attorney Diane Nicks, suggesting it would be better for the office to reconsider its charging decision than for this new evidence to come out in open court. Nicks agreed. On April 16, a week before Pankow's trial was set to begin, Nicks asked that the charges be dismissed, saying the investigation was being reopened:

"We're going to start fresh." Harlowe was magnanimous in victory, saying Nicks's decision "really reflects, I think, the system working."

Privately, Harlowe was disgusted by Woodmansee and Schwartz's investigation. "They were trying to tie the case up," he told me. "It wasn't a search for truth. It was a search for a defendant." And now this "substandard police work" would greatly complicate any attempt to charge the actual perpetrators.

The police, however, were apparently determined to affirm their original judgment. As I was preparing an article on these events, Madison Police Lieutenant Cheri Maples called to give me a "heads up." There was, she said, a "strong potential" that Pankow would be charged again: "I'm going to warn you right now." She didn't want me to have egg on my face. But despite their best efforts, the Madison police were never able to rebuild their case against Pankow. No one was ever charged for breaking little Alicia's legs, again and again.

14

Discovery

On April 24, 1998, a candlelight vigil was held for Patty outside Madison Police Department headquarters. Organized by a campus antiviolence group, it drew about two dozen people and one television news crew. Patty attended but at Harlowe's urging did not speak or call attention to herself. Several women shared stories of unsympathetic treatment from local law enforcement. Afterward Patty sent organizers a thank-you note, which read in part: "I was tearfully moved by the overwhelming presence of support. I no longer feel I'm going through this horrible experience alone. I'm sure you can imagine the last six months have been hell for me."

In many ways, however, Patty was more isolated than ever. Some of her friends and family members, for whom denial was a primary coping mechanism, had pulled away because of all that had happened. Her relationship with Misty, who after a brief hiatus had resumed seeing Dominic, remained bitter and contentious. And Patty's former landlord sublet her old apartment on Fairmont for significantly less than what she had been paying, then sued her in small claims court for the difference. When the matter came to trial in early April, the landlord's lawyer brought along one of the initial newspaper articles about a woman on her block who admitted lying about being raped. He said he would introduce it if Patty tried to use the rape as a reason for moving before the end of her lease. She made no such claim and the court commissioner ordered her to pay $701. Patty, crying, told the lawyer to add this to "the rest of the shit this has cost me" and walked out. The judgment was never satisfied.

Among the people at the vigil was a woman named Cami, a former welfare mom who had gone on to become a successful computer technician. Cami was appalled that Patty was being charged with a crime and called District Attorney Nicks to demand an explanation. Nicks said her office believed that the obstruction charge could be proven. As Cami interpreted this, perhaps a bit harshly, the office didn't care whether Patty was guilty or innocent and had no concerns about the public policy implications of prosecuting a woman who said she was raped. All that mattered was whether it could win.

Cami wrote Patty a note, which I passed on, commending her courage. Patty wrote me back: "I wish I was the strong and brave woman she thinks I am. The truth is, I'm feeling pretty weak and profoundly sad these days. I am working hard at being the woman she thinks I am. I feel that when I can actively participate in this fight, it will change me drastically. I am looking forward to that day." This was, in the truest sense, a self-fulfilling prophecy.

Detective Schwartz received records of phone calls from Patty's former residence, from mid-August through mid-October. The numbers were traced to a host of individuals, from Patty's family members to the assistant at her coffee shop. But one number—which the records showed was dialed at 4:12 on the morning of the alleged assault—proved elusive. Schwartz's file documents multiple efforts to track this number down by checking with cellular and paging service companies. They all said it wasn't theirs, frustrating the police inquiry. Later, Harlowe employed a different investigative technique: dialing the number. The person on the other end answered "911." It was the phone company's seven-digit analog for an emergency call.

My complaint against Riley was moving forward, or so it seemed. The PFC scheduled four evidentiary hearings, in June and July. The city hired a local attorney, Paul Schwarzenbart, to defend Riley, as state law required for cases not initiated by police. Schwarzenbart issued a curt, two-page answer to my complaint. It denied that Patty's letter was a citizen complaint under department rules or that Riley had made untruthful statements when he claimed to have no recollection of having received it.

The next step was discovery. With some help from James Friedman, a local attorney who had represented *Isthmus* on open records issues, I drew up a set of interrogatories, requests for document production and requests for admission. Schwarzenbart, in turn, subpoenaed me to appear at a deposition in late April and to produce "any and all notes or documents of any kind" related to Patty's letters or discussions I had with others about them. I complied, submitting a stack of photocopies as well as a letter that decoded my handwriting. The deposition took place at Schwarzenbart's office. Riley, a solidly built, square-faced man a few months shy of fifty, glared at me from across the conference table. It lasted about two hours and consisted mainly of going over the material I had produced.

Three days later Riley responded to my discovery request. He — or rather, Schwarzenbart — refused to provide any documents and frustrated my requests for admissions whenever possible. But Riley acknowledged having discussed Patty's letters with Woodmansee and Captain Jeff LaMar at the time they were received, only to later completely forget not only the letters but also these conversations.

Using the power afforded under PFC rules, I served subpoenas on eight individuals: Detectives Woodmansee and Draeger, Lieutenant Malloy, Captain LaMar, Police Chief Williams, Deputy District Attorney Karofsky, and Jill Poarch and Colleen O'Brien at Meriter Hospital. I subsequently served Karofsky with a second subpoena, ordering her to appear at a deposition and produce copies of primary case records, including police reports.

Karofsky filed a motion to quash both subpoenas, citing Wisconsin Supreme Court rules barring attorneys from "extrajudicial statements" that may affect a pending case. She also said my request for documents was "more encompassing then [*sic*] what the State is required to disclose to defendants in criminal cases," warning that if the PFC denied her motion "there would be little to stop every defendant in Madison from filing complaints with the commission in order to get discovery to which they would not otherwise be entitled." While expressing skepticism over this claim, I narrowed my request to only those documents that had already been provided to Patty's lawyer.

Schwarzenbart backed Karofsky's motion, saying the documents I sought were not relevant to my causes of action. He also moved to disallow any testimony or evidence related to the police investigation into Patty's sexual assault. At a PFC hearing in late May, Schwarzenbart, appearing via speakerphone, argued that I was trying to turn my complaint against Riley into "a mini-trial of the criminal case against [Patty]." I countered that the basic facts and documents regarding Woodmansee's investigation were key to assessing what Riley knew and when he knew it. The PFC decided to postpone hearings on the Riley complaint "until resolution of the criminal matter" against Patty.

Around this time, the Dane County District Attorney's Office came under fire for two other cases involving sexual assault. In the first, prosecutors cut a deal to let a forty-two-year-old city of Madison parks employee get off with one year of work-release jail time and probation for raping a nineteen-year-old coworker on the job. ("It just came over me," he told police.) In the second case, the office declined to prosecute a UW–Madison athlete and his friend who allegedly raped a female student, saying the case was too hard to prove. The student, Danielle McGuire, went public with her story, enlisting the support of the National Coalition Against Violent Athletes and appearing as a guest on NBC's *Leeza*, a daytime talk show. A second woman came forward to report being assaulted, two months before McGuire, by the same athlete. But the office still declined to press charges.

McGuire alleged that her assailant's status as an athlete afforded special protection. District Attorney Nicks, Deputy District Attorney Schwaemle, and victim/witness specialist Mark Kerman all insisted this had nothing to do with it. "What we decided," said Schwaemle, "was that this was not a case which can be prosecuted, which is to say that there was not evidence beyond a reasonable doubt." But McGuire remembered Kerman stating that because the man she accused was an athlete, "it would be a high-profile case and we don't want to put you through that." She also claimed Schwaemle had said, "Sometimes when a woman says no, she means yes, and coercion is a natural part of sex." Schwaemle declined to confirm or deny this remark; Kerman said his "high-profile" comment was "taken totally out of context."

Rather than making the office eager to demonstrate its enlightened approach toward sexual assault, these controversies seemed to make it more intransigent. Nicks was especially offended by media coverage of these cases, feeling that her office had been unfairly tainted. Patty's prosecution became an opportunity for vindication, wherein the office could prove that it was taking a stand against false reports, not genuine victims. It could not back down without running the risk of looking bad, a primary concern.

Dominic, meanwhile, was having public-relations problems of his own. In mid-June he and a friend were arrested for attacking a stranger outside a Madison convenience store. Dominic had accosted the man, an African American, saying, "You're a fucking nigger and you need to die," then tried to hit him with a twenty-eight-inch black aluminum baseball bat. Dominic's buddy, Kenneth, egged him on, shouting, "Whoop that nigger, whoop his ass." The man managed to get the bat away and police arrived in time to nab both attackers. Dominic was charged with disorderly conduct while armed; Kenneth, who had tried to run, was charged with disorderly conduct, resisting arrest, and violating probation. Interestingly Dominic as charged faced a lower maximum penalty for this incident than did Patty for obstruction—ninety days as opposed to nine months. (In the end, he got a $330 fine and no jail time.)

Patty's trial was originally set to begin the second week of May, but the date was pushed back several times. One delay happened at the prosecutor's request. "The State would not be prepared to go to trial in June because it has yet to receive test results from the State Crime Lab that are vital to its case," Karofsky wrote the court. "In addition, I will be on my honeymoon during the month of July. As a result, I respectfully request that this case be scheduled some time in August." Jack Aulik, the reserve judge assigned to Patty's case, agreed. The new trial date: August 6.

In preparation, Harlowe asked Patty's ophthalmologist, Dr. Thomas Stevens, to put his conclusions about her visual acuity in writing. After a fresh examination, Stevens wrote a letter stating that Patty "has a central loss of vision which would make it impossible to identify a face in good or bad light." Although her peripheral vision allowed her "to get around and avoid bumping into large objects," she was "considerably worse than legally blind in both eyes."

Harlowe also researched the issue of involuntary confessions. Earlier that year the *New York Times* ran an article headlined, "Police Refine Methods So Potent, Even the Innocent Have Confessed." Many of these methods, the paper said, are delineated in a manual, *Criminal Interrogations and Confessions,* used by police departments across the country. The manual instructs interrogators to methodically heighten suspects' level of anxiety, often by lying about evidence, to the point where they make incriminating admissions just to take the pressure off. Harlowe also located scientific papers on this topic and found case law regarding confessions obtained through heavy-handed and coercive tactics. He planned to file a motion to exclude Patty's confession on these grounds. But before he could do so, there was a development that threw the prosecution's case into a tailspin.

On June 29 the Wisconsin State Crime Laboratory reported the results of testing that the police had initially not bothered to do. It was a shocker: semen had been found on Patty's bedsheet, in quantities sufficient to allow for DNA testing.

15

"The Enemy"

It might seem reasonable to assume that the belated discovery of semen at the scene of a reported rape would cause police and prosecutors to waver in their insistence that the alleged victim was lying. Instead, this development was viewed as an obstacle to overcome. Deputy District Attorney Karofsky, on learning about the crime lab's finding, contacted Detective Lauri Schwartz, who launched an investigation apparently aimed at finding some explanation for this evidence that would allow the prosecution to proceed. She started with the primary suspect, Dominic, but seemed mainly interested in ruling him out, conjuring farfetched theories about how his semen may have found its way into Patty's bed without his having been there.

Schwartz's investigation, as detailed in her reports, represented a dramatic escalation of the Madison Police Department's efforts to discredit Patty. These reports were filled with self-serving accusations from highly questionable sources whose credibility was never doubted or motives impugned. "This lady is crazy," she quoted Dominic saying about Patty when she called to ask him to provide samples for DNA testing. Dominic initially declined, on the advice of his attorney. Schwartz persisted, driving to a residence on the outer reaches of Dane County where Dominic was then living with his mother, Carol. No one answered, so she waited in her unmarked squad. After a while Dominic arrived, and it was discovered that Carol had been home all along. Schwartz and Carol conversed at the kitchen table while Dominic stayed within earshot in an adjoining room.

Carol told the detective about a call she claimed to have gotten from Brenda. Brenda was angry that Dominic was now dating her niece and announced her plans for revenge, saying, "That son-of-a-bitch is not going to get away with this because I will do anything it takes to see him rot in jail." Carol was positive that Dominic was innocent because he had spent the night of the alleged rape at her apartment, along with her daughter Dora. Of course, Carol could not vouch for this personally because she was in jail at the time. She had only recently been released, after ten months, with Hal Harlowe's help. Carol claimed Harlowe admitted he had a "vendetta against the police department or some police officer."

When Schwartz explained that she wanted to collect hair and blood samples from Dominic, he joined them at the kitchen table. "I'm scared, this is a setup," he declared, noting that he had stayed over at Misty's place and that Patty could have moved things between rooms, perhaps with Misty's cooperation. "I wouldn't put nothing past either of them," said Dominic. He described Patty as a chronic alcoholic who abused Misty. His only examples: the time she banged on Misty's door, accusing her of being with someone; and the time she confronted Misty about letting Dominic's nephew sleep over, and the two had fought. Dominic speculated that Patty had procured one of his used condoms, and Carol scolded him in front of the detective for not being more careful.

In the end Dominic agreed to provide samples. And why not? Even if his DNA matched, the police were apparently willing to believe that Patty had surreptitiously obtained his semen, dumped it onto her bedsheet, and then never sought to call attention to it, even after she was told there wasn't any evidence and she was charged with a crime for reporting the rape. Dominic followed Schwartz in his own vehicle to Meriter Hospital, where head and pubic hair samples were collected and blood was drawn.

That same day, June 30, Schwartz met with Mark at his place of employment. He said he remained friends with Patty and believed "something really happened" to her the previous September. The last time he and Patty had sexual relations in her room was "at least a few weeks or possibly up to two months" before this. Schwartz, assuring Mark that he was not a suspect, asked to obtain blood and hair samples. Mark begged off, citing a prior commitment. He said he would call later to arrange a time.

The next day Schwartz met with Dominic's sister Dora at police headquarters. This was, apparently, the police department's first attempt to check out his alibi. Dora stated that on the night of the alleged assault, she and Dominic were at their mother's apartment. She was certain he was there all night because she was up frequently breast-feeding her new baby. Besides, Dominic was still so wasted from partying the night before that he was "in no condition to drive." Dora, whose car Dominic had damaged in an earlier fit of substance-induced rage, stressed that she did not approve of his drinking.

By striking happenstance, Dora said Brenda had also spoken to her about Dominic, vowing "to do whatever I can to put him in jail." (Brenda later denied saying any such thing.) After passing on hearsay about Patty, Dora produced two handwritten documents, two pages each, that Misty had found while digging through her mom's belongings. One was Brenda's list of reasons to suspect Dominic. The other was Patty's never-sent note accusing Dominic and warning him against harming her daughter. These Misty had given to Dora, who now turned them over to the police.

Schwartz also met that day with Misty, at Carol's home. Misty provided names and numbers for other family members and identified individuals whose numbers appeared on Patty's phone records. She gave the full names of two men—Russ and Doug—whom Patty had dated the previous year. She said that, before the assault, her mother never came home with any man Misty didn't know, but that this had happened since on one occasion. Misty confirmed that her mother had damaged Mark's car. She described the incidents where Patty had pounded on her door and fought with her after finding Dominic's nephew asleep on the couch.

According to her report, Schwartz told Misty "there was some concern about her mother having access to body fluids and/or hair belonging to Dominic." Misty agreed this was possible but did not think her mother was trying to set up anyone. She reiterated that Patty always locked the door to her room when she was away, ruling out a setup perpetrated by someone else. Schwartz asked about Patty's alleged childhood sexual abuse and past suicide attempts, about which Misty knew little. But she said her mother drank quite a bit and was seeing a thera-pist, whose name Schwartz now recorded as "Linda Mauston."

On July 2 Schwartz met with Doug, who confirmed having dated Patty the summer of the alleged assault. He said he had spoken to Patty after the rape and "thought it strange [that] absolutely nothing was taken" from her bedroom. Schwartz put this statement in her report without noting that it was false: Patty had always maintained that the intruder robbed her. Schwartz asked Doug for samples; he had been drinking and requested a ride to Meriter Hospital, which she provided.

Schwartz then went to pick up Mark, who also agreed to give sam-ples but was, by his own reckoning, too drunk to drive. Before she ar-rived, Mark spoke to an attorney, Marcus Berghahn, who urged him not to comply until he had a chance to investigate. Mark, intoxicated, turned Schwartz away from his door. She closed out the day with an 11 p.m. call to Patty's remaining former suitor, Russ. He said the last time he and Patty were intimate was in mid-February 1997, more than six months and presumably quite a few sheet washings before the alleged assault. He was not asked for samples. Russ told the detective he considered Patty a decent, reliable person and had no doubt that she was telling the truth.

Attorney Berghahn spoke to Harlowe that evening and sent him a letter the following day. Berghahn had since spoken to Schwartz, who "was quite adamant and lost her cool surprisingly quick." He outlined two "scenarios" for why Schwartz was "running around late at night col-lecting samples from Patty's male friends and acquaintances." The first was that "the State is seeing the light and is now looking for the assail-ant." The second was that it was trying to tie the semen to someone with whom Patty had consensual relations so this discovery could be "accounted for and explained away" and potentially even used against her. Berghahn noted that under this second scenario, submitting to sampling did not expose Mark to significant risks. Several days later, Mark provided the requested samples.

Schwartz delivered materials from all three men—Dominic, Doug, and Mark—to the state crime lab for analysis, which would take about three weeks. Meantime, the case against Patty was being challenged on another front.

In a motion filed July 7, Harlowe sought to exclude all state-ments stemming from Patty's October 2 interrogation, saying she "was subjected to improper techniques and influences that were both intimidating and coercive." The detectives, he alleged, failed to issue Miranda warnings and set out to "coerce and control" his client's mind, undercutting her ability to think rationally. Harlowe zeroed in on their assertion that Patty's vision was not noticeably bad, contrary to the findings of her ophthalmologist, which he attached.

"Imagine the extraordinary fear and disorientation of a blind person," Harlowe wrote, "being placed in an interrogation room and confronted by accusing officers" who say they know she is lying and is not really blind. Such tactics overwhelmed Patty's ability to resist, to the point where the statements she made could not be considered voluntary.

The motion would be decided by Reserve Judge Jack Aulik, a balding, jowly jurist then in his midsixties. Aulik had a mixed reputation. He had helped pioneer Dane County's drug court, where first-time offenders can avoid jail time or a criminal record if they complete a regimen of drug treatment and testing. Earlier that year, he had dispensed a merciful sentence of probation while bestowing personal praise on one of Harlowe's clients, an African American community activist who had fraudulently obtained prescription drugs. But Aulik had also been suspended for ninety days for having improper communications with an attorney in a civil case and, more recently, was forced to apologize after calling a probation agent a "broad" and "a typical left-wing, communist, two-bit probation officer" in remarks inadvertently recorded on a voice-mail message.

Perhaps the best harbinger of Judge Aulik's role in Patty's ordeal was a case he handled a few weeks before. Patricia Davis—a single mother with no criminal record—was charged with a felony after a police handwriting expert concluded she had signed a check that was stolen from an elderly patient at her workplace and cashed by someone using her identification. Davis spent a night in jail and was soon fired from her two jobs. Her attorney, Dan Stein, argued that her ID was likely stolen by a coworker convicted of a spate of nearly identical crimes, including one involving the same elderly patient. But Judge Aulik shut down this defense, saying, "There's no relevance that I can see." Another judge later ordered additional handwriting analysis that proved the coworker's guilt. Davis never received restitution or even a public apology.

Harlowe considered it unlikely that Aulik would disallow Patty's confession. What little hope he had was predicated on two factors: that the conduct of police was especially egregious and that Aulik might be open to an appeal to his sense of decency and compassion. Earlier that month, the judge had been diagnosed with liver cancer, after battling colon cancer the year before.

But mainly, Harlowe told me, he wanted to "have a crack" at questioning Woodmansee under oath. He was also curious about how Patty would do on the witness stand but planned to call her only if he sensed a strong chance of winning. Harlowe, on the eve of Patty's hearing, marveled at the lengths to which the police were going to account for the newly discovered semen: "They've spent more time and energy on this case than several homicides I've seen." He said the other side had adopted a "war mentality" in which Patty had become "the Enemy" and the goal was to vindicate Woodmansee's poor police work. "This case," he reflected, "is a rape victim's worst nightmare." It was about to get worse.

16

In Search of the Truth

The hearing on Harlowe's motion to suppress Patty's confession began at 8:30 a.m. on July 9, 1998. The state was represented by Karofsky, fresh from her Independence Day nuptials, and Brian Brophy, a very tall, brash, and ambitious young prosecutor. Patty, looking frightened, sat beside Harlowe at the defendant's table. Lieutenant Cheri Maples, Detective Schwartz, and Becky Westerfelt of the Rape Crisis Center were also present.

Karofsky began by asking Judge Aulik to dismiss the motion on grounds that it lacked specificity. Harlowe countered that it was clearly about the lack of Miranda warnings and the use of coercive techniques: "I don't think there's any mystery why we're here." Aulik denied Karofsky's request.

Woodmansee, clean cut and earnest looking, was called to the stand. Karofsky asked the detective to recount his police training and his investigation into Patty's alleged assault. Early on, Harlowe objected to Woodmansee's tendency to give long answers designed to put his police work in a good light, like saying he discontinued his initial interview with Patty after three to three-and-a-half hours because "we were both tired." Aulik instructed the witness to "respond only to the question asked."

For Patty, the tone of Woodmansee's testimony was set when, in recounting his investigation, he acidly remarked that she had canceled their second scheduled meeting "to go out with some friends to a tavern." She flashed back on how he had assured her it was okay to attend the concert for which she had advance tickets and urged her to have a good time, and was beset with apprehension. She really had become the Enemy, and her accusers were prepared to say anything they could to make her look bad.

The hearing focused on what happened October 2. Woodmansee said he got Patty to come to the police department by saying he needed to collect some samples. He described the tiny room where he and Draeger conducted the interview. Karofsky then asked a series of questions. Was the defendant "ever restrained in any way?" No. "Did she ever have handcuffs on?" No. "Did she ever have leg shackles on?" No. "Did she ever have a belly chain on?" No. "Was your weapon ever shown?" No.

Karofsky was seeking to establish that Patty was never formally in custody, one of two prerequisites for Miranda warnings, the other being the asking of questions intended to elicit an incriminating response. Police everywhere commonly avoid informing defendants of their rights in situations where only one of these two factors is present, by questioning suspects who are not technically in custody or letting those who are implicate themselves with statements made in the absence of probing questions. Woodmansee testified that when Patty offered to take a polygraph, he had said, "We're done with the investigation, you can leave, you can walk out, I don't care, we're done." This statement was offered as evidence that she was free to leave at any time.

Woodmansee recalled how he and Draeger had confronted Patty with various "inconsistencies," including problems with the time frame, Patty's apparent ability to see better than she claimed, and the lack of physical evidence. Woodmansee also admitted employing a "ruse," saying a test showed no latex residue from the alleged assailant's condom. He said he used this ruse "in conjunction with saying there were no signs of rectal trauma," itself a misrepresentation. He told Patty the SANE exam had found "no sign of trauma consistent with a sexual assault." After all this, Woodmansee related, Patty broke down, saying, "What do you want to hear from me? Want do you want me to say?" He asked for the truth, to which she answered, "I'll say what you want me to say if you'll drop this." Patty then confessed to fabricating the rape but could not explain why.

There was one more major admission. Woodmansee said he discussed his concerns about Patty's mental health with his supervisor and was given two options: Patty could be taken to the Dane County Mental Health Center for an assessment or "we could arrest her for obstructing and place her on a suicide watch." Did he discuss these options with the defendant? "Yes."

Woodmansee had no choice but to admit certain things, such as the highly equivocal nature of Patty's "confession," since he had put these in his report. But he also admitted to lying about his need for samples and the test for rubber residue, which hardly made him look good. In fact, these admissions were integral to the prosecution's strategy. Harlowe was alleging that the detectives set out to undercut Patty's ability to think rationally, which the courts had deemed improper. Karofsky wanted to shift the focus to the use of police trickery and deceit, which the courts had upheld.

Harlowe, in his cross-examination, ridiculed the detective's conclusion, based on his own observations and what others had told him, that Patty's eyesight was not noticeably bad: "And, in your opinion, the very best way to determine somebody's visual acuity is to kind of ask around the neighborhood, right?" He asked whether Woodmansee had tried getting the opinion of Patty's ophthalmologist.

"Objection, relevance," exclaimed Karofsky. "Sustained," said Judge Aulik. Harlowe, believing this was essential to his case, asked whether the detective ever determined that Patty was legally blind. Karofsky again objected on grounds of relevance. Harlowe threw up his hands in frustration.

"What's that about?" demanded Aulik. "What was that gesture about?" Harlowe pressed his point: "If it is not relevant that this woman is legally blind and then she is subjected to an interview where she is told, among other things, that she is not blind and they know it, then there's nothing relevant. And I'm sorry, I shouldn't have made that gesture." Aulik sustained Karofsky's objection.

Harlowe then tried asking what effect Woodmansee expected his various statements to have on Patty. Aulik shut him down again, saying the detective's opinion was not relevant. All that mattered, the judge said, were "the conclusions and findings as a matter of law that can be made from the conduct and facts that ensued." Harlowe zeroed in on Woodmansee's conduct, especially the things he told Patty to get her to confess.

In the ensuing barrage of questioning, Woodmansee admitted telling Patty that every other detective he had talked to about her case thought she was lying. He confirmed bringing up Patty's childhood sexual abuse, past suicide attempts, history of depression, and use of Prozac. He couldn't remember if she asked to leave and come back the next day but denied that she asked to come back with a lawyer. And Woodmansee stated that, after recanting, Patty went "back and forth a couple times" as to whether she was really raped.

Finally, Harlowe probed Woodmansee's representations that the state crime lab had found no evidence of sexual assault. "You didn't tell her anything about other evidence out there that might, despite everything you were saying, confirm that she had been raped?" he asked, making an oblique reference to the newly discovered semen. Woodmansee replied, "No, I didn't tell her about other evidence that had not yet been processed." Harlowe had no further questions.

Karofsky, on redirect, tried to undo the damage. Had Woodmansee lied in telling Patty the evidence that went to the crime lab came back negative? No. Why did he say there was no physical trauma consistent with sexual assault when the SANE nurse had not reached this conclusion? This was, he said, "my interpretation" of the evidence. (Harlowe, on recross, got Woodmansee to admit he had not made this clear to Patty.) Why hadn't he mentioned the ruse in his report? Because it seemed to have "no impact." Had Patty wavered in her recantation? The detective, moments after saying she had done so, now claimed she really hadn't: "She wasn't—she wasn't wavering that this happened, she was wavering that—she was wavering that maybe we could try this, maybe we could do this. It wasn't—she would admit to lying and then she would try to think of something else like the hypnosis or the polygraph. There was a consistency that was present during her confession." Except when she wavered.

Woodmansee closed out his testimony by saying he knew the techniques he had employed "might be perceived by people as trickery and deceit." He agreed this was what it amounted to but insisted, "I didn't do it with any malice. I did it in search of the truth."

In her closing argument, Karofsky focused on Wisconsin case law regarding police deceit: "I think it's pretty clear, judge, that police officers are allowed to use deceptions and ruses in their investigations."

One case she cited was about how police conned a confession out of a murder suspect. Another involved a drug kingpin. Patty, hearing this, was astonished: Did this woman not realize how ridiculous she sounded? Did she really see no difference between lying to killers and drug lords and lying to women who say they've been raped, to see if they crack?

Karofsky, drawing from Woodmansee's testimony, asserted that the defendant had "fifteen to seventeen prior police contacts." Like him, she did not clarify that these included times Patty called police to report a theft or disturbance, or that she had no adult criminal record. She said Patty was free to leave and was never threatened with going to jail. Karofsky then contradicted herself, saying Patty was told, "We could put you upstairs and arrest you on an obstructing charge and put you on a suicide watch." The prosecutor said the evidence was "uncontroverted" that Patty never asked for an attorney. For all these reasons, she said, the motion to suppress should be denied.

Harlowe, in his closing, appealed to Aulik's "experience and common sense," saying the judge needed to take into account the totality of circumstances under which Patty recanted. Over Karofsky's objections, he endeavored to reconstruct these circumstances.

Police summon Patty—who, according to Dr. Stevens's letter, was beyond legally blind—to a surprise interrogation. They put her into a tiny room with a toilet and say they know she lied about being raped. They confront her with alleged discrepancies, including the extent of her visual impairment. Said Harlowe, "They're telling her, these two cops in a closed room at night, that we know you can see, you're lying about seeing. And then they add to that that we've talked to your daughter, we've talked to your boyfriend, every cop that's had anything to do with this case, they all know you're lying."

Patty offers to take a polygraph and is refused. She's told the test for rubber residue proves she's lying. She's told the nurse who examined her found nothing. "What she's being presented with," said Harlowe, "is a world gone mad. It is truly a Kafkaesque situation. *I'm blind.* No you're not. *I was raped.* No you weren't. *There was physical evidence.* No there wasn't."

The detectives, said Harlowe, isolated Patty. They lied to her. They conveyed to her "that no matter what the truth was, no matter what she knew, she was lying and nobody in the world would believe her." They made her feel that "there is no hope because rationality is gone." Harlowe pulled a rhetorical arrow from his quiver and aimed it between Aulik's eyes: "Judge, under those circumstances, *you* would confess."

When Patty did recant, Harlowe noted, she framed it in terms of a willingness to say whatever the detectives wanted to hear: "Does that kind of give you a tip that maybe her will is overborne, that we're not dealing with deliberateness of choice?" Harlowe, visibly angry, called what happened "one of the most rotten interrogations I've ever seen. It's an embarrassment to me as a citizen." He said Aulik's duty was not only to apply case law and constitutional principles, but "to respond to this as a decent human being getting a sense of what this citizen was put through."

Karofsky, in rebuttal, saw it differently. "The police officers in this case ought to be proud of what they did," she told the court. While no one wanted a society where rape victims are "psychologically isolated and coerced," she said, "we certainly also shouldn't be living in a society where someone's allowed to finger someone and say that person sexually assaulted me and drag their name through the mud, and that's the basis of this charge."

It was an audacious distortion. Patty had never "fingered" anyone as her assailant—her identification of Dominic to police was always equivocal. And until Woodmansee brought it up at this suppression hearing, Dominic's name had never been mentioned publicly in connection with the case. And yet it was Dominic, a drug-dealing petty thug, to whom Karofsky's sympathies flowed, and not at all to the Enemy.

The hearing lasted three-and-a-half hours. Aulik promised a written decision. Afterward Harlowe met with Patty and others in a small conference room. "What you were subjected to," he told her, "pisses me off more than anything I've seen in twenty-eight years of practice." He was pretty sure Aulik would rule against him, as he suspected all along. But he thought Woodmansee's admissions regarding the ruse and nurse Poarch would be helpful at her trial. And he told Patty that nothing from this point on would be as bad as what she just endured. Harlowe was wrong on two out of three.

Karofsky left on her honeymoon. Brophy, commenting publicly on the case, defended the police methods used as "unfortunately necessary."

He also said Patty's prosecution was proceeding because her initial rape report "created an enormous amount of fear in her particular community."

On July 14 Judge Aulik issued his decision, which came down squarely on the side of the police. "Making up stories to induce suspects to confess is not improper conduct," he wrote, ruling that Patty's admissions were voluntary and not the result of any "coerciveness." How else, he wondered, could Woodmansee "have gotten to the exact reason [the] defendant was being questioned, to extract the truth, other than to outright accuse her of lying?" Harlowe, he claimed, wanted the court to conclude "that because the defendant suffered from a physical disability she should not be subject to questioning about a very serious accusation she had made against another person." He said Patty deserved no special consideration since "the record is undisputed that the defendant had 15–17 previous police contacts." Finally, Aulik repeatedly stated that the "rouse" [*sic*] employed by Woodmansee was "about the lack of prints on the condom."

The judge hadn't even been paying close attention. Yet his ruling would acquire a life of its own, as a kind of Magna Carta for those eager to affirm that the police officers in Patty's case did everything right.

17

Honest Mistakes

Cheri Maples had had enough. After fifteen years on the job, the Madison police lieutenant felt her commitment to the enlightened treatment of crime victims had been clearly established. A lesbian, vegetarian, and practicing Buddhist, she had previously worked with a local battered women's group and served as director of the Wisconsin Coalition Against Domestic Violence. She now headed one of the Madison Police Department's outpost districts and oversaw its handling of sensitive crimes. In this capacity, she had looked into the case involving Patty and had become thoroughly disgusted. Maples believed police enjoyed enormous power and discretion that could be abused. She credited media exposés of police wrongdoing with helping clean up departments across the land. But my reporting on Patty's case? That was going too far.

Maples, no doubt expressing a majority view among her colleagues, felt I was unfairly besmirching the Madison Police Department and especially Tom Woodmansee. She saw Aulik's ruling as a complete vindication of the methods used to secure Patty's confession and thus was irked that my article on the suppression hearing focused on Woodmansee's admissions about the ruse and Harlowe's expressions of disgust.

A few days after this article was published, Maples delivered a fourteen-page, single-spaced letter attacking my reporting to my editor, Marc Eisen, with copies to people in the police department and district attorney's office. It accused me of "self-serving mudraking" and "self-righteous insistence" that I was right while "everyone else is wrong." It compared me to Kenneth Starr, the independent counsel whose crusade to bring down President Clinton was then in full flower. Maples said I had set out to "purposely manipulate and distort facts." She even asserted that I had "dragged" Cathy, the East High student, into "this drama" for my own selfish purposes.

"I have stood by and watched a number of people that I have tremendous admiration and respect for be attacked," wrote Maples. "None have been more viciously attacked than Tom Woodmansee, a person I have only known to be honest, ethical and compassionate in his dealings with the citizens he serves." At worst, her colleague was guilty of "an honest mistake." And "if it turns out that an innocent victim was falsely accused, no one will feel more sick about it than Detective Woodmansee."

The most significant statement in Maples's letter, however, was that Patty was being prosecuted not because she confessed to making a false report but because she returned to her original story: "Without the recantation of the recantation she never would have been charged." Another factor, wrote Maples, was Patty's "going to the press." This was a point-blank admission of retaliatory intent, one substantiated by subsequent revelations.

Maples appealed to Eisen: "I believe that in your role as his supervisor, you have a responsibility to rein him in." Eisen, a fair-minded and deliberate fellow with whom I had worked for a decade, met with Maples, Woodmansee, and Nicks for three hours in late July. I was not allowed to attend. Eisen felt the trio raised some valid concerns about my lack of objectivity—I had become vocal in my belief that Patty was telling the truth—but was not persuaded that my reporting was inaccurate or unfair. He declined their demand, and my offer, that I stop covering the case.

On July 29 the state crime lab reported the results of its DNA testing. Mark, Doug, and Dominic were all conclusively excluded as the source of the semen found on Patty's bedsheet. The police and prosecution had failed to explain away evidence suggesting that Patty was raped.

Harlowe's reaction was to demand that the charges be dismissed and insist that Patty receive a public apology. He even considered refusing to accept a dismissal and force the case to trial, unless an apology was received. He soon backed down from this when he realized, much to his dismay, that dismissal was not assured.

"The posture they're taking is one of concern that she falsely accused Dominic," he told me. "They're still treating her as a defendant and that's an outrage." During an August 4 meeting with Karofsky and Nicks, Harlowe argued that the district attorney's office, which he once headed, had a moral obligation to right the wrong that had been done to Patty. Their response, he related, was "mechanical"—a reiteration of Aulik's ruling that the police tactics were proper. Harlowe set up a meeting between Nicks and Patty, whom no one from the district attorney's office had ever met or spoken to. Nicks agreed, then canceled.

By all outward signs, the office still planned to take the case to trial, the date of which had again been pushed back, to September 1. Subpoenas were sent to sixteen people—an amazing number for a misdemeanor obstruction charge—including all of the police officers involved as well as Carol, Dominic, Dora, Mark, Misty, and Brenda. Jill Poarch was summoned to a trial-preparation session in the district attorney's office, where it was explained to her that the police sometimes use ruses in the course of their work.

Meanwhile Schwartz took her investigation to a new level, in a call to Patty's sister Sue. As Harlowe related this contact, the detective "asked if Patty made up being molested as a child" and tried getting the phone number for Patty's former stepfather, to check this out with him. (Sue would later testify that Schwartz also asked whether her sister might fabricate a sexual assault.) Harlowe was furious: "This has gone too far."

For Patty, the idea that police would try to find the man who molested her when she was a little girl to give him an opportunity to say she lied about that, too, was more than she could bear. Sobbing, she told Harlowe she was willing to do anything—even plead guilty and go to jail—to end this nightmare. Harlowe called Nicks to voice his outrage. Her reaction: "She groaned and said, 'Oh, my God.'" The district attorney, to her credit, brought an immediate end to this line of inquiry. "I think she was genuinely offended," said Harlowe.

Still, Nicks's office refused to concede that Patty was not a criminal. Harlowe, frustrated, filed a motion seeking to compare DNA from the recovered semen against a data bank of convicted sex offenders. A match, he argued, "would further exculpate the defendant by establishing not only that she had been raped but the identity of her assailant." The police, through Detective Schwartz, made an effort to have this done. But she was told the sample was insufficient for such analysis.

Woodmansee's reaction to the DNA results was even more strident than that of the district attorney's office. He told Eisen, my editor, that on top of all the other things Patty lied about, she apparently had a lover whose identity she failed to disclose to police. When I shared this with Patty, she laughed. If only finding boyfriends were as easy as he imagined.

Patty, for her part, was devastated that her suspicions about Dominic were apparently incorrect. She had to admit to Misty that she had been wrong. Patty also felt as though she had let down people, myself included, who had regarded her suspicions as credible, and issued heartfelt apologies.

The state's criminal prosecution of Patty ended not with a bang but a whimper. On Friday, August 21, eleven days before the scheduled trial, the Dane County District Attorney's Office dismissed the obstruction charge. At Harlowe's insistence, the words "with prejudice" were added in handwriting to the dismissal order, meaning the charge could not be refiled. The office, in trying to fax this dismissal order to Harlowe, accidentally faxed it to *Isthmus*—a fitting conclusion to this tragedy of errors.

Harlowe said the dismissal had the same significance as an acquittal and was pleased about that: "It's over. She's not going to be prosecuted anymore." But he was troubled by the reluctance of the district attorney's office to admit error and apologize, saying prosecutors "missed an opportunity to resolve this with a little more class."

In response to my requests for comment, the district attorney's office issued a statement saying that the charge against Patty had been based on "the totality of circumstances" surrounding her reported sexual assault. This included a "lack of physical evidence," "repeated changes in the account" she gave police, and the fact that she "subsequently behaved in a manner that was wholly incompatible" with her claim of sexual assault—that is, she didn't act like a rape victim. When confronted, the alleged victim made what Judge Aulik deemed to be a voluntary confession. The discovery of semen at the scene, the statement said, did not prove that Patty was raped, only that "at some point someone left semen on the sheets." Indeed, the only thing the semen established for sure was that the man she "named as her assailant" was innocent. But because the state could not prove its case beyond a reasonable doubt, the charges were dropped.

Patty wasn't willing to let it go at that. She wanted the investigation into her rape reopened. "That sperm belongs to somebody and it isn't anybody I know," she remarked angrily after the charges were dismissed. "We have evidence that I was raped. What are they going to do about that?" There was, she noted, no apology of any sort. "They're not even admitting they made a mistake." Instead the district attorney's office was proclaiming that she behaved like no rape victim should, kept changing her story, and falsely accused an innocent man.

Instead of feeling relief, Patty was overcome with pain. In the year since the rape, she had not been able to process what happened, to mourn. "I was never allowed the time," she said. "I went straight from the terror of rape, right into working with police, right into defending myself. I got robbed of that chance to grieve." Her ordeal was not over. She had to reclaim her dignity and find the man who raped her.

On August 28, a second rally in support of Patty was held on the steps of the City-County Building. It was planned before the charges were dismissed, in anticipation of Patty's trial, and about forty people turned out. One protester wore a T-shirt inscribed with the words, "You don't act like a rape victim." The main organizer, Theo Lesczynski of the campus-based Violence Prevention Advocates, said the local justice system was not serving victims: "Time and again we see them not believed when they go to the police, we see them intimidated . . . we see their cases not prosecuted." Danielle McGuire, the Madison student whose reported rape was not pursued by the district attorney's office, agreed, based on her experience: "No one wanted to listen. No one really cared." Patty's brother Bobby and sister Sue also spoke, with lingering anger, about what had happened.

Maples also did not feel as though the matter should be put to rest. She wrote a column, at Eisen's invitation, that was published in *Isthmus*. It was, like her earlier missive, an impassioned defense of the lead detective, who "did absolutely nothing wrong in investigating this case." Maples asserted that "some parts of Patty's story were not true, and any reasonably trained detective would have come to the exact same conclusion that Tom Woodmansee did." She expressed no sympathy or concern for Patty, who even the prosecution admitted may have been raped.

For Patty, this column was one of the sharpest slaps she had yet endured. She wrote Maples a letter saying that while there may have been inconsistencies in her account, she had been truthful to Woodmansee, except for her recantation. Patty recounted how Woodmansee, in questioning her, had been "forceful and impatient," suggesting they might have to go into the bedroom and "role-play this thing." She described how she recanted only after the detectives subjected her to "psychological terrorism." She noted that she never decisively named Dominic as her assailant, despite pressure from Woodmansee to do so. It was only after he abandoned her case, without looking into other suspects, that she reached this conclusion, an honest mistake: "Mind you, I am in the restaurant business, not police science and, more important, it is not my job." Patty closed by asking Maples to provide a list of things she had lied about.

Maples never provided this list, or even a single example, but she did leave a message on Patty's answering machine offering to meet. Patty, at Harlowe's emphatic urging, did not respond. But Maples's longing to justify the actions of police found another outlet: she arranged for me to meet with Woodmansee, face-to-face.

18

A Question of Standing

Detective Woodmansee and Lieutenant Maples arrived at *Isthmus* at 1 p.m. on the last day of August 1998. Eisen, who was present at their insistence, led the pair into a basement conference room. No one shook hands. The purpose of the meeting, Maples explained, was to tell me the many reasons police had for concluding that Patty was lying.

During the next several hours Woodmansee proceeded to go through a long list of reasons, working off of several pages of typewritten notes. My attempts to ask questions or make counterpoints were mostly rebuffed. I did manage to ask whether Woodmansee had said, on October 2, "If you thought I was good working for you, you should see me working against you." He admitted saying something to this effect but implied it had a softer cast. I also inquired about Susan Pankow, who four months after the dismissal of charges still had not been recharged, contrary to what Maples had indicated was likely. Woodmansee, in derisive reference to the district attorney's office, said that "if they want to let her get away with it," there was nothing he could do. This was his perspective: not that he messed up in getting a child-care provider to think she broke an infant's leg in a scenario a doctor immediately discredited, but that prosecutors had deliberately decided to let a dangerous criminal go free.

Woodmansee went through his list of reasons, one by one. Patty had said the wrong things and had the wrong reactions. There were all sorts of discrepancies in her account and no evidence in support. I noted that I was familiar with many of these points, since Harlowe had shown me a copy of Woodmansee's forty-eight-page report. He insisted on going through the list. After about two hours, Eisen left the session, citing a prior commitment. Later, he expressed bewilderment with Woodmansee's performance, how he seemed not to distinguish between major and minor points, as though what mattered most was how many he could cite.

When Woodmansee finally finished, I asked whether he thought my own impressions of the case, based on my contacts with Patty and others, might have some validity. He allowed for this possibility. I said I considered Patty credible and consistent, and that my reading of his report led me to conclude that he had botched the investigation. At this, both Woodmansee and Maples stormed out of the office. (Later, when he was asked under oath about this encounter, Woodmansee replied, "I wouldn't describe it as much of a conversation. It was a discussion in which he did most of the talking. . . .")

Now that the charges were dismissed, few people wanted to revisit what had happened. Mayor Bauman followed through on her earlier pledge to seek an investigation into the matter but asked that it be done internally, by the police. Becky Westerfelt of the Rape Crisis Center declined to push the issue, saying her agency's ability to do its job depended on maintaining good relations with the police and district attorney's office. Westerfelt even directed Erin Thornley of the Wisconsin Coalition Against Sexual Assault not to comment publicly about Patty's case. Thornley found this typical of the frustrating concessions advocates for assault victims had to make to maintain funding.

Patty, however, was having a harder time putting this matter behind her. Now, besides a painful personal history, debilitating disability, fractured relationships, and struggling businesses, she had to deal with the emotional fallout from her experiences with the police and justice system. She began seeing a clinical psychologist, Nina Bartell, whom Harlowe had recommended. Bartell did forensic work as well as psychotherapy and had extensive experience with survivors of sexual assault. She tried to help Patty deal with her stress, trauma, and need to pursue justice in a way that did not consume other aspects of her life.

As part of this process, Patty began writing a journal to help her sort out what had happened. In her large, downward-slanting script, she penned a detailed account of the rape, sexual assault exam, the day at Mark's house, and her initial meeting with "Detective Tom." That was as far as she got. The rest—including October 2—was still too painful. Later, this journal would be used as a weapon against her.

Now that the "criminal matter" had been resolved, I asked the Madison Police and Fire Commission to resume proceedings against Riley. His attorney, Paul Schwarzenbart, responded by seeking dismissal of my complaint, claiming I lacked "standing"—that is, sufficient connection to the core events to bring an action. His argument: whether or not Riley followed department rules in how he handled Patty's letters was not my concern.

I felt confident this reasoning would be rejected, since early on PFC attorney Scott Herrick explicitly assured me that standing would not be an issue. State law said the process was open to any "aggrieved person," a seemingly broad category. Besides, as I noted in response to Schwarzenbart's motion, my status as a named plaintiff in an open records lawsuit that led to a judge ordering police to release citizen complaints gave me "standing galore." What good had it done to win this legal battle if police supervisors could suppress the most serious complaints without consequence?

Schwarzenbart, in his briefs to the PFC, reiterated his claim that Patty's letter to Riley was not really a complaint "within the meaning of [police department] rules." And, after seeking to exclude all information about the alleged rape and subsequent investigation as irrelevant, he attached Judge Aulik's ruling as proof that the police used no improper tactics. But his main contention was that "aggrieved person," as defined elsewhere in the statutes, applied only to those who have sustained "a distinct and palpable injury" to their interests. My only interest was as a journalist who had made Patty's "claim of sexual assault, and her prosecution for obstruction, *causes célèbres* in *Isthmus,* as a component of what appears to be an obsessive pattern of attacks on the professionalism of the [Madison Police Department] and the Dane County District Attorney's Office." The PFC said it needed time to decide this issue, but time was running out: Riley was planning to retire in January, after which the PFC's authority to impose discipline would end.

On October 2, one year to the day after her forced recantation, Patty took a major step toward dealing with her pain and isolation. She attended the Take Back the Night antiviolence rally on the steps of the Capitol. Mayor Bauman was one of the invited speakers, and afterward

Patty walked up to her and introduced herself. The mayor looked away as Patty talked, then left without listening to Patty and others in the portion of the program devoted to testimonials from survivors of sexual assault. It was the first time that Patty had spoken publicly about her experience. She joked about being glad she was visually impaired, since it meant she couldn't see her audience. In halting, extemporaneous remarks, she talked about the hurt that came from not being believed and the toll it had taken. "I can't get over what they've done to me," she said. "It scares me to death that this goes on."

That same week, the PFC issued its decision. It denied Karofsky's motion and allowed the part of my complaint that charged Riley had lied to me in denying knowledge of Patty's letters to proceed. But the commission granted Schwarzenbart's attempt to limit the scope of the issues, declaring the alleged sexual assault and police investigation irrelevant, and agreed that I lacked standing to complain about Riley's possible violation of rules regarding complaint acceptance and investigation. "From the face of the complaint we conclude the complainant's interest in these matters is generally not distinguishable from the interest of any other observer," wrote PFC president Alan Seeger. "Our action does not preclude [Patty] from prosecuting her own complaint before us if she chooses to do so."

Eisen, my editor, was incensed. He wrote a column lambasting this decision as contrary to "common sense and good public policy." Henceforth, he noted, using a real-life example, a citizen who saw a cop urinate in a drunk's bottle could not complain to the PFC, since only the drunk had "standing." Eisen said the commission's five members had gotten "lost in the gossamer of lawyerly web spinning" and expressed doubt that I would win the remaining part of my complaint: "Riley is using the 'I forgot' defense, which is notoriously hard to puncture." Privately he urged me to drop the whole thing. But, taking a cue from Patty, I didn't.

19

Losing Battles

"Like it or not, we are a society of rules. We set expectations for behavior, and prescribe consequences when these are violated. This is why we have police departments, to enforce the rules we have established. To this end, police have tremendous power—the power to arrest, to detain, to use deadly force. Because the police have so much power, it makes sense that police departments have their own set of rules governing how officers and supervisors are expected to behave."

Thus began my opening remarks before the Madison Police and Fire Commission on October 15, 1998. They were the same words I had planned to use four months earlier, when hearings on my complaint against Riley were originally slated. Now, of course, the matter before the PFC was much narrower and harder to prove. I cited the Madison Police Department's rule that officers "tell the truth at all times and under all circumstances, whether under oath or otherwise." This was the obligation Riley was under the previous February, when he denied knowing about Patty's letters. I intended to show this was not a true statement, since Riley had received these letters and discussed them with at least two others: Woodmansee and Captain Jeff LaMar. Moreover, just days before my call, Riley had spoken to two health-care professionals in response to issues I had raised, which were the same as those in Patty's letters.

"Lieutenant Riley's peers will affirm that he is a good and distinguished officer," I told the commission, Patty seated at the table beside me. "I don't dispute that. But I believe Lieutenant Riley did lie to me. He told me something that was untrue in order to cover his involvement in an investigation in which a lot of untrue things were said, and a lot of rules were broken. I urge you to hold him accountable."

None of the PFC's five citizen members, appointed by the mayor to three-year terms, had any expertise in police or fire issues. Seeger was a UW–Madison library services assistant and twice-unsuccessful candidate for city council. The others were an attorney, a utility executive, a state analyst, and Margaret McMurray, the former head of the Wisconsin chapter of the National Organization for Women. Earlier, McMurray had told Kilmark, the financial consultant, that the PFC would welcome a chance to weigh in on Patty's case. Kilmark passed this on to Patty, who was heartened.

Schwarzenbart, in his opening remarks, called Riley a "trustworthy and honest" officer with thirty-one years on the job and ridiculed my remaining cause of action as alleging "a Machiavellian cover-up that belies common sense." Riley, beside him, looked indignant.

During the next several hours I called six witnesses, five of whom—including the chief of police—were on Riley's side. (The exception was Jill Poarch, who was neutral.) Schwarzenbart made dozens of objections, usually to allege I was straying into issues the PFC had declared off-limits. Several times the entire commission and attorney Herrick retired into an adjourning room to deliberate before issuing a ruling. The PFC gave me more latitude than Schwarzenbart wanted, but the hearing was fractured by constant interruptions.

LaMar, Riley's immediate supervisor, testified that he had gotten calls from concerned residents of Patty's neighborhood and thus told Woodmansee he wanted to put out a press release if the rape report proved false, "which isn't all that uncommon." Pressed to be specific about the volume of calls, which Woodmansee had reputedly called "a ton," LaMar placed the number at "two or three." Shortly after this release was issued, Riley had come to him with Patty's letters. LaMar instructed that this correspondence, which they discussed, be put in the case file "so that the district attorney would be aware of it."

Woodmansee, taking his turn on the witness stand, confirmed that Riley had left him Patty's letters along with a note. They subsequently had a "sixty-second-or-less conversation" about the letters and concluded they were "indicative of the concerns that we had" about Patty's mental health. Woodmansee said he misunderstood Riley's instruction to forward the letters to the district attorney's office and instead put them into a file that remained at his desk. Schwarzenbart asked whether Woodmansee's report was by this time already "in the hands of the DA's office," to underscore that forwarding the letters would be an additional task. "That's correct," answered Woodmansee.

Lieutenant Patrick Malloy of the department's Professional Standards Unit said it would have been "appropriate" for Riley to have given the letters to him. He even told Riley, when the letters were located after my inquiries in early February, that he wished he had known about them earlier.

Poarch confirmed having spoken with Riley about Patty's case shortly before he had denied knowing about the letters. Chief Williams had trouble recalling his encounters with Riley, in part because he had suffered a mild stroke that June. (This happened just days after he drew national attention when a 9-millimeter handgun he had stashed in his oven for safekeeping went off as he roasted a turkey, firing a bullet into a banister.)

I asked each police witness whether Riley had an unusually poor memory; all said he did not, even as they recalled, in detail, conversations he had completely forgotten. Schwarzenbart, in turn, asked each witness about Riley's "reputation within the department for truthfulness." It was, said Woodmansee, "outstanding."

Perhaps the most extraordinary witness was Deputy District Attorney Jill Karofsky, who said it would have made no difference had she gotten Patty's letters at the time they were sent, instead of several months later. She would have taken into account "all the inconsistent statements in the police reports" as well as the fact that Patty confessed and would have "come to the conclusion that she lied." After her testimony, Karofsky walked to the back of the hearing room and received a high five from someone who had come to watch.

The hearing adjourned until the following week. I was discouraged. None of my own witnesses supported the conclusion that Riley lied; I couldn't be sure of it myself. Besides, whether or not a police supervisor fibbed to a reporter was hardly the most urgent issue. I was only fighting this battle because the PFC threw out the rest of my case—and because James Friedman, my attorney helper, thought I might not be able to appeal that decision until this part was played out.

I considered dropping my complaint and almost did. But then Herrick told me I was doing "a really good job" presenting my case. I decided to stick it out; after all, Herrick knew what the commissioners were saying when they scurried off behind closed doors. Perhaps they were finding significance in the large number of conversations that Riley would have had to forget in order to draw a blank when asked about Patty's letters.

That week Patty wrote a note to Karofsky, with a copy to Nicks. She expressed her objections to Karofsky's "public speech on all my wrongs," saying she was "horrified to hear how little regard every last one of you admitted to giving my very serious complaint." Patty told her former prosecutors that the "financial and emotional devastation" she endured, as well as damage to "the reputation of the DA's office," could have been avoided if police had sent her bedding to the crime lab for analysis early on. "The delivery cost would have been the same," she noted. Karofsky and Nicks did not respond.

The second and final PFC hearing took place on October 22. Colleen O'Brien of Meriter Hospital said she had spoken to Riley about Patty's case on February 4, the day before my call to him. My own account of Riley's response when I asked him about and read portions of Patty's letters was submitted as an affidavit, on which I was cross-examined. Then it was the defense's turn.

Schwarzenbart called several police witnesses to testify about contacts they had with Riley regarding my call. His office mate, Lieutenant John Davenport, said Riley was "upset" after this conversation. Why would he be upset, unless he knew what he told me was untrue? After all, he supposedly had no recollection of these letters, and I did not contradict him, since I had not yet learned that he was the person who received them.

Riley, testifying in his own defense, explained it like this: "My concern was that if I had a complaint against one of my detectives I was upset that I didn't know about it." He said he personally retrieved the letters—contrary to what Malloy said about locating the letters himself—and contacted both assistant chiefs and Chief Williams to let them know what transpired. He never tried setting the record straight with me because he didn't think it would make any difference.

At the end of this hearing, both Schwarzenbart and I asked to make oral closing arguments. But the PFC insisted on written briefs. I argued that it was not plausible that a police supervisor who no one thought had a bad memory would completely forget letters alleging serious misconduct that he read and discussed with others. Schwarzenbart, in a twenty-five-page brief and twelve-page reply brief, said there was no reason for Riley to remember, since there was nothing unusual about a suspect recanting a confession. Moreover, Riley had "no logical reason to lie," since he never considered the letters a complaint. And again, after blocking me from exploring these issues, Schwarzenbart cited Judge Aulik's ruling as proof that Patty's confession was properly obtained.

I anticipated losing, but I didn't know how badly. The PFC's decision was scathing. Some cases, it said, came down to conflicting evidence or a complainant's proof falling short of what's needed, but not this one: "In this case, we find *no evidence other than the Complainant's opinion testimony* that Respondent lied to the Complainant, that is, deliberately misrepresented a fact. In our view, *all* evidence is fully consistent with Respondent's explanation that he may have had a lapse of memory." (Emphasis in original.) The PFC found Riley's "explanation of forgetfulness or inadvertence fully credible and reasonable."

Schwarzenbart sent Eisen a letter demanding a retraction of *Isthmus*'s "false and defamatory" statements regarding Riley. Having fought to keep the PFC from considering whether Riley broke the rules in his handling of Patty's letters, he now wanted the paper to declare that Riley did no such thing. Eisen declined, although *Isthmus* ran a just-the-facts article on the PFC outcome. Schwarzenbart ended up billing the city for $22,226 in legal fees to defend against an action I spent $81 to present.

Even before the PFC issued its decision, Patty expressed interest in filing her own PFC complaint. I warned against it, knowing that she lacked the skills to navigate the commission's user-unfriendly process. In search of an alternative, I wrote Mayor Bauman, calling her attention to Patty's efforts to protest how she was treated and force a new investigation into her sexual assault. I also indicated that Patty was considering her own PFC action. Was there maybe another way that was less costly and confrontational?

Bauman, in reply, declined my suggestion that she meet with Patty, but suggested there was indeed another way: the case could be turned over to the Division of Criminal Investigation, part of the state Justice Department. Patty, apprised of this, immediately sent the police a written request, dated November 2, seeking a state investigation "of both my rape and the Madison Police Department's handling of this case."

Harlowe didn't think this was a good idea, and he advised Patty against it. One of the "basic principles of criminal defense," he told me, is "never invite an investigation." There was no guarantee such a probe would lead to a satisfactory result. But Patty disregarded Harlowe's advice. She wanted something done, even if it meant taking the enormous risk of trusting someone in law enforcement.

In mid-November Bauman released the results of the Madison Police Department's internal probe into Patty's case, conducted at her request by Assistant Chief Ted Balistreri. It was a remarkably threadbare report, barely more than a page. Balistreri said that, after talking to Nicks, Karofsky, Malloy, and Maples—but not to Patty or anyone who supported her—he was "confident that no wrongdoing occurred." He said the tactics used to secure Patty's confession were deemed legal by Judge Aulik and justified because "it was the opinion of our detective that 'Patty' was not assaulted and, hence, not a victim." Riley did not appear to have broken any rules with regard to his handling of Patty's letters, which did not strike Balistreri as being a complaint. Finally, he said, Patty had spurned Maples's offer to discuss "the 41 points which led us to believe she was lying." (These, I surmised correctly, were the notes Woodmansee had used during his meeting with me.) In conclusion, Balistreri said, "This entire matter has been taxing on many of us, including Patty. I can only hope that at some point we can all put this behind us and move on."

Patty, after reviewing this document using a machine that magnifies type size, faxed the mayor a note: "I have seen the poor excuse for an investigation letter written to you by Ted Balistreri. Again, I cried. I'm terribly disappointed and I hope you are too. What investigation? I haven't been interviewed yet, nor has anyone I know. What are the 41 points against me? No one has told me yet or questioned me for explanations." She bristled at the "insensitive conclusion that I should simply put this behind me and move on," saying she lived in fear for her safety, compounded by her fear of asking the police for help. She appealed to Bauman to reject "this joke of an investigation" and hold someone accountable for what occurred. "I honestly didn't do anything wrong. I'm the victim here."

Bauman replied by letter, dated December 9: "I am, of course, deeply concerned about your situation. The fact that you will never feel safe again and find yourself frightened to ask for help is not an acceptable situation. I hope that you will, at some time, be able to find closure with respect to many of these issues." But not with any help from Bauman, who went on to "clarify" that Balistreri was asked to investigate only whether there was "any inappropriate action by any Madison police officers." He found there was not, as did Judge Aulik: "As such there is nothing further that the Madison Police Department can or should do." Bauman said the matter was now in the hands of the Division of Criminal Investigation, which by this time "should have" contacted her. It had not.

Patty decided to file PFC complaints against Riley and Woodmansee. Patty's brother Bobby, having no legal qualifications or skills, agreed to represent her and I agreed to help in a limited capacity. The three of us got together to draft the complaints. Patty's complaint against Riley was mostly a reiteration of my original, only this time from someone with "standing." Her complaint against Woodmansee alleged violations of department rules against lying, discourtesy, "overbearing, oppressive and tyrannical" conduct, and failing to file complete reports—that is, not mentioning his use of lies and deception. Bobby had gone to the public library and reviewed the police department's policies and procedures manual, jotting down the rules he felt had been broken.

Patty delivered both complaints to the PFC in mid-December, along with a note. "I've tried [sending] letters to anyone I thought would listen, to no avail," it said. "I've asked the department to investigate, but they haven't. I've asked the mayor to help, but she's refused, urging me to 'move on.' My New Year's resolution is to quit crying over this devastating year and fight back. Only then will I 'move on.'"

PART THREE

AGAINST ALL ODDS

20

Healthy Outrage

Patty was in over her head, and she knew it. The Madison Police and Fire Commission, contrary to its statutory charter, had evolved into a forum that only a lawyer could love. Patty and Bobby were ill equipped to conduct discovery, defend against motions, prepare legal briefs, and subpoena and question witnesses. Riley and Woodmansee each had lawyers, paid for by the city and police union, respectively, authorized to devote as many billable hours as necessary to defeat Patty's complaints. And that's what they set out to do.

Riley, through attorney Schwarzenbart, submitted a baleful affidavit: "I am surprised in her decision to file charges given that she was present during undisputed testimony in the [earlier] matter that upon my receipt of her letter in late October 1997 I had spoken to my commanding officer, Captain Jeff LaMar, [who] agreed with my assessment that the letter should not be treated as complaint requiring referral to the Professional Standards Unit." Riley's recollection of this conversation was now fully restored. Chief Williams, also via affidavit, echoed "disappointment" over Patty's complaint and certified Riley's recent retirement, meaning he was no longer subject to PFC discipline.

Patty and Bobby prepared a discovery request. It asked whether Woodmansee was aware of and obliged to follow department rules regarding truthfulness, discourtesy, "tyrannical, overbearing and oppressive conduct," and filing complete, accurate reports. It also asked about the various things he'd done that appeared to violate these rules, such as lying about rubber residue and then not mentioning this in his report. Finally, it sought certain documents, including his list of forty-one points. Woodmansee's attorney, Gary Young, thumbed his nose at this request, contending that making his client comply with discovery was like compelling him to testify against himself.

But Young did produce a voluminous reply to Patty's complaint. It denied that she was a victim of sexual assault, saying she had admitted lying about this in what Judge Aulik deemed a voluntary confession. It confirmed that Woodmansee had brought up Patty's past suicide attempts and raised the prospect of holding her on "suicide watch," but claimed this was done in a caring rather than coercive way. Young's filing argued, essentially, that the Madison Police Department rule requiring officers to be truthful "at all times and under all circumstances" did not mean what it said, in light of police practice and Judge Aulik's ruling, which was attached. And it challenged her standing to complain, saying she was not an "aggrieved person" within the meaning of the law. Was anyone?

Even before she undertook the painstaking task of reading this document on her visual-aid machine, Patty knew she needed help. "I don't think I can do this," Bobby confided, perhaps a bit late. Patty asked an attorney friend if he could represent her. He declined, but suggested an acquaintance named Mike Rieselman, formerly an attorney in California. Rieselman, on hearing details of Patty's case, was immediately interested—not in the PFC process but in filing a lawsuit.

Rieselman, then thirty-five, fancied himself a "civil rights lawyer" and boasted that he had taken eight cases to jury trial in three years in California, winning one of them "without any evidence." But then his marriage ended, his luck went south, and he ended up in Madison, doing odd jobs. Rieselman thought the PFC was a waste of time, especially since complainants could not get compensation from which to pay attorney fees. He was also worried about his ability to appear before it, because he was not licensed to practice law in Wisconsin. Late in the afternoon of January 11, 1999, less than an hour before the PFC's initial hearing on Patty's complaints, Rieselman called an acquaintance, Mike Short, who had a Wisconsin bar card.

Michael John Short, also thirty-five, was a Wisconsin native and UW–Madison graduate who had tried his hand at various jobs before heading to Gonzaga University in Washington State for his law degree. He put in a year each with the public defender's office in Spokane and as a criminal defense lawyer in Reno. Returning to Madison in late 1997, he passed the Wisconsin bar exam and began taking cases, working out of his apartment. When Rieselman called out of the blue to see if Short could hightail it to the PFC proceeding, Short said he didn't think so. But the call piqued his curiosity—he was aware of Patty's case from my articles—and his sense of obligation. He found himself rushing to the City-County Building. Rieselman was surprised to see him.

At this hearing, Schwarzenbart sought dismissal of Patty's complaint against Riley on grounds of "jurisdiction and mootness," since the PFC's authority to impose discipline ended when Riley retired. The PFC was inclined to agree, but gave Patty's attorneys—already she was treated as a nonplayer in her own complaint—a couple of weeks to object. Young asked to delay setting a hearing schedule because Woodmansee was out of state. The PFC granted this request but sought assurances from both sides that the matter would be handled expeditiously. Short piped up: "Our intention is not to drag this thing out any longer than necessary."

And so it was that Short found himself getting pulled into Patty's ordeal. Part of it was personal: his sister had been sexually assaulted nearly two decades earlier by a member of the state legislature, and the incident turned into a painfully high-profile case. Short met with Patty privately and became convinced she was telling the truth. He was shocked when he read the police reports, suppression-hearing transcript, and Aulik's ruling, and angered when he watched a videotape of the PFC hearing at which Karofsky gave her imperious testimony and received the high five. In short order, Patty's determination to fight back became his own.

Others were also taking up the cause. Bobby sent a scathing letter to Mayor Bauman, saying her lack of willingness to get involved left him "completely disgusted." He challenged her to conduct "a truthful and complete investigation." Bauman did not respond.

Cami, the local woman who had taken an interest in Patty's case, also sent the mayor a letter, with copies to thirty-eight city officials and members of the media. "I am afraid for our community," she wrote. "I've read documents and transcripts concerning the case, attended Patty's [suppression-motion] hearing last summer as well as the recent PFC hearings. I've listened to police officers contradict themselves and

each other. In the meantime, Patty's story has withstood scrutiny."
Cami concluded by declining to apologize for appearing overbearing:
"At this point, I prefer healthy outrage to the sickening cynicism and
indifference which has so far prevailed."

On February 5 Bauman wrote Patty offering "the opportunity to
meet with me, one-on-one, so as to, if possible, bring closure to some of
your issues." On the same day, the mayor asked Assistant Chief Balistreri for an update on the involvement of the state Division of Criminal Investigation. The agency had yet to contact Patty, more than four
months after she requested an investigation. Bauman also replied to
Cami, tersely declining to discuss the case "with you or any other unau-
thorized representative" of Patty. She demanded that Cami identify
"your interest in this matter."

Cami wrote back to Bauman (and the thirty-eight others), expressing "surprise that I should need to identify myself as anything other
than a citizen of this community in order to be heard and answered by
my elected representative." She blasted the mayor's attempt to dodge
the issue and chided her "inability to believe that there are members
of this community who actually care whether or not a rapist is on the
streets due to the police department's persecution of one of his victims." Bauman also answered this letter, saying the matter had been
thoroughly reviewed: "While you, Patty, and perhaps I may not agree
with the manner in which Patty's case was handled, the fact appears
that it was handled in accordance with normal policing policies." (Cami
remained outraged, but subsequently fell away from involvement in
Patty's case.)

The meeting between Bauman and Patty took place in late February. Rieselman and Short accompanied her and met with the mayor
beforehand. Rieselman mentioned the possibility of a federal lawsuit
and said he wasn't sure how much influence the mayor had on such
matters. Bauman replied that she was the Madison Police Department's
"commander-in-chief." The mayor then met with Patty. She said she
could empathize with Patty's enduring fear, since she herself was afraid
of elevators and store escalators, due to past bad experiences. She made
no promises to do anything and suggested that the way for Patty to
achieve "closure" was to leave the past behind. Then she gave Patty a
hug. The meeting was over.

The PFC dismissed Patty's complaint against Riley, saying it lacked "subject matter jurisdiction" to discipline a retired officer. Young filed a motion seeking to limit the issues in Woodmansee's case to those "not already decided by Judge Aulik." At a subsequent hearing, Short objected, noting that Aulik's ruling was "not a final adjudication." It could have been appealed and overturned, had the dismissal of charges against Patty not made this unnecessary. The PFC asked both sides for briefs on whether it should relitigate issues "already decided" by Judge Aulik.

Rieselman and Short agreed to work together as co-counsel, which proved immensely difficult. They had markedly different personalities — Short was likable and optimistic, Rieselman dour and peculiar — and different notions about how to proceed. But both were driven by a sense of outrage. "The whole thing's offensive to me," said Rieselman. "With these guys still claiming she's lying, she has to be vindicated." And they both saw the PFC as a weak means to this end. "I don't think the Police and Fire Commission has any credibility to be ruling on this matter," said Short. "I don't think we should be monkeying around with the PFC."

On February 26 the two Mikes withdrew Patty's complaint "due to limited resources and the PFC's legal responsibility to fully investigate this matter." Their client, they said, "simply cannot afford the cost of discovery disputes, trial preparation and trial, especially given that the Respondent apparently intends to spend unlimited amounts of time and money in an effort to keep the PFC from hearing evidence in this case." They asked the commission to investigate on its own authority, as state statutes and the Madison PFC's own rules expressly allowed.

"Woodmansee's report on this case and his testimony at the motion to suppress hearing in the criminal case prove his misconduct beyond any doubt," the attorneys wrote, calling on the PFC to "appropriately punish" the detective "for the outrageous injustices visited upon and suffered by the Complainant." They promised that Patty would "cooperate fully with such an inquiry." The PFC scheduled another hearing to take this up.

In the meantime, I set out to obtain Woodmansee's list of forty-one points. The police department initially rejected my request, saying these were "the personal notes of Detective Woodmansee to refresh his recollection in separate meetings with you and the district attorney's office," and as such were exempt from the open records law. But eventually the department, whose previous interpretations of the law had resulted in two lost lawsuits and $96,000 in assessed legal costs, relented.

The released document was as insubstantial as I remembered from my session with Woodmansee. Among the items: "Expressed no emotional reaction to being in the room where the alleged assault took place"; "We spoke for over 40 minutes when she tells me that she made a mistake and is talking about the previous week"; and "Stated that she went to bed with her clothes on and this was unusual for her."

Some of Woodmansee's points were factually incorrect. He said the rapist, if one existed, had mysterious prior knowledge that Patty's brother picked her up for work; yet, according to Woodmansee's own report, this was something Patty told the rapist. Some were absurd, including Patty's failure to "call out" to Misty—as though waking her daughter while a knife-wielding assailant was still in their apartment was clearly the most logical thing to do. Several centered on Patty's re-actions, like calling her assailant "almost sympathetic" and laughing as she related embarrassing details.

In early March, five months after her request, Patty was contacted by Elizabeth Feagles, a special agent with the state Division of Criminal Investigation. Feagles said she was reopening Patty's original sexual assault. And while she would not be investigating the detectives' conduct, as Patty had wanted, Feagles promised there would be no further in-volvement by the Madison Police Department. Replied Patty, "That would be nice."

Feagles, a twenty-two-year veteran, and another female agent, a trainee, met with Patty at her apartment on March 9. (Misty had re-cently gotten her own place, resulting in greatly improved relations be-tween mother and daughter.) Short was also present. It was the first time Short had heard Patty describe the assault; he was struck that it was identical in every particular to what she earlier told police. For a person who had been raked over the coals for alleged inconsistencies, Patty was remarkably consistent.

The meeting lasted about three hours. Patty again identified Misty's former boyfriend Lonnie as a possible suspect. Both Patty and her at-torney came away thinking that Feagles believed Patty and was deter-mined to conduct a thorough investigation. But Feagles was skeptical of

Patty's account. She would note in her case report that, in relating how her assailant seemed to almost fall asleep when she was gratifying him orally, Patty had joked, "Don't tell any of my future dates." Was this the kind of thing a rape victim would say?

Rieselman produced the first draft of a complaint for a federal lawsuit. It named five individuals—Woodmansee, Draeger, Riley, Schwartz, and Maples—as well as the city of Madison. It listed fifteen grounds for action, including civil rights violations, false arrest, violations of the Americans with Disabilities Act, negligent and intentional infliction of emotional distress, defamation, and civil conspiracy. Short felt the suit was overreaching and underresearched—one of many areas of disagreement between the two Mikes—and wanted to take his own crack at it. They both agreed to hold off on filing; obviously, if the PFC disciplined Woodmansee or if Feagles found the man who raped Patty, there would be stronger grounds for a civil case.

The final PFC hearing on Patty's complaint against Woodmansee took place on March 31. The PFC skeptically inquired why it should pursue the matter on its own authority, and, at one point, Short asked Patty to speak to this issue. It was the first time anyone from the PFC had heard a word pass her lips. "I was told by many people that I could take a complaint to the PFC free of charge, and when I did I found I was objected to on everything by this attorney," said Patty, pointing to where Young was sitting. "So I had to try and hire an attorney with limited resources. I didn't have any money, as I am still paying off the . . ."

"I guess we're kind of getting off the path here," interrupted Short, snatching back the reins. In fact, Patty's inability to frame her appeal to the PFC in terms of legal arguments was itself a perfect argument for why the commission should exercise the independent authority the legislature had been so clear to grant. Short said Patty was "willing to take the stand" regarding any such action. The PFC agreed to consider this appeal and issue a written decision.

It would take the commission, which had voiced concern about the expeditious handling of Patty's case, seven more weeks to do so. The PFC harshly rejected Patty's appeal, saying that while it had the statutory authority to file charges, "we have no practical or institutional resources for investigation and prosecution." The commission, ignoring the promise of full cooperation made by Patty's attorneys, claimed Patty had withdrawn her complaint "at least in part in order to avoid being deposed" and called her willingness to submit to examination "very uncertain." In light of this, the PFC said it would "decline to test the limits of the statute and reconstruct our rules and policies in order to investigate and prosecute this Complainant's case."

It was a familiar outcome: Woodmansee was off the hook, and Patty was left dangling.

21

Filing Suit

For more than a decade, Axley Brynelson had been the city of Madison's law firm of choice. Axley attorneys handled most of the municipality's outside legal work and represented its insurer on disputed liability claims. During a five-year period in the early 1990s, this generated more than $1.5 million in fees. There was no competitive bidding, no performance reviews, and city officials were not allowed to see the firm's itemized billing statements on liability claims. Asked in 1996 why Axley enjoyed this favored status, longtime City Attorney Eunice Gibson replied, "I don't know." But she was pleased with the quality of representation and felt the firm helped save the city money.

Key to these savings was Axley's reputation for deliberately turning even minor claims into full-fledged legal fights to discourage people from seeking compensation. "I have seen a complete and utter reluctance by the law firm to discuss settlement," said attorney Jeff Spitzer-Resnick, who represented a Madison man injured by police responding to an anonymous—and false—911 call. "The only reason I can see for this is to continually bill the client by extending cases." Axley rang up $86,888 in fees defending against an action Spitzer-Resnick had offered to settle for $10,000.

In another case, Axley billed $177,027 fighting a wrongful termination suit by Madison's former affirmative action officer. The law firm lost, resulting in a major judgment against the city (it eventually paid $441,000) and a withering rebuke from Circuit Court Judge Moria Krueger. The judge said Axley attorneys led by Michael Modl "tried to unduly complicate the task at hand" by bombarding her with arguments and case law "immaterial to the issues needing resolution." She said the attorneys engaged in "obstinacy, mischaracterizing, and repetition to the brink of apoplexy"; their arguments were "lacking in sense and integrity"; and they "over-litigated the last stage of this case so dramatically that it tried one's patience even to read their endless submissions."

On the same day that Krueger delivered this scolding (she later entered a formal finding that Axley attorneys presented a frivolous defense), another judge sanctioned the firm for filing a specious legal action, ordering it to pay restitution. In yet another case, Axley collected $22,284 in fees to defeat a $3,000 claim from a man whose recovered stolen car was junked after Madison police sent notification to the wrong address.

Axley's fondness for smash-mouth litigation was even turned against the city's own employees. In the mid-1990s the firm went after Bob Brown, a Madison firefighter who retired after twenty-eight years of service when he was diagnosed as having suffered a heart attack while fighting a fire. A doctor who reexamined the case had raised questions about this finding but later reversed himself, saying he acted on the basis of incomplete information. Axley nonetheless tried to terminate Brown's disability benefits and force him to repay two years of benefits he had received. Brown spent thousands of dollars of his own money fighting the firm before succumbing to a fatal heart attack that the former head of the city's workers' compensation program attributed to stress from this ordeal.

None of these cases forced reconsideration of the city's allegiance to Axley. Not a single local politician raised a fuss. Madison's risk assessment manager, Kevin Houlihan, proclaimed that insurance premiums kept coming down year after year—which was, from the city's perspective, the only thing that mattered. Although other attorneys viewed the firm with derision ("There are normal ways of doing things," one said, "and then there's Axley Brynelson's way"), it was solidly ensconced as Madison's defender against civil litigation. If Rieselman and Short followed through on their plan to file a lawsuit in federal court, it was Axley they'd be up against.

As it was, the two Mikes were having enough trouble just putting up with each other. Rieselman, broke and down on his luck, seemed to vacillate between impatience that the case was not moving forward and doubts about his ability to stay involved if it did. He quarreled with Short over strategy. He heard secondhand about a man who claimed he had consensual relations with Patty, making him potentially the source of semen on her sheets. Patty told Rieselman, truthfully, that she hardly knew this person and never had sex with him. But after getting into a spat with this man, Rieselman reported him as a suspect to special agent Liz Feagles. She tracked him down and obtained samples to be tested against the diminishing supply of recovered DNA. Patty, angered, said she didn't want Rieselman to have anything more to do with her case. Rieselman accepted this graciously and played no further role. Short was not sorry to see him go. Still, Rieselman's impassioned belief that Patty was entitled to justice was instrumental in moving the case forward.

Feagles, meanwhile, had broken the code that kept Madison police from figuring out that "Lonnie Alvord," whom both Patty and Misty identified as a suspect, was really Alonzo Elvord Jr. At the time, Elvord was in prison, serving a five-year sentence for the armed robbery he committed with his cousin Joey shortly after Patty's assault. Feagles visited Elvord at the Kettle Moraine Correctional Institution. He said he knew Patty was blind and described her as "nice." He denied involvement in her assault and said he was willing to submit samples for DNA testing. Feagles eventually did obtain samples, which were sent to the state crime lab for analysis, as were those from the man Rieselman had named. The results: negative for both.

In August, at Short's urging, Feagles began checking out a new suspect: Kenneth. This was the man Dominic had been with the year before when he was arrested for attacking a stranger with a baseball bat. Kenneth, it emerged, had past criminal convictions for battery, drunk driving, disorderly conduct, and child neglect. One previous domestic incident, which led to Kenneth being charged with battery and victim intimidation, had been investigated by a Madison police officer named Tom Woodmansee.

"I really think this is the guy," said Short, disregarding the fact that Kenneth was Caucasian and would have been thirty-three at the time Patty reported being raped by a light-skinned black or Hispanic man in his early twenties. Feagles, in her pursuit of this angle, spoke to Dominic and others. Kenneth, who had been jailed for driving after revocation (fourth offense) and obstructing an officer, was released before Feagles could obtain samples for DNA tests. He then missed a mandatory court appearance on theft charges in Dane County, and a bench warrant was issued for his arrest. Feagles asked to be notified the next time he was in custody.

As summer turned to fall, Short put the finishing touches on his complaint for Patty's federal lawsuit. He opted against including Riley and Maples as defendants, although his complaint still cited the failure of police to properly handle Patty's letters and Maples's assertion that Patty was charged because she recanted her recantation and went to the press. The final draft named Woodmansee, Draeger, and Schwartz as defendants and listed eight causes of action, including false arrest, denial of right to counsel, coercion, retaliatory prosecution, and civil conspiracy. The main points: police did not adequately investigate Patty's assault, failing even to test bedding that was later found to contain semen; they used lies, threats, and psychological pressure to get her to confess; and they caused her great emotional distress through such actions as Schwartz's call to Patty's sister.

On November 17, 1999, Short walked into Madison's federal courthouse—an imposing, dark-blue building adorned with a whimsical dash of red neon—and delivered Patty's complaint. He filed Patty's name and address under seal and obtained a protective order requiring that these be omitted from any public filings. For the purposes of her lawsuit, she would be known as Patty Doe. "She's pursuing this because she's gotten no satisfaction from the system," Short told *The Capital Times*. "She wants the truth to once and for all be known."

Short had some idea what he was up against. He had discussed the case with Hal Harlowe as well as Jeff Scott Olson, a prominent local civil rights attorney. As Olson saw it, Patty's confession and Aulik's ruling presented nearly insurmountable obstacles. Harlowe also advised against a lawsuit. But Patty wanted to go forward, and Short was willing to help. Their already slim chances were further diminished when the case was assigned to Federal Judge John Shabaz, one of two jurists in Wisconsin's Western District.

Shabaz, a former Republican state lawmaker appointed to the bench in 1981 by President Reagan, was a staunch conservative with a reputation for siding with law enforcement. Wisconsin's Western District, according to the U.S. Sentencing Commission, ranked as either the first or second harshest district in the nation from 1997 through 1999, as measured by the number of times defendants received sentences that exceeded set guidelines. As an arbiter of civil cases, Shabaz had moved to block student fees from going to campus groups he said advanced "the homosexual agenda" and rubber-stamped the nation's most restrictive law against so-called partial birth abortion; both actions were overturned. That summer Shabaz had dismissed a lawsuit against police officers who doused a pregnant woman in labor with pepper spray because her husband, in trying to rush her to the hospital, had tried to keep driving after being stopped for speeding. Shabaz said the woman had no grounds to sue even though she was sprayed, because her husband was the primary intended target.

Two weeks before Short filed his complaint, Judge Shabaz presided over a jury trial in another case of alleged police misconduct. Two black men, brothers Victor and Tre McNair, filed suit because officers from a Madison suburb drew guns on them and placed them in handcuffs after stopping them for a suspended license plate; at least seven squad cars responded. The McNairs, who were on their way to church, charged that police used excessive force; the jury agreed, awarding $10,000 in damages. Shabaz would mull this over for several weeks before substituting his own judgment—that the police did nothing wrong. He not only threw out the jury award, he ordered the brothers to reimburse the defense for $8,714 in legal fees. A federal appellate court later reversed Shabaz, saying "the police treated the McNairs like desperadoes who had been firing Tommy guns out the windows." Ultimately, the police ended up with a $103,292 bill, including fees for the attorneys who fought to overturn Shabaz's ruling.

Kenneth did end up behind bars again, and Feagles was able to obtain samples for testing. She also contacted Patty's former boyfriend Russ to get samples from him. Both Patty and Russ had told police their relationship ended many months before the assault, so he could not possibly be the source of semen on her sheets. Patty found this development disconcerting. "Liz is not believing what I'm saying," she lamented. "Why is she doing this now that news of the lawsuit is out?"

In early February 2000 both tests came back negative, and Feagles's investigation went cold. The state crime lab, in testing these samples, utilized a newer scientific method that required only minute amounts of genetic material to create a DNA profile. As a result, the profile from the semen on Patty's bedsheet was uploaded into a federal data bank that also contained profiles of convicted sex offenders. No match was found. Patty's case remained an open file but was no longer actively pursued. Feagles's case activity reports—thirty in all, totaling about seventy-five pages—were provided to the attorneys from Axley Brynelson but not to Short.

Three Axley attorneys were assigned to counter Patty's complaint, including senior partner Brad Armstrong and associate Mike Modl, who handled many city of Madison cases. The two men were a study in contrasts. Armstrong, who turned fifty-nine the month Patty's lawsuit was filed, was robust and domineering. A former UW–Madison football player, his style, honed over three decades of practice as a civil defense attorney, was to box his rivals into a corner and bully them into submission. Others in the firm feared him, with good reason: he was fiercely intelligent and capable of great cruelty. He was also deeply religious, and a leader in his church, Bethel Lutheran.

Modl, then forty-four, was a slight, mousy man with gray hair and an irrepressibly cheerful disposition, sometimes bursting into song. He wore thick glasses and could not see well enough to operate a vehicle; his wife drove him to and from work. Although he had gotten his law degree just twelve years before, Modl had a brilliant legal mind and numerous areas of expertise; he was the firm's go-to lawyer for all kinds of questions. He was friendly, approachable, and well liked by others, even opposing counsel. Modl's talents were almost always plied defending the powerful against the weak: municipalities facing civil rights claims, financial institutions accused of discriminatory practices, employers charged with workplace harassment, prisons sued by inmates. He was the system's best friend.

Two days after Christmas, Short met with his rivals at their offices in downtown Madison to discuss scheduling and discovery. Armstrong warned him about the resources that Axley was able and willing to employ in the detectives' defense. Short was not intimidated, but perhaps he should have been. Several days into the new year, Axley filed an impetuous answer to Patty's complaint. It admitted that Woodmansee made a false representation regarding rubber residue but denied almost everything else. It denied that Woodmansee at some point began investigating Patty for the crime of obstruction. It denied Patty was taken to a "small" interrogation room, saying the dimensions of the room "were approximately 12 x 8 foot." It even denied things Woodmansee had put in his report and admitted under oath, such as telling Patty her vision was not noticeably bad. At times, the querulousness of the Axley attorneys defied comprehension. Paragraph 61 of Short's complaint read, in its entirety, "Plaintiff then stated, 'Okay, I made the whole thing up.'" Axley's answer: "Admit only that Plaintiff admitted, 'Okay, I made the whole thing up' and deny the remaining allegations in paragraph 61 of Plaintiff's Complaint."

This filing was followed in late January by Axley's "first set" of interrogatories and requests for production, which filled twenty-four pages and contained dozens of demands, such as: "Please identify all documents in your possession, custody or control which you contend support your allegation that Defendants subjected Plaintiff to retaliatory criminal prosecution as alleged in Plaintiff's sixth cause of action." Among other things, Axley demanded that Patty identify every occasion in her life in which she received "any treatment from any health or mental health provider." It wanted the names of providers, the dates of each treatment, and "your entire medical history as it relates in any way" to these visits.

Short showed me Axley's discovery demands and asked if I had any ideas. I suggested crying. The responses he eventually submitted were past deadline and incomplete; in most cases, he declined to answer Axley's interrogatories, saying he first needed to conduct discovery. But he did open up his files to Axley's inspection, including turning over a copy of the journal that Patty had begun writing about the assault and its aftermath. Patty was deeply distressed: this was something she produced for her own use, to help sort out her experiences, and now it was being given to people looking for things to use against her. She also signed releases to let Axley obtain medical records from every doctor or mental health professional she could remember visiting.

Axley Brynelson was not satisfied. Andrew Clarkowski, the third attorney assigned to defend the city against Patty, filed a motion in early March 2000 to compel Short to comply more fully with the firm's discovery demands. This led to a hearing before Judge Shabaz. The defense, said Clarkowski, was merely seeking answers to "standard contention interrogatories" so that it could prepare its defense. Short said his own efforts to obtain discovery had been frustrated by Axley, and thus the interrogatories were "premature." Shabaz came down firmly on Axley's side, granting the motion to compel and ordering Short to pay the costs of bringing it. The judge also strongly signaled that he would respond favorably to a motion to dismiss.

"I don't understand the modern practice of law, obviously," said Shabaz, noting that if he were a lawyer in private practice facing a similar situation he "would have immediately moved for summary judgment." The judge expressed his belief that Short's failure to fully comply with the discovery request was essentially an admission that he had no case. "The fact is that this is the best response the defendant could have received. So I don't understand what's going on here, unless there's an awfully deep pocket and the defendant is interested in running up the meter." As if this were too subtle, Shabaz expressed his "hope that the comments of the court would be pursued," reminding the Axley lawyers that "you don't have to wait" to file a motion seeking dismissal.

The Axley lawyers did not bite, instead preferring to keep open the spigot of billable hours through an exhaustive series of depositions and filings that in the end, arguably, would help achieve Patty's goal of letting the truth be known, once and for all.

22

Patty's Depositions

Brad Armstrong got right down to it. Less than four minutes into his deposition of Patty on March 15, 2000, having ascertained only her name and that of her biological father, the Axley attorney sized up the frightened woman across the conference table and asked, "Did [your father] ever physically or sexually abuse you?" It was the kind of question—tactless, insolent, abrupt—he would pose again and again during Patty's first deposition that day and two more to come. Armstrong asked about her past suicide attempts. He asked about the sexual abuse inflicted by her stepfather. Interspersed were comments insinuating that Patty was a complete imbecile, caught up in a drama she lacked the capacity to comprehend. To wit: "You are involved today in a lawsuit. Do you understand you're involved in a lawsuit?"

Throughout these depositions, Armstrong subjected Patty to the kind of questioning most defense attorneys representing rapists would never try in court, because it would be barred under rape shield laws and alienate juries. His strategy was clear: to batter Patty psychologically in order to get her to make incriminating admissions, just as the police officers he was representing had done. None of the information obtained by rummaging through the painful details of Patty's past was used in pleadings to the court; Armstrong's purpose was apparently to exploit her emotional vulnerability. Part of this involved heightening her level of discomfort. All three depositions took place on his turf, in the offices of Axley Brynelson in downtown Madison. Mike Modl was present for the first two, Woodmansee for all three. The detective, whom she could not see, made his presence known by sighing frequently.

165

There was not much that Short could do to protect Patty. Depositions are open discovery, and even questions that draw objections must still be answered. Short did repeatedly object, on grounds of relevance and the manner in which questions were framed. Armstrong, in response, sprayed him with venom. "Be quiet now," he demanded early in the first deposition after Short objected to a question phrased as a statement. "Excuse me?" replied Short. "I said be quiet now," repeated Armstrong, warning of likely "counseling sessions with the judge" if Short kept interfering.

Armstrong went through Patty's entire history of relationships, with a particular interest in whether they involved abuse. "When did you first have sexual intercourse?" he asked, over Short's objection. "I was thirteen," said Patty. "And with how many men have you had sex in your life?" Patty wasn't sure. "Hundreds?" asked Armstrong. Actually, she said, it was more like fifteen.

"And how many men have sexually abused you in your life?" Only her stepfather. "And in your life how many times have you claimed that you have been raped?" Just once, but she had on two occasions extricated herself from situations where she thought an assault was about to occur, including the time a strange man walked into her house and she pushed him back out. Armstrong found this incredible, asking if the man was "some kind of a dwarf." He also asked, "Did you have any voluntary sexual contact before you insisted he leave?"

Next Armstrong wanted to know how many men Patty had sexual intercourse with since the alleged rape. Patty, in answering, admitted she had on one occasion come home with a man she met in a bar. Armstrong unloaded: "Do you know your daughter Misty has told various people that after September 4, 1997, you would go to the bars, get trashed, and bring home strangers and have sex with them?"

"There was that one," answered Patty.

"She said you did that with regularity," insisted Armstrong, misstating what Misty had told Detective Schwartz. "Do you deny that?"

"I deny that," said Patty. She speculated that Misty was trying to make her look bad because she had implicated Dominic. Armstrong seized on this: "Assuming she felt she was in a position where she had to protect her boyfriend, what has that got to do with her saying that you would go to bars, particularly on weekends, get trashed, and bring home strangers and have sex with them?" He asked whether Patty was now claiming there were "only two times" she came home with strangers, distorting her testimony that it had happened once. Short objected to this and to Armstrong's use of the word "stranger." But Patty, putting honesty before self-interest, interjected, "He actually was a stranger. Yeah, I did just meet him."

Armstrong asked about Patty's past use of drugs and current use of alcohol, saying "every counselor you've had" as well as "Becky from Rape Crisis" described her as alcohol dependent. Patty disagreed, noting that she didn't drink at all during the week and no longer used any illegal drugs. He asked about Patty's ongoing fear of police. She recalled what Draeger had said about police not believing her next time. Armstrong derided this: "So you're saying that in your heart of hearts you really believe that if you call the police tonight and said 'Somebody is here, I want him out,' that nobody would come and help?" Replied Patty, "I'm working on it psychologically."

After several hours, Short requested a break. When he and Patty were alone, she broke down and wept. She was shocked by Armstrong's meanness and unnerved by Woodmansee's presence in the room. Short tried to reassure her, saying she was doing fine.

When the deposition resumed, Armstrong delved into information he gleaned from Patty's psychological records. "Do you have a hatred for men?" he inquired. No, Patty answered. Then why were there "several references in your stuff, your counseling records, indicating that you have a deep distrust and hatred of men?" "I don't know what you're talking about," answered Patty. "In counseling it's an emotional time. . . . I hate, love a lot of things in counseling."

Armstrong flared. "So what are you saying to me?" he exclaimed. It was "documented in the records" that Patty had a hatred for men. "Are you unable to say at this time what you meant by that?" Patty, flustered, tried to explain: "I'm saying if I said it, which I don't doubt, I certainly didn't mean it. I don't hate men." Armstrong used this to suggest that Patty had lied to her counselors and, probably, to lots of other people too.

He then asked again about Patty's stepfather, her past use of drugs, times she had been hospitalized, boyfriends who had mistreated her. It was like a medley of blues tunes, meant to focus Patty's attention on bad things in her life. Having established this soundtrack, Armstrong for the first time asked about the issues at hand: "You claim, as I understand it, Patty, that on September 4, 1997, you were raped at your place on Fairmont?"

"Right," Patty answered.

"Why do you say you wouldn't make up that story?" wondered Armstrong. Patty couldn't imagine anyone making up such a thing and would never think to do this. Armstrong continued: "Have you ever made up *any* stories before?" Probably, answered Patty. He had her there.

Armstrong asked about Dominic, saying Patty had contended "for several years" that he was the man who raped her. When Short pointed out that it had not even been several years since the assault, Armstrong opted for another falsehood: "For two or more years, has it been your position that you were certain that [Dominic] raped you?" No, answered Patty, she was never certain but he was "my best suspect" until July 1998, when the DNA tests excluded him. Armstrong asked how that made Patty feel, "after having made all these accusations." Patty expressed regret over the strain it had caused between her and Misty. Did Patty hate Dominic? No, she said, "I actually feel kind of sorry for him." Armstrong went on to ask: "Patty, have you ever had sexual intercourse with [Dominic]?"

For Patty, the most painful moments were when Armstrong produced her rape-account journal. Short argued that this document might fall under a work-product exemption if Patty had prepared it on advice of her criminal defense attorney. But Patty, again being perhaps a bit too honest, said she had not. Armstrong quizzed her at length, reading passages she never intended anyone to see, such as how, "in hopes of getting him to climax sooner, I sensuously moved my tongue around the tip of his penis and gently caressed his testicles."

"You're making fun of it," Patty protested. "I'm asking questions about it," said Armstrong. "I'm sorry however you feel about it." He kept reading: "I could hear him responding positively as if he were my lover." "Right?" asked Armstrong. Patty was crying. "I'm going to object again," said Short. "Correct?" asked Armstrong, ignoring him. "I just wish I never wrote that thing," said Patty. Short renewed his objection. Armstrong blew it off: "You can have a standing objection to every single question on every conceivable grounds relating to this document." He was still going to ask.

"And what was there about his response," asked Armstrong, "that seemed as if he were your lover?" Patty: "He just made a couple of groans, moans." This "strategic move," he read on, caused her shame and embarrassment. "I'm not sure what you mean there," he said. "Is it the rape that shames and embarrasses you or your strategy to help him have an orgasm and caressing his testicles that embarrasses you, or is it something else?"

"Yeah, the method of helping him," answered Patty, humiliated. But this strategy didn't work because the rapist didn't climax? "No, he didn't," said Patty. Armstrong did not relent: "But it was your plan that he would have an orgasm and he would ejaculate in your mouth?" "Right," said Patty.

Why, if "you didn't want to have sex," had Patty positioned herself so the man could enter her vaginally? "I wasn't fighting the guy at any time," she said. "I know I should have but I wasn't." On those two other sexual assault attempts, Armstrong noted, Patty had successfully fought back, even though she was alone. But during the alleged rape on Fairmont, where "you had another person in the apartment to help you fight the assailant," she did nothing to resist. "Why is that?"

The man had a knife and Misty was pregnant. "I didn't want him to hurt anybody," she said. "But," exhorted Armstrong, "he never did hurt anybody, did he?" Patty: "I didn't know at the time what he was going to do." Armstrong kept at it. "This person never did hurt you at all, did he?" Short objected, but Armstrong paid him no mind. "*Did he?*"

Patty knew what was expected of her: to give in, to back down, to concede defeat. To say all right already, you win, I give up. I'll say whatever you want. I'll do whatever you want. I'll let you to walk all over me. Almost her whole life, this was how things had gone. But not this time.

"No," she answered. "But I didn't know he wasn't going to. If I fought, he may have." Armstrong ridiculed this: "Was there *anything* that this person did that was forceful in the course of this event?" Said Patty, "Just the fact that he had a knife I felt forced." Persisted Armstrong, "Did he *ever* in touching you physically force *anything*?"

Patty's hurt was turning to anger. "I don't know what you're saying," she retorted. "Did I want him to have sex with me? Is that what you're saying?" Replied Armstrong, peevishly, "I assume the answer is no."

"Right," said Patty.

Armstrong remained on the offensive. Did the man, with any part of his body, use force on her? "He did hold my hair, my head," replied Patty. "He pulled my hair. I felt the knife a couple of times. It didn't hurt. So he didn't beat me. Is that what you're asking?"

"Well, he didn't do that, did he?" crowed Armstrong. "No," said Patty.

Armstrong then asked about the anal assault and whether the rapist may have had an orgasm during this part and remained hard. Short objected, saying this "calls for a medical conclusion." "Or experience," wisecracked Armstrong. In fact, he said, Patty really had no idea whether the man climaxed in her anus. Patty responded: "I know from the hospital he didn't."

The deposition ended past 5 p.m., after more than eight hours. Armstrong was nowhere near finished, but Short insisted on calling it a day.

Patty's second deposition, on March 21, was just as brutal. Again, Armstrong read from her journal, which he insisted on calling a "diary." When Short objected, he renamed it "this writing which I call a diary." Armstrong also repeatedly described the gathering at Mark's house on the day of the rape a "party." When Short protested, Armstrong replied, "If a number of people referred to this event . . . as a party, do you say they're not telling the truth?" Actually, it was Armstrong who was being dishonest; while Misty had told Woodmansee she was upset to see people drinking and laughing, she had not called it a "party," nor had anyone else who was there.

Once again, much of the deposition was devoted to exploring personal areas that had nothing to do with the conduct of police. Patty was grilled about her relationship with Mark. "Did he sexually abuse you?" "Did he physically abuse you?" "Did you sort of stalk him?" "Was he afraid of you when you were jealous and angry?"

Armstrong also lambasted Patty about how, after September 4, she let Misty stay "back in the rape apartment, alone." What steps had she taken "to protect Misty" during this period of time? Patty had urged Misty to also stay at Mark's, but she declined. By the way, said Armstrong, this "prompts me to ask a question I forgot to ask last time. After you had your [older] daughter [at age fourteen] and you had had those seven, eight, nine years of sexual abuse by your stepfather, why did you leave [this daughter] in the home with your stepfather to be raised?"

Short objected. Patty cried. "I was a kid," she pleaded. "I thought I was the only one being abused." Armstrong showed no mercy: "And at that time, recognizing that you were a kid, you had no concern that your stepfather might sexually abuse your first daughter?" "I didn't," said Patty, adding that she was never aware of any abuse. "Have you asked her?" pressed Armstrong. "No," admitted Patty.

A moment later, employing his parallel tack of treating Patty as though she had the IQ of shrubbery, Armstrong asked, "Do you understand that you filed a complaint in the federal court suing Woodmansee and some other people?" He called Patty's attention to the section of her "diary" where she described her first meeting with Woodmansee, and how he seemed to exude "obvious arrogance." What did she mean by that? Well, for one thing, said Patty, Woodmansee told her straight off that he was going to do a better job than the police who had already questioned her.

This set Armstrong off. "Weren't you real happy," he asked, "that somebody was going to do a better job in questioning you to find out who raped you?" He then chided Patty for writing that Woodmansee, during this first encounter, was frustrated with her inability to remember details. Wasn't this to be expected from someone "working very hard with the victim to get some answers that might help solve the crime?" Patty said she thought Woodmansee's "pressuring" was counterproductive. He made her feel as though "I can't remember" and "I don't know" were not acceptable answers and expressed his frustration by sighing a lot.

"So what?" interrupted Armstrong. Replied Patty, "What do you mean, 'So what?'" She couldn't believe she had to justify her opinion that Woodmansee's sighs were inappropriate for a detective interviewing a rape victim, even as he was sitting right there in the deposition room sighing up a storm. Armstrong erupted: "You have an officer trying to solve your rape and he's frustrated by your answers and he's sighing. *Who cares?*"

Patty said she felt intimidated, recalling how Woodmansee had suggested the two of them might have to "role play" the rape if she couldn't get it right. Armstrong berated Patty's discomfort with this suggestion: "And you are upset that he's trying to be very thorough and do whatever is necessary to help you remember to the best of your ability what happened?"

After hours of this sort of questioning, during which he continued to denigrate Patty about "the rape you claim happened," Armstrong turned his attention to the events of October 2, which were at the heart of the lawsuit. It was here that his efforts to break Patty's spirit paid off.

For a long time she held firm, maintaining that the entire time she was at police headquarters and, even afterward, at the mental health center, she felt she was in custody. She recounted that she wasn't allowed to leave to smoke a cigarette and that when she asked to come back the next day with a lawyer or counselor Woodmansee had refused, saying, "You'll just change your story." But then, in a rapid-fire exchange, Armstrong succeeded in strong-arming Patty into a series of admissions that would undermine her cause of action.

ARMSTRONG: "Did you ever ask Tom or Linda if you were free to leave?"
PATTY: "No."
ARMSTRONG: "Did you ever tell Tom or Linda that you wanted this interview or interrogation to stop and you wanted to go home?"
PATTY: "Not in those words, no. I told him I was telling him what they wanted to hear so that I can leave."
ARMSTRONG: "Did you ever attempt to get up and walk out, announce you were leaving and make the move to leave?"
PATTY: "No, I didn't feel—they wouldn't have let me."
ARMSTRONG: "So is that the answer?"
PATTY: "I never made the attempt to get up and leave."
ARMSTRONG: "And you never announced that you were now going to leave?"
PATTY: "No."
ARMSTRONG: "Did you ever demand to call a lawyer?"
PATTY: "Just the one time."
ARMSTRONG: "The one where you said you want to maybe come back the next day with your lawyer or Linda Moston?"
PATTY: "I didn't say maybe. I said I wanted to come back the next day with my lawyer or my psychologist."
ARMSTRONG: "Now let's talk about this day when you're actually with the detectives. Did you ever demand to have an attorney present on that day?"
SHORT: "Objection, asked and answered."
PATTY: "No."

The questioning went on for several more hours, until about 6 p.m. Armstrong scoffed at Patty's testimony that she feared the two detectives, based on their threat to put her in jail overnight on suicide watch. Why should this make her afraid? he wondered. Wouldn't being jailed really be more of "an inconvenience or annoyance"? He again questioned her indelicately about the assault ("Did this person ever kiss you?" "Did you kiss him?"), challenging and doubting her account. But Armstrong's purpose was already achieved. Once again, Patty had been too honest for her own good. If only she had said, "Yes, I demanded an attorney; yes, I got up to leave but they physically prevented me."

Patty's third deposition took place a few days later. Armstrong, who was billing the city's insurer at the rate of $120 an hour, painstakingly went through Patty's itemized claim for damages. It listed twenty-one hours of lost work time, at $8 an hour, for a total of $168. In all, Patty sought actual damages of $5,528, including Harlowe's $5,000 fee, plus unspecified punitive damages.

Toward the end of this deposition, Patty expressed that Wood-mansee seemed single-mindedly focused on a single suspect, Dominic. He kept asking whether she thought it was him, which struck her as beside the point: "There's evidence. Get it. I thought the evidence [would show] that he did it or he did not." Woodmansee, from his place at the table, issued a sigh so loud that Short complained. Said Wood-mansee, "I'm doing my best not to react to her accusations that are lies."

23

The Police Defendants

Parties to a civil action who are being deposed should remember, first and foremost, to abandon hope. They cannot possibly help themselves or their side; they can only minimize the hurt. Depositions are fishing expeditions in which opposing lawyers cast about for incriminating admissions. Statements that serve the interests of the person being deposed are tossed back into icy waters. Smart deposition witnesses are correct but not candid, responsive but not forthcoming. The police defendants in Patty's case understood this, and it made them formidable witnesses, although Woodmansee's powerful need for self-justification would create a few chinks in the armor.

Due to his lack of financial resources, Mike Short deposed only three people: Woodmansee, Draeger, and Schwartz. Since he didn't have an office of his own, these depositions took place on enemy turf—the offices of Axley Brynelson. His six deposition sessions, including recesses, took a total of seventeen hours, compared to the nineteen and a half hours that Axley spent deposing Patty.

The first defendant deposed was Lauri Schwartz. The earnest young detective, Modl told Short, had been calling him to complain about her inclusion in the lawsuit. Short agreed to consider dropping her depending on what he was able to learn. Schwartz's depositions—a three-hour session followed by an hour-long one—were mostly a waste. Schwartz said she consulted with Woodmansee during his initial investigation and suggested that he employ a ruse, although not specifically the one regarding rubber residue. Later, she was assigned to do follow-up work on Patty's obstruction charge. She could not remember if she made it clear to the people she spoke to that this was her purpose. She did not contact any of the family members whose names and numbers Misty provided, except for Patty's sister Sue.

Schwartz made this call to obtain contact information for the sisters' former stepfather, whom she wanted to question about Patty's allegations of past sexual abuse. Determining whether this abuse occurred, she said, was relevant in assessing "the credibility of the person in the current investigation." After this contact caused a fuss, District Attorney Nicks "informed me that she believed that my investigation was concluded."

Short sought more specifics, but Schwartz did not provide them. He was left sputtering that she "can't remember the substance of any of her conversations." That sparked an argument with Modl, after which Short called it quits. He later agreed to drop Schwartz from the suit, focusing his efforts on the police conduct that led to Patty's confession.

Linda Draeger had helped secure this confession, so her testimony was critical. But Short deposed her for barely two hours before throwing in the towel. Draeger used the phrases "I don't recall," "I don't remember," or "Not to my recollection" more than forty times, not counting her "no" answers to questions beginning, "Do you know . . . ?" The veteran detective couldn't remember the circumstances under which she assisted Woodmansee on October 2. She couldn't remember him bringing up suicide or sexual abuse in Patty's family history and said no mention was made of suicide watch—all things Woodmansee had admitted. Draeger did recall lecturing Patty about "The Boy Who Cried Wolf" and letting her smoke inside rather than endure the (make-believe) inclement weather. Did Draeger also smoke, as Woodmansee and Patty attested? Draeger couldn't remember.

Woodmansee, in his three depositions, also suffered from the severe memory lapses endemic among Madison police. Indeed, he could not even remember what *year* it was—1997 or 1998—when Riley gave him Patty's letter complaining about his use of lies and threats. This was especially perplexing, since this letter and the one to the *Wisconsin State Journal* that accompanied it were central to the Police and Fire Commission proceeding at which Woodmansee testified.

Back then, it was not disputed that these letters were received on October 23, 1997, the day after the *State Journal* article they referenced.

And Woodmansee, explaining his failure to forward these letters to the district attorney's office, as Riley had intended, testified that his report on the case had already been sent. But now, in March 2000, he could not remember "if the letter was in my possession" at the time he sent his report. When Short pressed him on this, Woodmansee got testy: "I did not intentionally hide this letter as it feels like you're insinuating."

Woodmansee said he completed his forty-eight-page report "sometime soon after" the last event it describes, on October 10. The exact date "should be easy enough to figure out if we look at the case intake form, because that's when I forwarded the report to the DA's office." He located the form among the files he had brought along. "The date presented was the twenty-fourth of October."

This did not ring any bells for Short, who moved on to other questions. Nor did the significance of this date occur to him when a copy of this intake form was included in a court filing several weeks later. Short was trying to hold his own against three attorneys as well as a judge who had announced his eagerness to throw out the case. He was juggling depositions and discovery demands in addition to handling other cases for which he was actually getting paid. And he was not fully aware of the timeline and testimony regarding Patty's letters. Thus it never dawned on him what this date revealed: Woodmansee did not seek obstruction charges against Patty until *the day after* he was presented with the letters she had sent to his boss, accusing him of misconduct. This revelation powerfully substantiated one of Short's causes of action—that Patty's prosecution was commenced as an act of retaliation. But Short was too overwhelmed to notice.

Woodmansee's report did say he notified the district attorney's office of his intention to seek charges two weeks earlier, on October 10. And the police department's October 21 press release indicated its inclination to seek prosecution. But this did not actually happen until after Woodmansee received Patty's letters, making his failure to give these to the district attorney's office, as his supervisor had wanted, even more suspicious. It also meant that Woodmansee's testimony before the PFC had been untrue.

Throughout his depositions, Woodmansee exuded what Short would later describe as "monumental arrogance." His memory was selective, his answers self-serving and evasive, his reinterpretations of reality audacious. When not attacking Patty's credibility, he pegged himself as her ally: "She's had horrible things happen to her. She's had a great deal of dysfunction in her life." He saw her decision to fabricate a rape as a cry for help, to which he was seeking to respond by having her charged with a crime. "I felt that I was trying to help her," he said. "I still feel to this day that I was."

During his first deposition, Woodmansee testified that Patty was unequivocal in naming Dominic, saying she was "sure he did it" and "very sure he did it"—statements that appear nowhere in his forty-eight-page report. During the second deposition, he admitted, "She never said she was positive throughout the entire contact I had with her." Woodmansee then expressed amazement that Patty was upset when he confronted Dominic: "It makes no sense to me." Perhaps, Short suggested, she was bothered that he told Dominic she had, in no uncertain terms, named him as her rapist. "Why did you say that to him?" asked Short. Woodmansee: "Because she did!"

Woodmansee's third deposition was devoted to his list of forty-one reasons for not believing Patty. Short went through the list, item by item. He asked about Woodmansee's representation that Patty reported no odor, including any alcohol odor, from the suspect, then changed her account. Short noted that, according to Woodmansee's report, one of the first things Patty said about her assailant was that he had "a strong smell" of alcohol on his breath. So why did Woodmansee put this on his list? "I don't know what I'm trying to say," he answered.

Another item: during her 911 call, Woodmansee alleged, Patty "indicated that the knife used in the assault was one of hers but she never mentioned this to me." Short, reading from a transcript of the call, notes what Patty actually said: "He had a knife but I believe it was just like one of mine." She never said it *was* one of hers. Woodmansee thought she had. Was it possible, asked Short, that he got this wrong? Woodmansee would not concede the point: "I listened to the tape closely. What I heard was her indicate that it was one of her knives possibly."

Short continued through the list, establishing that each item could be the result of some error or misunderstanding. Woodmansee protested that it was unfair to focus on specifics when what mattered was "the totality of the investigation with all the inconsistencies." The detective admitted including discrepancies in the accounts given by Patty and Misty without ascertaining who was right and who was wrong. He could not name any of the "several" women who told him it was not possible to feel a condom fill. Short found this hard to believe: "I mean, those are pretty personal questions." Barked Armstrong, "What's the point?"

Many items weren't inconsistencies at all, just things Woodmansee considered strange, like Patty's offer to go into the closet. Wasn't this, asked Short, a rather smart idea? Woodmansee didn't think so: "I found it highly unusual that someone going through the incident . . . described would make any suggestions to the suspect to help the suspect rather than just do nothing and be told what to do."

Woodmansee had also listed that Patty only belatedly revealed the intruder had touched her on the shoulder and asked if she wanted more sex, to his mind a "very unusual and blatant fact." Asked Short, "Doesn't that go to her credibility, though, that she would tell you such an odd thing?" "No," said Woodmansee. "It goes to her consistency of saying very odd things of her alleged account of what took place." When Short suggested Woodmansee's assumptions of how Patty should react might be erroneous, given that he was not a blind rape victim, he replied acidly, "Neither was she."

Under other circumstances, a rookie detective who mishandled a rape investigation might have acknowledged, even learned from, his mistakes. But the unwavering allegiance of the police department, district attorney's office, and now the city's hired attorneys caused Woodmansee to commit himself entirely to defending his actions and defaming Patty. In the process, damage was done not just to Patty but also to Woodmansee's potential to become as good a detective as his self-image.

On April 17 the attorneys for Axley Brynelson filed a motion seeking summary judgment—dismissal of the case. It was accompanied by a 90-page brief, a 55-page document called "Proposed Findings of Fact and Conclusions of Law," a 10-page affidavit from Tom Woodmansee, and more than 250 pages of exhibits, all made part of the case's public record. These included police reports that revealed Patty's last name in violation of the protective order, excerpts from Patty's depositions, and, of course, Judge Aulik's ruling. "Plaintiff has failed to provide any factual support for her claims," the motion said, referring to Short's ongoing failure to respond fully to Axley's interrogatories. And it claimed Patty's causes of action were all barred by "the doctrine of qualified immunity" that protected police officers in the performance of their duties.

Woodmansee's affidavit, like his list of forty-one points, mainly itemized his reasons for doubting Patty's account. They ranged from the fact that no condom or condom wrapper was found to Woodmansee's belief that Patty's demeanor "was not consistent with that of a sexual assault victim." There was one freshly minted reason: Patty's failure to force her adult daughter to break up with the chief suspect. "In my opinion, it is inconceivable for a mother to allow her daughter to be alone overnight with the individual who the mother believed had sexually assaulted her."

Short had just three weeks to submit his response. In the meantime, the attorneys for Axley Brynelson proceeded with plans to depose nearly everyone on his list of potential witnesses. It was an exercise that would prove helpful to Patty's case but be devastating to Patty.

24

A Strong Case

Patty's agreement with Mike Short required her to pay all expenses as the lawsuit progressed. These included filing fees, copying costs, and, most onerous, depositions. While the court reporter was hired by the party doing the deposition, both sides ordered transcripts, and the tab soon ran into thousands of dollars. Patty, having nowhere else to turn, began borrowing from her businesses. It was a dangerous strategy, but she was desperate.

In early April 2000 Hal Harlowe expressed his concern about Patty's circumstance: "The inarticulate term of art for it is, they're 'costing her to death.'" He feared her case would not just be dismissed, which he expected, but that she would be assessed costs. Short brushed this off: "Patty is as judgment-proof as any person I've ever seen in my life." She made eight dollars an hour. Her businesses were struggling. There was no way she could ever repay the vast sums of money Axley Brynelson was expending, as Judge Shabaz had put it, "running up the meter" on its deep-pocketed client.

Axley tapped two outside experts—Ray Maida, a local investigator of sensitive crimes who had worked for both the police and district attorney's office, and Joseph P. Buckley, president of John E. Reid and Associates, a Chicago-based interrogation-training outfit—to review Patty's case. Buckley, as coauthor of *Criminal Interrogations and Confessions*, literally helped write the book on techniques used to extract sometimes-false confessions from recalcitrant suspects. Maida was paid $55 an hour for his time; Buckley got $150 an hour, or $1,500 per day, "plus expenses." Maida, in his written report, found "nothing in the documents" or his interview with Woodmansee to indicate any "wrongdoing" or violations of common police practices. Buckley, in a three-page report accompanied by a six-page list of materials he professedly reviewed, concluded that police had done "a reasonable investigation," that Patty's interviews and interrogation were "conducted in a reasonable manner," and that her resulting confession "appears to be a voluntary and truthful statement." That she promptly and consistently repudiated it was not given any credence, or even addressed.

In the latter half of April 2000, nine more people were deposed in Patty's case. Most sessions were brief, averaging just under two hours. The longest were for Misty and Debra Kuykendall, a "direct services supervisor" at the Rape Crisis Center. The shortest were for Dr. Thomas Stevens, Patty's ophthalmologist; and Nina Bartell, a psychotherapist she visited after the charges were dropped. Also deposed: Connie Kilmark, Linda Moston, Patty's sisters Brenda and Sue, and Jill Poarch.

The Axley attorneys, Modl and Armstrong, divided these depositions between them. Both routinely attacked witnesses when they supported Patty or called the conduct of police into question, as all of them did.

For instance, when Misty testified that she had been offended by some of Woodmansee's questions—like how often she and her boyfriend had sex and in what positions—Modl tore into her. "Did you understand, Misty, that [Dominic] was a suspect?" No, not at that point. "Do you know now that [he] was a suspect?" Yes. "And you understand that your mother said the person who assaulted her assaulted her anally, orally, and vaginally?" Yes. "And knowing what you know now, do you find Woodmansee's questions to you about positions . . . to be offensive?" Well, no, but he could have explained himself better. "Did you ask him why . . . he was asking it?" No.

Misty, in response to Modl's leading questions, admitted being surprised that, after the assault, her mother was not more upset. But this had not caused her to doubt that an assault occurred. On this point, Misty was a rock: "I don't believe my mom would make up a rape."

What made this testimony more compelling was Misty's insistence that this was *always* her position: "I never doubted her being raped at all, period." This meant that while Woodmansee and later Schwartz were pumping her for information to support an obstruction charge,

Misty believed her mother was telling the truth. The only point of dis-agreement was whether Dominic was to blame. And, from Misty's per-spective, it wasn't clear "who was focusing more on Dominic between the two of them"—her mother or Detective Woodmansee.

Kuykendall's deposition, conducted by Armstrong, was even more contentious. Although Kuykendall had not met Patty, she reviewed records of her contacts with the Rape Crisis Center. A ten-year center employee, Kuykendall had provided sexual assault training to law en-forcement officers, at times working alongside Woodmansee. She con-sidered him knowledgeable and "somewhat" sensitive, but had raised a concern with him—just prior to Patty's case becoming public—about the use of ruses. He had mentioned this during a training session as a possible tool, and Kuykendall and two other Rape Crisis workers took him to task on it, saying they didn't think it was a good idea.

This riled Armstrong, who demanded to know whether Kuykendall was aware that "essentially . . . all jurisdictions in the United States" allow police to use ruses. She reiterated that such tactics could "back-fire" in sexual assault cases by creating a climate of distrust. She added that Woodmansee, on hearing these concerns, still "didn't get it," so the Rape Crisis Center told the state Justice Department it didn't want him teaching these classes.

Armstrong asked if Kuykendall was aware that "the police depart-ment uniformly believes" Patty did not tell the truth. She thought this might have changed, due to DNA evidence. "Well," said Armstrong, "there is DNA evidence that demonstrates that the person she claimed raped her [did not]. Is that what you meant?" Kuykendall didn't know enough to say. Armstrong railed against her ignorance. Had she or any-one at the Rape Crisis Center seen Woodmansee's "fifty-page" report? Had they reviewed Patty's "prior medical or psychological records"? Had they seen the record of the SANE nurse or those from the Dane County Mental Health Center? Was Patty's behavior—confessing that she lied about being raped and then not telling the mental health work-ers differently—"consistent with a victim of rape"?

"Yes, it is consistent," answered Kuykendall, to whom it made "per-fect sense" that Patty would not be candid with the mental health work-ers with Woodmansee present or even later "if she felt she was still somehow under his jurisdiction because he had taken her to the center." Moreover, Patty's actions squared "with what she told our counselor."

Armstrong bore down on the particulars. Was it "consistent with a rape experience" for a victim to use the word "sensitive" in describing her assailant? "It can be," answered Kuykendall. "So you're saying more often than not," misstated Armstrong, "the victims will say that their brutalizer was sensitive?" No, she wasn't saying that. But Kuykendall had heard other victims say similar things, which made sense because "very often someone who was being brutalized would want to seek out any semblance of kindness or sensitivity on the part of the person doing this to minimize the impact of what was happening."

What about laughing? Is it typical, Armstrong asked Kuykendall, for a victim to laugh while describing a sexual assault? Yes, as a matter of fact: "Laughter is a nervous response that many people have, especially describing such intimate and graphic things." What about getting drunk, as Patty did that night? This was not surprising, given "some people's extreme desire to block out the reality of the assault." What about a victim who would "party with the alleged perpetrator"? This, said Kuykendall, is not uncommon in cases of domestic abuse.

Armstrong, exasperated, said he had presented what he thought were "some extreme examples" and yet Kuykendall was not troubled by any of them: "Is there anything that I could say to you that Patty did or said during the course of the alleged rape where you would say, gee, I haven't heard this before and that seems inconsistent?" Kuykendall replied that she would have thought it peculiar if Patty had framed some things to police the way she put them in her so-called diary. But given that this was written strictly for her own benefit, her representations were "consistent" and "understandable." Armstrong asked a few more questions, then cut Kuykendall off in midsentence and ended the deposition.

Linda Moston's deposition, which Armstrong also handled, took place at her home in rural Waunakee. Short had trouble finding it and arrived late; Armstrong, much to Short's displeasure, had begun without him. Moston proved nearly as astringent as Armstrong, whom she accused right off the bat of "trying to put words into my mouth."

Armstrong asked whether Patty's pain and sense of powerlessness owed partly to her stepfather's sexual abuse of Patty's older daughter, "assuming that Patty testified to that under oath." Moston knew of no such abuse, which no one had testified to. She also rebuffed Armstrong's claim that Patty suffered from "alcoholism and drug dependency," saying her main problem was depression. And when he began a question by saying, "And if Patty was not raped," Moston would not stand for it: *"Patty was raped."*

"You personally don't know that," began Armstrong. "I do," Moston interrupted. "In my heart, in my body, in my soul, I know that [she] was raped, beyond a question of doubt." Armstrong kept expressing skepticism, but Moston remained adamant. "Patty's not lying about the rape." "I just don't believe Patty is capable of making up a story like this." "Patty would not want to call this kind of attention to herself." Eventually he gave up.

Modl, in deposing Patty's sisters, also tried to shut down unwanted testimony. When Brenda expressed anger over the tardy testing of Patty's bedding, he demanded: "Do you have any experience in law enforcement?" "Any training in law enforcement?" "Have you had any experience in your entire life with the Wisconsin crime lab and their processing of evidence?" When Sue lamented that Patty had no support person during her October 2 interrogation, she got the same: "Do you have any special experience or training in dealing with rape victims?" "Have you ever had any employment that involved counseling rape victims?"

Yet both sisters affirmed Patty's truthfulness and attested to the emotional trauma she had endured—a key element to her pursuit of damages. Since the rape and its aftermath, they said, Patty had become more withdrawn and afraid. "Her spirit is gone," said Sue. "She's mistrustful. She's frightened. She is worried, worried about relying on anyone anymore."

Other witnesses also gave supportive testimony. Dr. Stevens affirmed that even at a short distance, Patty could not likely discern a person's facial features: "Her central loss is too great to make out any details." Kilmark, after outlining her extensive experience and training in psychology and sexual assault (including having lectured at national conferences for survivors of sexual abuse), said she believed Patty was raped and, due to that event and others that followed, "lived in a constant state of stress and fear." Bartell had "no reason to disbelieve" Patty's account, based on their therapy sessions. The psychotherapist was personally familiar with cases in which women made false claims of sexual assault, but Patty did not fit the bill.

The last person deposed was Jill Poarch. This took place in two sessions, with Short posing questions during the first. This was the only deposition, besides her own, that Patty attended; she couldn't afford to take more time off work. Poarch gave detailed accounts of Patty's sexual assault examination and her subsequent encounter with Woodmansee, who "thought that there should have been more injury" and asked whether the injuries found "could have been self-inflicted."

During her first deposition, Poarch wouldn't comment on the appropriateness of the tactics employed by police, including Woodmansee's ruse. But during the second, after Armstrong rudely dismissed her ("Other than what you've heard from Patty, you don't know anything about the investigation in this case, do you?"), Poarch spoke up: "It just doesn't feel right that you would use an interrogation tactic like that with a victim." Sexual assault was already an underreported crime and the way Patty's case was handled, she felt, made victims more reluctant to report. Indeed, after what happened to Patty became "very public knowledge," Poarch said, "we saw fewer patients and there was also a greater percentage of patients that decided not to report to law enforcement." Armstrong's rejoinder: "In your view, is it okay for an alleged rape victim to have lied about the rape?" No, replied Poarch, that was not what she meant.

Short was heartened by these depositions, feeling they might get the case past summary judgment and into court. In fact, he thought he had a strong case. Patty and her witnesses had stood up well to opposing counsel, collectively affirming that she was credible. The police, clearly, had conducted only a cursory investigation before using lies and psychological pressure to get Patty to recant. A jury might regard this as unfairly coercive, whether or not she demanded a lawyer or tried bolting for the door.

Getting to this point, however, came at a huge cost for Patty—not just in terms of the emotional battering she endured but also in dollars and cents. Her quest for justice did not deplete her courage or resolve. But it left her flat-busted broke, and then some.

On the morning of April 28 two representatives of Wisconsin's Business Enterprise Program arrived without warning at Patty's coffee shop. They shut it down and confiscated her supplies. Patty had fallen too far behind in her payments. Patty called Moston, who got word to Short. He tried reaching her, to no avail. Devastated and ashamed, she left this message on her answering machine: "I'm here. I have to take the day off. I can't talk to people today. Please don't call me." Short stopped by Patty's place to make sure she was all right. He found her grieving the impact of these events on her chief assistant, who had been with her for fourteen years. That was just like Patty, Short related, "always concerned about somebody else."

Hal Harlowe went to bat for Patty, arguing that Business Enterprise had not given proper warning and otherwise failed to follow its own procedures. Kilmark helped arrange a repayment plan. But Patty's coffee shop franchise was lost forever, and it would be five months before she was given a new vending machine run. In between, she got a part-time job at a neighborhood grocery store, and Short assumed the lawsuit's ongoing costs.

On May 9, a day past the deadline, Short filed his response to Axley's motion for summary judgment. He recounted Patty's assault and subsequent "humiliating interrogation," saying she was not allowed to leave the room or come back with an attorney. He disputed the defendants' immunity claims, saying "no reasonable officer would have conducted such a slipshod investigation and coercive interrogation." He said Woodmansee had disregarded his training regarding the proper investigation of sexual assault.

Accompanying this filing was an excerpt from the state sexual assault training manual used in sessions conducted by Woodmansee. It advised that victims' reactions are widely divergent and can include showing little emotion and even smiling and laughing: "Do *not* assume that a victim's behavior is a red flag for untruth." Short also submitted a response pleading that made prodigious use of Kuykendall's testimony that Patty's behaviors were not inconsistent with what one would expect from a victim of rape.

Short's pleadings were nowhere near as polished as those from opposing counsel. They contained minor factual errors and misspellings. But they identified dozens of instances in which the two sides had different takes on what occurred. Short's goal was to establish that there were fundamental disagreements over matters of fact, which a jury should decide, as opposed to disagreements over matters of law, which were in the judge's purview.

Several days later, Axley submitted a nineteen-page rebuttal to Short's objections to its findings of fact and a fifty-nine-page reply brief in support of its motion to dismiss. Included was a section that capitalized on Short's failure to notice that Woodmansee forwarded Patty's file to the district attorney's office the day after receiving her attempt to lodge a complaint against him. There was, Axley asserted, "*no* evidence that Detective Woodmansee's decision to refer [Patty] for prosecution was related *in any way whatsoever* to her letter to Woodmansee's supervisor." (Emphasis in original.)

Short, exhausted, did not respond to this latest set of filings. He and the Axley attorneys filed a joint final pretrial report that disclosed each side's prospective witnesses. Short listed eighteen names, including all of the people deposed as well as Mark and several additional members of Patty's family. Axley listed twenty-four witnesses, including Maples, Riley, Thiesenhusen, Maida, Buckley, and Dominic. Both sides named the principal players: Patty, Woodmansee, Draeger, Schwartz, and Feagles. There were, it was agreed, five major factual issues:

1. Whether Defendants falsely arrested Doe in violation of her constitutional rights.
2. Whether Defendants retaliated against Plaintiff in violation of her First Amendment rights by prosecuting her for activity protected under the First Amendment.
3. Whether Defendants coerced a confession from the Plaintiff in violation of her constitutional rights.
4. Whether Defendants had probable cause to recommend prosecution of Doe for obstructing an officer.
5. What sum of money, if any, should be awarded to Doe to compensate her for the alleged violation of her constitutional rights.

No jury ever got to decide these issues. On May 18, 2000, Judge Shabaz threw out the lawsuit "with prejudice and costs," saying the plaintiff "has not demonstrated any violation of her constitutional rights." He found that Woodmansee had probable cause to believe Patty had lied given "the lack of physical evidence" and discrepancies in her account. The detective's alleged failure to contact potential witnesses or analyze evidence was immaterial since he had "no duty to further investigate" once he came to believe that Patty had committed the crime of obstruction. Whether or not she requested an attorney was irrelevant since her statements on October 2 were "never used against her as evidence in a criminal trial." Even if Patty's confession was coerced, "her due process rights would not have been violated unless the confession was used against her at trial."

In other words, Shabaz held that any police misconduct in securing Patty's confession was absolved when prosecutors dismissed charges after their case fell apart. Police could deny citizens the right to counsel or coerce them into confessing so long as the evidence obtained was not used at trial. This interpretation, if consistently applied, opened to acute vulnerability one particular class of criminal defendant—the demonstrably innocent.

Shabaz, in reaching his decision, cited a 1992 federal appellate court case, *Mahoney v. Kesery*, which holds that even coerced statements do not violate the Constitution until they are introduced against a defendant in a criminal proceeding. But an equally applicable 1994 case, *Weaver v. Brenner*, says "use of the statement at trial is not required," only that there be some "use or derivative use of a compelled statement at any criminal proceeding against the declarant." Arguably, charging a person with a crime counts as a criminal proceeding.

But Patty's opportunity to argue her case had come to an end. She was out of money, and thus, in terms of her ability to navigate the justice system, out of luck. Short conveyed to Modl that his client could not afford to pay the defense's legal costs, as Shabaz had ordered. The Axley attorney agreed to accept $1,500—on condition that Patty relinquish her right to appeal. Patty had to sign a document to this effect, and Short paid this amount.

The lawyers at Axley Brynelson billed the city's insurer $98,617 to defend against Patty's lawsuit, most of which went to pay their hourly fees. But picking this deep pocket was not a risk-free proposition. For one thing, it generated reams of information that supported Patty's version of events. For another, although it continued to hire Modl for certain cases, the city's insurer began referring most of its liability claims to another Madison law firm, which had argued that it could do the job for less. And this, from the point of view of the city and its insurer, was the only thing that mattered.

25

"Shocked and Hurt"

In deposing Patty's therapists, attorney Armstrong had shown keen interest in two areas related to Patty's lawsuit. The first concerned his suspicion that someone else had put her up to it. "Do you know who told her to bring [this] lawsuit?" he asked Bartell, as though this could not possibly be her own decision. He also questioned Bartell and Moston about the psychological impact of suing—or being manipulated into suing—the police.

Moston said Patty's ongoing legal battle "is making it very difficult for her to go in and really do the work that she needs to do" regarding the rape and her problems with depression and self-esteem. Instead, she had to be "on defense all the time," unable to deal with anything else. Bartell said what mattered most to Patty was not whether she won or lost but that "she tried as hard as she could to present what she believed to be the facts of her case," in hopes that others would believe her.

As it turned out, Moston was right that Patty needed to process a lot of pain, and Bartell was wrong in thinking she would derive comfort in having done her best. Instead, the punishing ordeal that Patty endured, only to lose her livelihood and then her case, filled her with rage. Several days after Shabaz's ruling, she sent an angry letter to Mayor Bauman.

"Congratulations!" the letter began. "As you know, the attorneys your city hired to protect the police officers who turned on me after I reported being raped did a fine job. They held back nothing, spent money like water, and used every rotten spiteful tactic in the book." These lawyers, she noted, brought in Woodmansee, presumably at city expense, to sit across the table during her depositions. They "repeatedly suggested that I must have enjoyed being raped by my attacker, since I didn't fight him" and "sarcastically mocked the heartfelt journal I wrote about the rape." They grilled her about sex partners and other private matters.

"Even after all I've been through," wrote Patty, "I was shocked and hurt that these tactics were used against me by lawyers representing the city of Madison." She urged Bauman to ask the lawyers if they thought she was lying about being raped: "If not, why was it so important to you to make sure I didn't even get so much as an apology over how I was treated?" She said the mayor ought to "hang your head in shame. The message you're sending to the women here and even the cops is unacceptable."

Bauman, predictably, did not reply. It was typical of the indifference that would ultimately end her political career. (In the next election, she placed a distant fourth in the primary, garnering a mere 12 percent of the vote.) Patty sent a copy of her letter to *The Capital Times*, which did not publish it.

Kilmark wrote a letter of her own to the *Wisconsin State Journal*, detailing how Patty had been "doubted, accused, ridiculed, threatened — all on top of being raped." She urged the city "to publicly examine the whole process that occurred in this case. The citizens of Madison deserve to have their confidence in the system restored." Kilmark's letter was not published either.

The year after Judge Shabaz's ruling would be one of the hardest in Patty's hard life. Her business was lost, and her debts from the lawsuit would take many years to retire. There was no vindication, no partial victory, no sense that she had succeeded in holding the cops accountable. The experience taught Patty that right and wrong has little to do with how the justice system operates. What matters more is the ability of lawyers to manipulate the inherent biases of the system.

And yet there was a bright side. Patty had not buckled under nor caved in to Armstrong's bullying. She remained steadfast and consistent, while demonstrating a far greater commitment to honesty than the police defendants or their lawyers. Mike Short had stood by her, as had Harlowe, Kilmark, her therapists and sisters, and even, for a change, her daughter.

Moreover, Patty believed that people on the other side knew she was telling the truth. How could they not? Which was more likely — that an emotionally fragile woman momentarily buckled under police pressure to confess? Or that she told the truth on just this one occasion and everything else—her reported rape, recanted recantation, private writings and therapy sessions, letters of complaint, appeals to public officials, charges with the PFC, lawsuit against the department, and deposition testimony—was a lie?

Some months after the civil case, Kilmark was introduced to Armstrong at the annual assembly of Lutheran church representatives at a conference center in Lake Geneva, Wisconsin. Kilmark was president of her congregation, St. Stephen's, and Armstrong was representing Bethel Lutheran. Because Modl had handled Kilmark's deposition, she and Armstrong had not previously met, although he recognized her name in connection to the civil suit. "How is Patty doing?" he inquired warmly. Kilmark was nonplused and didn't really answer. Armstrong hoped Patty was doing well. "I liked her," he said.

Misty, after several unproductive semesters working toward a police science degree, abandoned her quest for a career in law enforcement. She was evicted several times and was repeatedly charged with driving after revocation, which eventually led to her spending a week in jail. A would-be suitor began stalking her, and she had to get a restraining order. But despite it all, Misty managed to be a caring mother to her young son.

Dominic, sadly, proved himself unworthy of the concern prosecutors had shown over his unfairly damaged reputation. In September 2000 he was charged with nine criminal counts for a series of events involving a former girlfriend, whom he had moved in with several months *before* he and Misty broke up, as she put it, "for good." These charges included six counts of battery for times he beat her, one count of substantial battery for breaking her nose, and a felony reckless endangerment charge for holding a gun to the side of her head moments before it accidentally discharged. Dominic was convicted on four counts and sentenced to twelve months in jail.

That wasn't the end of Dominic's woes. In February 2001 he was charged in federal court for his role in a cocaine distribution ring that also involved his mother, father, sister, and former roommate Slim. The ring was busted by the Dane County Narcotics and Gang Task Force for which Woodmansee worked. Dominic was ultimately sentenced to

109 months and sent to the federal penitentiary in Terre Haute, Indiana. His mother, Carol, formerly Detective Schwartz's trusted source, was called "an evil, manipulative person" by the prosecutor and sentenced to thirty years.

Woodmansee, meanwhile, was a main player in a major undercover investigation of a local bar, Jocko's Rocket Ship, long known as a hangout for drug users. He posed as a customer and ingratiated himself to the bar owner and others, making repeated cocaine buys. After the bar was raided and closed, he conducted interviews with former patrons, including members of the Madison Fire Department. The firefighters were assured they were not targets of any criminal investigation and were warned about the dangers of not cooperating. Many ended up making admissions about their use of drugs, mostly marijuana.

The Jocko's investigation resulted in federal drug conspiracy charges against nine individuals; all drew stiff sentences from Judge Shabaz. In addition, a half-dozen Madison firefighters were terminated due to drug activity. On May 14, 2001, Woodmansee's work on the case earned him a Meritorious Conduct Award. Drug team supervisor Lieutenant William Housley called him "an individual of uncompromising personal integrity and a police officer who holds himself to the highest professional ethical standards." Woodmansee was not able to accept the honor publicly, given his ongoing involvement in undercover operations.

Within a month of this award ceremony, fate would deliver a crushing blow, one that made it appreciably more difficult for Woodmansee to claim that his handling of Patty's case had produced the right result.

26

Vindicated?

Most human DNA is the same from one person to the next. The science of using DNA (deoxyribonucleic acid) for identification purposes is based on finding genetic markers that show variation. In the early years of DNA testing, making matches was difficult and time consuming, although the results were highly accurate. A newer method, known as STR (short tandem repeat), can rapidly identify sequences of DNA from minute amounts of genetic material.

In moving to embrace this method, the FBI in 1997 selected thirteen core genetic markers on which to reconstitute its national database, the Combined DNA Index System. CODIS uses two indexes that can be compared against each other. The first contains DNA profiles from offenders in all fifty states. The second logs profiles from crime scene evidence.

Because the national data system based on STR loci did not become operational until October 1998, DNA obtained from offenders under existing state laws was entered only belatedly, as time and resources permitted. Thus a biological sample obtained in mid-1996 from a particular convicted Wisconsin sex offender was not analyzed for an STR profile and put into the database until five years later, on May 29, 2001.

On June 11 special agent Liz Feagles was contacted by Marie Varriale, a forensic scientist at the Wisconsin State Crime Laboratory. Varriale informed Feagles that DNA from semen found on Patty's bedsheet matched that of Joseph J. Bong. It was what's known as a "cold hit."

Bong, then twenty-five, was serving an eighteen-year prison sentence for armed robbery and false imprisonment stemming from events on September 12, 1997, eight days after Patty was raped. Also arrested in connection with this crime was Bong's cousin Alonzo "Lonnie" Elvord, a suspect in Patty's assault. The pair's preliminary hearing took place October 1, the day before Woodmansee obtained Patty's confession.

According to the police reports and testimony at this hearing, Bong and Elvord used a sawed-off shotgun to rob a hotel and abduct the female manager and her boyfriend, who happened to be present. Elvord drove the car, the boyfriend beside him in the front seat. Bong, holding the shotgun, sat in the back with the manager. Suddenly Bong grabbed her hair and pulled her head down toward his groin, just as Patty's assailant had done, and began fondling her breast. The hotel manager screamed. The boyfriend lunged at Bong and managed to pry the gun away. In the ensuing struggle, the hostages fled the car and the cousins drove away.

Within a week Dane County sheriff's deputies tracked down and secured confessions from both men. Bong, in his statement, sought leniency for Elvord. "I talked Lonnie into doing the whole thing," he said. "I got Lonnie drunk and high and he is not the type of person to do this." Bong explained that the crime occurred after the two of them bought a quart of brandy and twenty dollars worth of marijuana and polished off a twelve-pack of beer. He later summoned a deputy to his cell to amend his statement: the pair had not actually paid for the marijuana, he now said; they ripped the dealer off.

Bong's attorney, Mark Frank, tried to have his confession suppressed, saying his client, a diabetic, was questioned for more than four hours while authorities "failed to provide, refused to provide, or otherwise withheld insulin." He said Bong had substance-abuse problems, a history of mental illness, below-average intelligence, and learning disabilities, "reading at approximately the second-grade level." The deputies testified that he never said he was diabetic or asked for insulin. The judge declined to throw out the confession, and Bong pled no contest to one count of armed robbery and two counts of false imprisonment. The sex assault charge was dropped.

At Bong's sentencing, Frank was left grasping at such straws as, "Mr. Bong has never committed a crime sober." Bong also spoke on his own behalf. "I'm a good person. I've just done a couple of dumb things in my life. And I realize that I have a drinking problem," he told the court. "I want help and I want to be part of my family's life and I know that I need to do some time and it isn't going to probably minimize this at all. Whatever you give me I will have deserved it because it is a horrible thing." Bong's eighteen-year term was more than three times what Elvord received but less than half the forty-three years the prosecution requested.

With the DNA results in hand, Feagles connected the dots. At five feet ten and 180 pounds, Bong was a bit taller and heavier than what Patty described but in other respects seemed to match. He was a light-skinned biracial man with short hair who would have been twenty-one at the time of the rape. He had committed a crime with Elvord, a known suspect in Patty's rape. Besides the hotel robbery and abduction, Bong had previously been convicted of two counts of sex with a child age sixteen or older and one count of fourth-degree sexual assault, originally charged as second-degree sexual assault while armed. He also had felony convictions for car theft, receiving stolen property, and bail jumping.

In late June, Feagles obtained a search warrant authorizing her to take a swab from Bong's inside cheek—known as a buccal sample—for additional DNA analysis. This she did at Dodge Correctional Institution, about an hour from Madison. Subsequent testing confirmed the match.

Reporters for Madison's daily papers broke the story after they saw Feagles's public application for a search warrant to obtain additional samples from Bong and recognized the particulars. The application said the victim, identified by initials only, had "at one point during the Madison Police Department investigation . . . recanted her report because she [felt] pressured to do so." Feagles also set forth her belief that this victim was "credible and reliable in her account of the sexual assault." Both papers quoted Short as saying that Patty had been "vindicated."

Police Chief Williams continued to insist his officers did everything right. He claimed the state Division of Criminal Investigation had conducted an investigation into how Patty's case had been handled and cleared his detectives of any wrongdoing. "We accept their finding," he said solemnly.

This was a complete fabrication. Despite Patty's request that it do so, the state never investigated the conduct of Madison police, and it certainly never exonerated them of wrongdoing. The only such exoneration came from Williams's own assistant and arguably from Judge Aulik, who lost his battle with cancer the same week Williams told this lie.

In response to Williams's remark, the state Justice Department and Madison police were left trying to provide spin control. "We don't *know* that they did anything inherently wrong or deliberately negligent," ventured Justice Department spokesperson Mitch Henck, before admitting that investigating police was not a focus of its probe, as Williams claimed: "He's not correct there." Madison Police Department spokesman Ben Vanden Belt (later forced to resign after being charged with giving cocaine to and having sex with a minor) said the state had been asked "to reinvestigate this case as a whole" and thus would have presumably pointed out if Madison police engaged in misconduct or even "neglected to follow up on some great lead."

Actually, there was one great lead the police may have neglected. After Bong was identified as a result of the DNA match, Misty remembered a visit she'd had from a friend, John Quamme, shortly after the rape. (Patty remembered this too, as it was one of the first nights she spent back at the Fairmont apartment and she was startled by Quamme's knock at the door.) Misty said she and Quamme went for a walk, during which he told her about the hotel robbery and suggested she mention Bong to the police. This she recalled doing in a phone conversation with Woodmansee. "I know that I brought Joey's name up," she told me. "I know that I told Tom." Woodmansee would deny ever getting this tip. Quamme, when I spoke to him, denied giving this information to Misty. He said he was Bong's cousin and "trying to stay out of this."

Days after this new DNA evidence was revealed, former District Attorney Diane Nicks contacted Hal Harlowe. Nicks, who had since become a judge, asked him to pass a letter to Patty. It was brief and cautiously worded: "I write to express my sincere regret for the period during which charges were pending against you. Clearly, it was an extremely difficult time for you. I am sorry for the pain that you experienced." She hoped recent developments and the prospect of charges against the newly identified suspect "lead to a measure of closure and comfort for you."

Harlowe, in forwarding this to Patty, attached a note of his own. "Although the letter is not labeled an apology, it is clearly intended as one," he wrote, adding that this was not enough. "Before this is over, I intend that you receive an unambiguous public apology. You certainly deserve one."

From Patty's point of view, the new DNA evidence was nothing short of miraculous. She had thought, not without justification, that her case had been forgotten. Now, she assumed, the system would be forced to admit that she had told the truth. "I'm ecstatic," she said at the time. "It's absolutely the best news I could hope for."

But the identification of a suspect also meant that, even after almost four years, Patty's ordeal was not yet over. If the case went to trial, it would get ugly. The efforts of police and others to discredit her—to peg her as mentally ill, alcoholic, promiscuous, and untrustworthy—could and probably would be used against her. And all of the material collected by the lawyers from Axley would be potentially available for use in Bong's defense.

There was another complication: Misty, it turned out, had not only known Bong slightly, she knew him slightly in the Biblical sense. "I fucked him," is how she broke the news to her mom. This did not happen at the duplex on Fairmont, and certainly not in Patty's bedroom, which according to everyone was always kept locked. But after this information was reported to Feagles, people in the police department and district attorney's office began speculating about what "really" happened: Bong had used Patty's bedroom to have sex with her daughter and left semen on the sheet, an act purely coincidental to Patty's false claim that she was raped by an intruder matching his description. Short was angered by such speculation but knew it could provide the basis for reasonable doubt. "As a criminal defense attorney," he mused, "I'd *love* to try this case."

Harlowe also grasped how the defense could use Patty's momentary "confession" to argue that no rape occurred. It could highlight discrepancies in her account, real or imagined, as evidence that nothing she said could be believed. It might even get Woodmansee and Draeger to testify as defense witnesses. Harlowe wanted to make sure Patty was aware of these risks and that she was involved in deciding whether to press charges.

Dane County, by this time, had a new district attorney: Brian Blanchard, a former newspaper reporter, assistant U.S. attorney, and business litigator. He had defeated incumbent Brian Brophy, who was appointed to the post after Nicks was appointed judge. Brophy, despite being endorsed by nearly every prosecutor in the office, had the misfortune of running as a Republican in a Democratic-leaning county on the same ballot as a presidential election so hotly contested it took more than a month to call. (Afterward, Brophy became a defense attorney; his campaign treasurer, Jill Karofsky, also left the office, landing a job with the Madison-based National Conference of Bar Examiners, which sets professional standards for lawyers.) Blanchard was bright, thoughtful, and personable, but he lacked experience in Dane County's criminal court system. He was seen as an outsider, and he needed to win the trust of his staff—which had, after all, overwhelmingly favored his opponent.

In late July Harlowe met with Patty in his office. Feagles's case file, he had learned, had gone to Deputy District Attorney Judy Schwaemle. Harlowe had known Schwaemle for many years, going back to when he was district attorney and hired her as a prosecutor. He saw the choice before her as a double-edged sword: while charging Bong would be tantamount to admitting the office was wrong in prosecuting Patty, not charging him might look as though it would rather let a rape go unpunished than admit error.

Whether Patty wanted the case to proceed was another question. "My job is to keep you in control of what happens," Harlowe told her. "The rape, that was a loss of control. And that's what the system did—they took that and compounded it." Now she was at risk of further "public embarrassment and humiliation"—unless she declined prosecution. Harlowe urged her to consider this option. She could just say she was tired, she lacked faith in the system, she didn't want to keep fighting. It didn't matter, he said, what people in the police department or district attorney's office thought: "They weren't with you when it mattered." And there was nothing more Patty needed to do to be vindicated. "You've won already," he told her. "They now know you were telling the truth. You were raped, and the police screwed up."

But Patty was not inclined to walk away now. Earlier, she had asked for the rape investigation to be reopened, against Harlowe's advice, because she wanted the man who assaulted her brought to justice. Now, even though Bong was in prison, she didn't want him to get away with what he did to her, for fear this would embolden him, when he did get out, to assault someone else. She knew a trial might be brutal, but she couldn't imagine it would be worse than what Armstrong had put her through.

One thing soon became clear: the Dane County District Attorney's Office was in no hurry to make a decision and had little regard for Patty's peace of mind. In August, Schwaemle contacted Short to obtain transcripts of Patty's depositions. These he provided, knowing they contained nothing that damaged her credibility. But once again, it seemed as though the system was trying to find some reason to doubt Patty's account.

The fourth anniversary of Patty's rape came and went. The World Trade Center towers were obliterated by terrorists, and anthrax scares gripped the nation. Patty thought her ordeal suddenly seemed unimportant, and the district attorney's office seemed to agree.

On October 25 Harlowe accompanied Patty to a meeting with Blanchard, Schwaemle, and victim/witness advocate Mark Kerman. It was the first time anyone from the district attorney's office had met Patty. She said it was important to her that Bong be prosecuted and expressed surprise that charges were not already filed. Schwaemle and Blanchard said the case involved an inordinate amount of work, because of all the paper it generated. They did not commit to filing charges, saying this decision would be made within a month. If they did go forward, it would be a complicated and uncertain case.

In early November Cheri Maples of the Madison Police Department sent Patty a letter of apology. Earlier, when the new DNA evidence came to light, she had prepared a press release defending the police investigation but expressing regret; others in the department blocked its release. And so Maples, who now held the rank of captain, decided to act unilaterally. Her letter read in part: "I was wrong and your case will always serve as an important reminder to me that the police are not infallible and holding us accountable in a democratic society is extremely important. I can only imagine the additional trauma you were put through after being sexually assaulted and then having your story questioned, and then not being believed by the police officers and supervisors charged with investigating your case. Words will never be able to convey how sorry I am."

Maples, who after her promotion was put in charge of police training, assured Patty that as a result of her case the department would "reexamine how we provide training to police officers and sensitive crimes detectives. We will attempt to convene a group associated with the initial investigation and charging decisions to discuss what went wrong to try to avoid making the same mistakes in the future." In conclusion, she offered "my sincere apologies for any injustice that was done to you personally throughout this ordeal. The fact that it was a sincere and honest mistake does not and is not intended to diminish the pain and trauma that you were subjected to."

Woodmansee was angered by this communication, feeling it exposed him to legal action. Williams and others in the department shared this sentiment and subjected Maples to a disciplinary investigation. Maples, who a few months earlier had gotten Williams in hot water by objecting to his joking about "women with big breasts," indicated that she would not back down and would go public if discipline were imposed. None was.

Schwaemle summoned Patty and Harlowe to another meeting, on December 5. Kerman was also present. The district attorney's office was willing to press charges but, given the difficulties the case presented, was leaving the decision in Patty's hands. Schwaemle pressed Patty to explain why she had recanted to police despite having been raped. Patty said she thought it was the only way she would be allowed to leave. Harlowe, as at the suppression hearing, tried to explain Patty's disorientation and fear. Schwaemle warned that the defense might argue the sex was consensual, involving either Patty or her daughter, and that the police might not be on Patty's side.

Patty, after taking a couple of days to think it over, left a voice-mail message for Schwaemle saying yes, she wanted to go ahead. She asked Schwaemle to call her back, but the prosecutor did not. Weeks passed. In early January 2002 Blanchard told me the plan was to prosecute "unless we see something that causes us to rethink." His office wanted to review "all" of the material in Patty's case.

Soon after, Feagles obtained a signed release from Patty to access the medical and mental health records that Axley had unearthed during the civil suit. Short was bothered by this request, which again seemed to indicate a greater interest in checking out the alleged victim than the alleged crime. Had Patty really been vindicated, or was she being set up for another fall?

27

Wishing It Were Over

In journalism, as in quantum mechanics, the process of observation alters what occurs. People and institutions behave differently when they're being watched. As Patty's ordeal played out to growing media interest, a key question arose: were they behaving better, or worse, than if no one was paying attention?

Clearly the Madison Police Department, from Chief Williams on down, was mainly interested in justifying its actions. With the exception of Captain Maples, no member of the department had publicly acknowledged that any errors were made or had expressed any sympathy for Patty. And even Maples sought to exonerate the police and shift blame back to the person she now acknowledged was a victim. "This is not Tom Woodmansee's fault," she stated in one communication, calling him "an inexperienced detective in sensitive crimes [who] was not given enough managerial help and support." She also said Patty did not behave like "most sexual assault victims" and may have "exaggerated portions of her story because she is not used to being believed." No examples were given of this alleged exaggeration, a charge not even Woodmansee had thought to make.

Just as clearly, the desire to avoid looking bad had driven the extraordinary efforts of the district attorney's office to salvage its criminal case against Patty after the discovery of semen evidence. Might it now also affect whether and how aggressively it was willing to prosecute Joseph Bong, the man whom this evidence ultimately implicated?

As the weeks turned into months with no action taken, this seemed more likely. Privately Harlowe and Short expressed rising levels of frustration. For Patty, the delay was heartrending, oppressive. She couldn't understand what was taking so long, and this compounded her anxiety over the part of her ordeal that she knew was still ahead.

In mid-March of 2002 Patty contacted Kerman, the office's victim/witness advocate, imploring that the case move forward as quickly as possible. He explained that Schwaemle had many hats to wear and cases to attend to, but intended to file charges within the next two weeks. That meant the preliminary hearing would probably take place in April. By mid-April Patty still hadn't heard a thing. She was reluctant to make further inquiry: "It just seems like, what good does it do to keep calling them?" But she did call and she spoke with Schwaemle. Patty explained her anxiety and concern, saying she hoped to plan a vacation but was unable to, not knowing when the hearing might be. Schwaemle said she planned to come in that weekend to draft a criminal complaint.

Another week passed, and neither Patty nor her lawyers were apprised of any new developments. Harlowe drafted a letter to Blanchard, saying that unless action was imminent he planned to ask a judge to file charges directly and appoint a special prosecutor, as Wisconsin law allows. He finished the letter on Friday, April 26, but gave himself the weekend to think it over. It would be a shot across Blanchard's bow, a challenge to his authority, and it could be seen as an attempt to embarrass him. It was not Harlowe's style, but he felt he had no choice.

In other quarters, too, frustration was reaching critical mass. Short barely stopped himself from upbraiding Blanchard when he saw him in a public place that Saturday. Instead, he vented to Feagles: "I told Liz, basically, that what they've been doing is cruel. They have all the information to charge the guy, and then to let Patty twist in the wind is cruel." Feagles didn't disagree. She told Short she had awoken at 2 a.m. this same Saturday, distressed about Patty's case. Later that morning, Feagles called Schwaemle and found her at work, drafting the criminal complaint. On Monday it was presented to Feagles to sign, as a complaining witness.

Harlowe learned the news when he decided to place one last call to Schwaemle before sending his letter. He was delighted that he didn't have to: "I would rather have them feeling good about themselves than looking over their shoulders." He thought Schwaemle seemed committed to the cause, although he remained perplexed as to why the office took it on. It could have passed the buck to the state Justice Department, to avoid the conflict presented by its prior prosecution of Patty.

Schwaemle, in talking to Harlowe, mentioned that she thought Patty was on vacation. This is how Patty's remark about not being able to plan a vacation was misinterpreted. Patty, on hearing this, thought it was typical: the people who had put her life on hold were twisting her words to suggest she was taking off on vacation irrespective of what was happening with her case. "It will be so good to have this done with," she sighed.

The criminal complaint charged Bong with five felony offenses: one count of first-degree sexual assault while armed for each of his three acts (anal intercourse, vaginal intercourse, and fellatio), plus one count each of burglary and robbery while armed. Each count carried a maximum penalty of forty years, plus a ten-year penalty enhancer for "habitual criminality." That made for a potential but wildly unlikely sentence of 250 years. The complaint recounted the crime, drawing on information from Thiesenhusen, Woodmansee, and Kaddatz, and detailed the events that produced the DNA match.

Bong was brought back to Dane County from the state prison in Green Bay and made his initial appearance on May 17, 2002. It took place in a special secure courtroom, adjacent to the jail, where defendants and court personnel conduct preliminary business. In a separate chamber, members of the public sat in pews, watching the proceedings through thick glass and listening via crackling speakers. Among those present were Short, Feagles, and Misty, who had seen an article in the paper that morning and rushed down. Said Feagles to Short, "I wish I could say it was over."

Led in wearing a jail jumpsuit and handcuffs, Bong smiled thinly as he exchanged a few words with the court-assigned public defender. Since Bong was in prison, the bail was nominal—$10,000, or $2,000 for each count. A preliminary hearing was set for the following week.

This formal filing of charges against Bong was the first actual news event in Patty's case since the DNA link came to light a little more than eleven months earlier. And it was the first development *ever* that suggested that the district attorney's office considered Patty a victim, not a likely criminal. Harlowe, in his public comments, showered the office with praise, saying it had done "a commendable job." He attributed the long delay—felony complaints in Dane County are generally drawn up within a few days—to the office's desire to be thorough. Harlowe also publicly praised Patty's courage, telling the *State Journal,* "I'm honored to know her."

The Capital Times, in an editorial that week, called the charges "a step toward justice in a case where police and prosecutors failed [Patty] and the community." It added, "Patty is still owed public apologies by Madison Police Chief Richard Williams and the Police and Fire Commission, which failed to investigate police wrongdoing." Patty, wisely, did not hold her breath.

On May 22 Patty met with Schwaemle and Kerman to go over the testimony she would be asked to give at the preliminary hearing the following day. Harlowe had offered to accompany her, but Patty chose to go alone. Schwaemle explained that Bong's appointed public defender, Daryl Jensen, was not an especially abrasive fellow and the questions should not be punishing. Patty was given various pieces of advice, such as not to use the words "I guess" when answering questions. She was heartened to perceive that Schwaemle and Kerman were on her side.

The preliminary hearing was set for 9 a.m. Patty arrived early for a pep talk with Harlowe. Three other prosecution witnesses—Schwartz, Kaddatz, and Feagles—were on hand to document the chain of evidence that led to the DNA match. They gathered in a group in the hallway, but none of them said a word to Patty; because of her visual disability, she didn't even know they were there. When she learned of this later, she was surprised that Feagles had not greeted her, and irked that Schwartz did not take this opportunity to express regret over what police had done. "She should be ashamed of herself," said Patty. "I would have swallowed my pride and said, 'I'm so sorry.'"

Before the case was called, Judge John Albert asked Schwaemle whether the prelim would take place as planned: "Is this a go?" "No," she answered, explaining that the proceeding would have to be delayed. Just then Bong was led into the courtroom wearing a blue Dane County jail shirt, his hands cuffed in front of him. He took a seat at the defense table and leaned back in his chair.

The lawyers stated their appearance. Public Defender Jensen, sporting a Chia-like growth of short, curly hair, explained that his client wished to be represented by another attorney. This meant Bong needed to waive his legal right to a prompt preliminary hearing, which he did by softly answering "yes, sir" to a series of questions. Judge Albert, himself a former defense attorney, made the next scheduled event a status conference rather than a preliminary hearing, so the prosecution's witnesses would not have to show up again only to experience another delay.

The proceeding ended. Bong stood up, turned around, and peered at Patty with narrowed eyes, maintaining this focus all the while that he was led from the courtroom. She sensed, more than saw, that he was staring at her. At one point, he was just a few feet away, his eyes continuing their cold embrace. In the hallway afterward, Schwaemle explained that the new timeline probably meant the preliminary hearing would take place in late June or early July. Patty's hands were shaking.

Left: Attorney
Mike Short
(2002 photo by
Mary Langenfeld.)

Below left: Attorney
Brad Armstrong.

Below center: Attorney
Michael Modl.

Below right: Judge
John Shabaz.

Judge Gerald Nichol at the trial.

Defense witness Tom Woodmansee.

Defense attorney Mark Eisenberg.

The defendant.

Dane County District Attorney Brian Blanchard *(left)*, with victim/witness specialist Mark Kerman.

Deputy District Attorney Judy Schwaemle. (Trial photos by Mary Langenfeld.)

PART FOUR

FINAL JUDGMENT

28

For the Defense

Mark Eisenberg's career as a lawyer began just as his father's was falling apart. Self-confident to the point of arrogance and flamboyant to the verge of caricature, Don Eisenberg was once Wisconsin's best-known criminal defense attorney. In the early 1980s he represented the state's two most notorious accused murderers: Barbara Hoffman, a Madison massage parlor worker who allegedly conned sad sacks into taking out life insurance policies naming her as the beneficiary, then poisoned them; and Lawrencia "Bambi" Bembenek, a former Milwaukee police officer accused of killing her husband's ex-wife. Eisenberg lost both cases, in ways that brought infamy to his name.

In 1984, the year after his sons Mark and Stephen became lawyers, Don's law license was suspended over a conflict of interest in the Hoffman case. (He had simultaneously represented one of the key witnesses against her.) The original six-month suspension—imposed after he told the state bar association, as the press euphemized it, "to put its rules in a specific part of its collective anatomy"—was extended because he continued to practice and because, when Bembenek appealed on grounds of ineffective assistance of counsel, he proclaimed on Geraldo Rivera's national television show that she was most likely guilty. Bembenek, amid mounting evidence of her innocence, later cut a deal to secure her freedom following a successful prison escape. (Much later, as Patty's case neared its dénouement, she was back in the news, seeking to clear her name through DNA testing.)

Don Eisenberg's reputation went from bad to even worse. In 1987 he was indicted by a federal grand jury on conspiracy and money-laundering charges; he was acquitted, and moved to Florida. Two years later, his still-suspended law license was revoked by the Wisconsin Supreme Court over charges that he misused money in clients' trust accounts. His sons represented him in a 1996 bid to reclaim his license, but the court turned him down, saying he lacked "the necessary moral character." On his third try, in late 2000, Eisenberg got his license back. He remained in Florida but began doing legal work for his sons' Madison-based law firm.

It was a successful, well-regarded outfit. Both brothers inherited something of their father's passion and his fondness for flash and dazzle. In June 2002 Steve Eisenberg won a stunning $7 million civil judgment from a local hospital for its failure to stop his client from leaping into a wall during a psychotic episode, causing paralysis. The man died soon after the judgment was awarded. Mark Eisenberg, the older of the two, wore expensive suits and neatly coifed hair and exuded an aura of self-satisfaction. But he was known for being well prepared and for fighting hard for his clients. Word that he had been hired as Joseph Bong's attorney was considered a lucky break for Bong and bad news for Patty.

As a criminal defense lawyer, Mark Eisenberg gravitated toward tough cases in which the law and circumstance presented opportunities to win. He beat disorderly conduct charges against a sixty-year-old man who propositioned an undercover sheriff's deputy, saying there was nothing disorderly about one person asking another for sex. He sought, without success, to exclude statements his client, accused of being an accomplice to murder, had made to Detective Linda Draeger after initially asking for an attorney. He got a jury to reject a hate-crime charge (while returning a verdict of guilty for disorderly conduct) against a man who tormented his neighbors by, among other things, painting "Lesbians will go to hell" on an old vehicle and then crushing it with a monster truck a few feet from their property line. The man, said Eisenberg, was just objecting to the women being "unneighborly."

At the June 27 status conference, Public Defender Daryl Jensen broke the news: "Mr. Bong, through his mother, has now retained the Eisenberg law firm to represent him." Judge Albert was skeptical, noting that no one from the Eisenberg firm was present. Bong, his head shaved completely bald, had this to say: "I didn't know anything until when I got here yesterday that we even had court." The judge agreed to push back the preliminary hearing another thirty days but kept Jensen the attorney of record pending a formal substitution request. He also said the court would be "adverse" to further delays: "Out of consideration for the victim, this thing has to move forward."

Short was incredulous that anyone in Bong's family would have the financial resources to hire Eisenberg. The last time Bong was in trouble, his attorney was appointed by the state public defender's office. Retainer agreements are confidential, but it's possible Eisenberg agreed to a lower-than-usual fee because it was a high profile case.

On July 1 Mark Eisenberg formally became Bong's attorney. "I don't think this case is about Bong," he told me soon afterward. "I think this case is about Patricia and her daughter." He added brightly, "It's a pretty good case."

The preliminary hearing took place on July 22, 2002, before Judge Albert. A couple of reporters were present, as was Mike Short. The day before, Patty had met again with Schwaemle and Kerman to go over her testimony. She learned she would be the only witness. Eisenberg would stipulate that the DNA on the bedsheet belonged to Bong, so there was no need for police witnesses to establish the chain of evidence.

Patty was called to the witness stand and sworn in. She was quizzed, first by Schwaemle and then by Eisenberg, about the events of September 4, 1997. She spoke slowly, often pausing for long moments before answering. Her story spilled forth as on prior occasions.

"I was sleeping on my stomach and I woke up immediately to a knife to my throat and a guy in my bed," she testified. "He told me to be quiet and nobody will get hurt." And so on. The anal assault. The oral sex. The vaginal sex. The alarm going off, which "kind of scared both of us."

Schwaemle asked what was, for her semen-based case, a critical question: did the man ejaculate? Patty, who had endured abuse on this point from attorney Armstrong, answered equivocally. "It's hard to tell if he had an orgasm or not," she said. "I don't know if—I don't remember or couldn't tell, that part I don't know. But he did finish."

Eisenberg, in his cross-examination, returned to this point: "You couldn't tell if he ejaculated?" "I guess he did," she answered. He zeroed in on areas that had aroused police suspicion, like what time her alarm clock was set for and whether there was anything unusual about the man's penis. He tried asking about Bong's relationship with Misty, but the judge would not allow it.

Schwaemle, on redirect, asked one final question: "Did you know Mr. Bong at the time?" No, Patty answered, she did not. She was excused as a witness and made a beeline for the courtroom door. As she walked past the defense table, her composure faded and she began crying. Short followed her out of the room to give comfort.

"Based on the testimony I heard," ruled Judge Albert, "I find probable cause to believe that a felony was committed by the defendant." As was customary, he then assigned the case to another judge, Gerald Nichol, for future proceedings.

Nichol, then sixty-seven and still a regular hockey player, was considered one of the county's best judges. He had served a single term as Dane County district attorney in the early 1970s, then worked as an attorney in private practice before being elected to the bench in 1988. He presided over the first Wisconsin case in which a defendant was convicted of murder even though no body was ever found. He also conducted the first Dane County murder trial that hinged on DNA evidence. In the early 1990s, when a labor dispute between Madison teachers and the local school district ended up in his court, Nichol assumed the role of mediator and forced the sides to keep talking until an agreement was reached. He was not seen as having a great legal mind or a passion for pondering the fine points of case law, but he ran his court in a fair and evenhanded manner.

Judge Nichol's first exposure to the case was at Bong's arraignment in late August 2002. Schwaemle was late and another prosecutor had to be rounded up to fill in. Eisenberg, in the courtroom beforehand, was in a jovial mood. He joked that he might seek a dismissal because the prosecution was absent, and that, after his planned defense, the district attorney's office "might want to refile charges" against Patty. He also yukked it up with court personnel about how Bong was serving an eighteen-year sentence, saying "I want him out." (In fact, by this time, Bong was eligible for parole, although the severity of his crime made this unlikely.)

When Bong was brought into the courtroom, in handcuffs and jail garb, Eisenberg greeted him warmly: "Hi, buddy." The proceeding lasted less than five minutes. Not guilty pleas were entered on Bong's behalf and Judge Nichol gave each side twenty days to file motions. Eisenberg asked for thirty days, saying there was "a significant amount of discovery" as well as "some issues about the complainant's psychiatric history." The judge granted the extra time. Just as the arraignment ended, Schwaemle arrived.

The thirty-day deadline came and went, with no request for an extension. On the fortieth day, in early October, Eisenberg filed three threadbare, perfunctory motions. He sought exculpatory evidence and information on the criminal backgrounds of any prosecution witnesses, and he asked whether Bong's "other crimes, wrong or bad acts" might be introduced.

No one from the district attorney's office kept Patty posted on developments in the case. "Nobody really gives a shit," she concluded. Mike Short also felt the office was treating Bong's prosecution as a low priority. "If they screw this up, I'm going to be a bitter man," he told me. "I'm going to talk to every media outlet that gives me the time of day."

In late October and early November, Eisenberg filed two new batches of motions. Unlike his initial ones, these were substantive and intensely case-specific. He wanted Patty's psychiatric records. He wanted records of her sessions with therapist Nina Bartell, with whom Patty discussed "why she would lie about saying the sexual assault did not happen." He wanted lab reports regarding the DNA analysis. And he wanted Patty to undergo an independent psychological examination regarding the rape.

Accompanying these motions was an affidavit from Eisenberg recounting various juicy bits from Woodmansee's and Schwartz's reports. These included Mark's speculation that Patty might be capable of fabricating a rape and his diagnosis of her as having "a mental chemical depreciation," Dominic's considered opinion that "this lady is crazy," and Misty's purported statement to police that she "assumed her mother was hallucinating" about the alleged assault. This last point was a creative misstatement of Misty's comment to Schwartz that her mom had stopped taking Prozac because "she didn't want people to use that

[as] an excuse for saying she hallucinated the assault," as Draeger had insinuated.

Eisenberg's most significant motion sought dismissal of the charges on grounds that the criminal complaint "omitted material statements . . . which were necessary for a neutral and detached magistrate to determine probable cause." He listed four major omissions: Patty identified another man as her assailant; she recanted her complaint; Feagles abandoned her investigation for lack of evidence; and Misty admitted having sex with the accused "on at least one occasion." Eisenberg called it "very probable that the semen stain from Joseph Bong occurred when he was having intercourse with Misty."

Ironically, while seeking a dismissal due to omissions, Eisenberg neglected to mention a few things himself: Patty was equivocal in naming Dominic as a suspect; her recantation was momentary; Feagles's investigation occurred after the recantation, suggesting she found Patty's account credible; Misty's sexual contact with Bong did not happen in the Fairmont apartment and certainly not in her mother's bedroom, which multiple sources said was always locked.

In mid-December a pretrial hearing was held in Dane County court. The defendant was not present, in part because he had recently been transferred from Green Bay to the state's super-maximum security prison in Boscobel. This is where "the worst of the worst" Wisconsin inmates are locked down in tiny cells, which they are almost never allowed to leave, as part of a regimen meant to modify their disruptive behavior. Between late July and late November, Bong had received seven major conduct reports for such offenses as fighting, disobeying orders, possessing contraband, and theft. Three separate incidents involved attacks on fellow inmates. In one case, he allegedly beat a fellow inmate over a gambling debt; guards found clumps of the man's hair on the ground and blood on Bong's upper lip. In the final flare-up, Bong told a female guard to "Shut the fuck up" and "Shut up, you goofy ass bitch," saying "I don't give a fuck about a conduct report because I'm going to Supermax." He was right.

At the pretrial hearing, Eisenberg discussed the difficulties he had obtaining the "ton of discovery" done during the federal lawsuit. Attorney Brad Armstrong had refused to provide these materials, including Patty's "diary," saying these were covered by a protective order.

Schwaemle agreed Eisenberg was entitled to this information and promised to help him obtain it. Eisenberg said he might ask Patty to sign a release. "If she refuses," he told the court, "then I can argue she shouldn't be allowed to testify." Schwaemle offered no counterargument.

Eisenberg gave a brief, biased summary of the case for Judge Nichol, who admitted knowing nothing about it. Nichol agreed to a status conference in forty-five to sixty days, at which Eisenberg's motion to dismiss would be taken up.

"Delay, delay, delay," groaned Patty when she heard the news. "I feel it's going to go on forever and ever and ever." She feared the volume of material sought would give the defense grounds for further delay. But Harlowe felt it was important that the defense get all of the material it wanted, lest this later serve as the basis for an appeal.

In mid-January 2003 Schwaemle filed a two-page response to Eisenberg's motion to dismiss, saying any omissions from the criminal complaint did not meet the case-law standard of showing "reckless disregard for the truth." The inclusion of these facts, she argued, would have "merely provided the additional information that the complaining witness offered inconsistent accounts." She did not highlight any of Eisenberg's own omissions and misstatements.

The status conference took place in early February 2003. Again, Bong was not present. The judge agreed to make a written ruling on Eisenberg's motion to dismiss, probably within the week. Schwaemle said she and Eisenberg were "essentially in agreement" on his requests for discovery, though not everything had been provided. Nichol, noting that "this case is old," wanted to "hold everybody's feet to the fire" by setting a trial date. He asked both parties how long they expected a trial to take. "Three days," answered Eisenberg. "I was going to say two," said Schwaemle. The judge set jury selection for Monday, June 30, and the trial for the remaining three days that week before the long July 4 weekend. A motion hearing would be held at least a month in advance.

The following week, the same in which he was named Judge of the Year by the State Bar of Wisconsin, Nichol issued a decision on Eisenberg's motion to dismiss. He concluded that none of the information outlined in the defense pleadings was sufficient to warrant dismissal of charges. As he put it:

[That] the victim recanted, which is not all that uncommon in these types of cases, is an issue of credibility for the jury to decide. Because it was dark and the victim sight-impaired, she could not make an identification of the assailant, so the fact that the victim thought the voice of the assailant sounded like her daughter's boyfriend doesn't defeat the Court's finding. Finally, the fact that the victim's daughter had intercourse with the Defendant does not negate the evidence of the Defendant's semen being on the bedsheets of the victim and taken as evidence from the crime scene shortly after the incident happened.

For these reasons, the motion is denied.

Nichol's ruling heartened Patty and her advocates. While his mistaken belief that she implicated Dominic via voice recognition indicated a cursory review of case materials, the judge had framed things from her perspective, even imagining how her visual disability added to her disorientation. It was a good sign.

But it was followed by more delays. In early May 2003, shortly before the motion hearing was slated to take place, Schwaemle contacted the court to say she had a scheduling conflict. The motion hearing was pushed back to late July, with the trial now set to begin August 28. Said Patty, "It doesn't seem like it's ever going to happen."

In late July, four days before a scheduled motion hearing, Schwaemle called Harlowe with some good and bad news. The good news: the state crime lab had run additional tests and found Patty's DNA mixed with Bong's. That would make it harder to argue that the defendant's DNA was present because he and Misty had a tryst in her mother's bed. Harlowe was pleased with this development, as was Patty. The bad news: the defense wanted time to review these findings, meaning the trial would again be delayed, this time to November 17, the week before Thanksgiving.

There was a motion hearing in September. Bong, still completely bald, was brought into the courtroom wearing jail attire. He had continued to distinguish himself in prison, drawing 270 days of program segregation—solitary confinement—for an incident in which he had shouted strings of obscenities at guards and other inmates. Now he sat quietly as lawyers hashed out the remaining issues regarding discovery.

Schwaemle wanted to withhold some of Patty's therapy records that, she said, "are not relevant and contain no exculpatory information." Eisenberg wanted everything, arguing that Patty no longer had any medical privacy privilege, due to the waiver she'd signed in the civil suit. He asked the judge to review the records before making his decision; Nichol agreed.

A few weeks later Judge Nichol ruled that the defense was entitled to all of Patty's psychiatric records, saying she had "waived her privilege of confidentiality by executing signed releases" in the civil case. Eisenberg, around this time, filed a new request: that Dominic be brought back from Terre Haute to testify at trial.

Everything looked like a go for the November 17 trial date, more than six years after the rape and two and a half years after Bong was identified through DNA evidence. Subpoenas were issued. Plans were made for Patty to meet with Kerman and Schwaemle to go over her testimony again. Bong was sent back to the Dane County jail. Then, in late October, the trial was pushed back again, this time because Bong was not feeling well.

When Kerman called to break this news and discuss new trial dates, Patty snapped, "I don't have a calendar for 2010." She spent a sleepless night; we spoke the next day. Patty was crestfallen: "I thought this was going to be the year when I put this all behind me." I looked up this latest development as recorded on the state court system's online database: "Defendant is ill. Motion to pp [postpone] by defense atty. State has no objection." Responded Patty, "I object."

Harlowe arranged a meeting with Schwaemle, at which Patty was told there was indeed a way to put this all behind her. Bong, through Eisenberg, had offered to plead guilty in exchange for the prosecution's agreement to seek only a five-year term. Patty calculated what this meant: Bong could complete his sentence and be released, quite possibly to hurt someone else, while he was still a young man. She asked that this offer be rejected; it was.

The new trial date was March 8, 2004. During the months of waiting, sexual assault and the credibility of alleged victims became a national issue when a young woman reported being raped by a professional basketball player, Kobe Bryant. His attorneys played hardball, subpoenaing the woman's psychiatric records and forcing her mother to testify about her emotional troubles, creating a climate so extreme that the charges were eventually dropped when the woman withdrew her willingness to cooperate. What Mark Eisenberg set out to do to Patty was even more extreme.

29

"Expect the Worst"

Every family has its secrets, some darker and buried deeper than others. The secrets kept by Patty's family were very dark and very deep. "We don't talk about it," Patty's sister Brenda said matter-of-factly during her deposition in the civil case. Yes, she knew Patty alleged being sexually molested by her stepfather (Brenda's father) when Patty was young. Yes, she attested, "I would say I believe her." But mostly, said Brenda, "it's just not something—we just don't go there. It's fine that way." Patty, in her own deposition, put it like this: "We like to pretend nothing ever happened."

Mark Eisenberg filed his motion on Friday the thirteenth of February 2004. It sought "to allow the defense to introduce in its case prior untruthful allegations of sexual assault made by the complainant"— namely, her claims of being sexually molested between the ages of six and fourteen. The stepfather, Eisenberg told the court, "will testify that this never happened." Detective Schwartz, tellingly, had tried the same approach: find the stepdad and see if he'll say she lied about that, too. But Eisenberg, unlike the detective, had found the stepdad.

"Patty's going to be victimized all over again," sighed her sister Sue, in response to this news. A few days earlier, she had gotten a call from an investigator who did not initially volunteer that he was in Eisenberg's employ. Just like Schwartz, he wanted to know about these allegations involving the stepfather. He asked "if I believed Patty and everything she said." Her reply: "Of course I do."

Eisenberg and his investigator visited Patty's ex-husband, Misty's father, showing him her psychiatric records, the ones Judge Nichol had

222

turned over on grounds that Patty "waived her privilege of confidentiality" when she sued the police. They also spoke with Patty's former boyfriend Mark, perhaps to ask about her "mental chemical depreciation." But tracking down her childhood molester was Eisenberg's attempted coup de grâce.

Sue shuddered at the memories it brought back, the secrets it threatened to unleash. "We were all victims of inappropriate behavior by that adult," she told me. Patty, the oldest, got the worst of it, and by coming forward as a teenager might have spared her sisters. Police reports confirm that the authorities who removed Patty from the home never even spoke to these other children. Sue recalled being touched in inappropriate ways. A third stepdaughter, she related, would only say, "I know what he did to *me*." Another sibling, one of the man's daughters, would not let her own daughter be alone with him. Sue agreed this was wise: "He's a person who never should be around children."

Patty reacted to Eisenberg's motion with alarm: "I can't have it going that far." Denial had worked well for her family; it protected her mother, especially, from pain and guilt over these past events. And now this lawyer was stooping to this, "telling our family when and how to deal with it."

The impending trial and, perhaps, the throwing down of this gauntlet, seemed to energize Schwaemle. This would be her first trial in more than five years—her duties in the district attorney's office were largely supervisory—and she was excited by the challenge that the case presented. Eisenberg had so much to work with to confuse the jury and plant the seeds of reasonable doubt: Patty's recantation, her implication of Dominic, Misty's fling with the defendant, police witnesses more interested in justifying their decision to turn on a rape victim than in convicting her assailant. Schwaemle's job was to keep the issues simple: a woman is raped; the semen of a man she didn't know but who knew of her is found in her bed. "A lot," she told me, "will depend on what Judge Nichol lets in."

"I think I'll get a lot of stuff in," chirped Eisenberg to Schwaemle prior to the start of a February 27 hearing on his motion to dredge up Patty's "prior untruthful allegations of sexual assault." Patty was at this proceeding, the first she had been to in Nichol's court. Sue was also present, in case she was needed to testify. The stepfather was nowhere to be seen. Neither was defendant Bong, per his own wishes. This may have been a tactical error, since it underscored how distant the issue in Eisenberg's motion was from the question of his client's guilt or innocence.

Eisenberg argued that Patty's past history proved her propensity to fabricate claims of sexual assault to achieve her goals—in the earlier case to "get out of the house" after a fight with her mom. The stepfather, he said, would testify that he never had "sexual intercourse" with her. This was odd, since Eisenberg introduced as an exhibit the portion of Patty's deposition transcript where she said the childhood assaults did not include intercourse.

Schwaemle noted that these thirty-year-old accusations involved a very different kind of assault. She cited case law requiring that, for such evidence to be introduced, it must be beyond dispute that the alleged victim was lying. In this case, Patty and her siblings were prepared to testify that the abuse occurred, so the perpetrator's denial did not mean a thing. "Half the priests that are accused of it today aren't admitting that they sexually assaulted their parishioners," she noted. "That doesn't make those allegations false."

The judge sided with Schwaemle, but for a different reason. When Patty came forward with her prior allegations, she was an adolescent. Now she was a mature woman. Said Nichol, "I don't think I would want some things in my adolescence to be considered probative" of adult conduct. This testimony, he said, would be "unduly prejudicial." Eisenberg gave further argument, but Nichol stuck to his decision.

On the same day as this hearing, Madison Police Chief Richard Williams announced his imminent retirement, to pursue career opportunities outside Madison. This followed months of emphatic, unequivocal denials of rumors that he was planning to step down.

Both sides filed additional motions seeking to limit the scope of evidence, necessitating another hearing, on March 3. In the courtroom beforehand, a court worker told Eisenberg about a recent case in which a man masturbated in front of a woman, then wiped his ejaculate on her. Eisenberg laughed and said, "Yeah, there's a lot of sickos in this world, no doubt about it." Just then, Bong was led, handcuffed and leg-chained, to the seat beside him. He was no longer bald and had evidently recovered from the health problem that earlier delayed the trial.

Patty missed this hearing, but Brian Blanchard, the Dane County district attorney, did attend. After more than three years in office, Blanchard had grown into the job, acquiring competence and confidence. While some hard-bitten veteran prosecutors still saw him as an interloper, Schwaemle publicly proclaimed, "I think Brian could be the best district attorney Dane County has ever seen." This was high praise indeed, given that prior occupants included Wisconsin Governor Jim Doyle, Gerald Nichol, and Hal Harlowe. Blanchard's presence was a strong sign of his office's support.

The defense's motions were considered first. Schwaemle agreed to nearly all of Eisenberg's proposed exclusions. There would be no mention of Bong's prior sexual assaults and other crimes, unless he were to testify in his own defense. Schwaemle then asked, and Nichol later agreed, that there be no testimony over whether Misty had sex with Bong at "any other time and place" beside the bedroom where Bong's semen was found.

Schwaemle also sought to keep the police from testifying as to their "beliefs regarding the truthfulness" of Patty's report of sexual assault. This would be just as improper, she said, as having the state's witnesses expound on their opinions as to the defendant's guilt. But Schwaemle did want to solicit testimony regarding what Patty was told on October 2, 1997, when she recanted. Eisenberg argued that having the police admit saying they did not believe Patty would open the door for him to probe why. Schwaemle was adamant: "What they told her is relevant. But why they believed it is not relevant." Nichol declined to issue an immediate ruling, telling Schwaemle, "Ordinarily, I would agree with you, just out of hand. But ordinarily, you don't have a recantation."

Another area of dispute involved Dominic. Schwaemle did not seek to exclude that Patty identified him as a suspect, agreeing it was fair game to use this to impeach her credibility. But she did want to keep out the various reasons this seemed to make sense. These included his physical appearance and his history of violence against women. Eisenberg objected, saying this went to "the identity of the perpetrator." It thus became clear that Eisenberg planned to argue, as part of his defense, that Patty's initial suspicions were perhaps correct: she was raped by Dominic. The judge agreed to allow testimony on Dominic's appearance and habits, not his prior crimes.

A final matter was whether the defense could argue that Patty "behaved in a manner inconsistent with a victim of sexual assault." Eisenberg declared that Patty "had a party and was laughing and joking after the assault." Nichol found this "marginally relevant" but "unduly prejudicial" and ruled that it could not come in.

At one point, when discussing whether Madison police could testify as to why they did not believe Patty, Eisenberg asserted, "The jury is going to know anyway when we're done with the trial why they didn't believe her." Nichol smiled broadly and said, "At least you hope so."

Clearly, this was a case in which the jury's judgment would reign supreme. All the years of contention involving scores of players, all the thousands of pages of documents, would be superseded by the conclusions of twelve ordinary citizens after a few days of exposure to selected evidence.

Patty spent much of the Friday before trial going over her testimony with Schwaemle and Feagles. They listened to the tape of Patty's 911 call and heard something that others had managed to miss: during the call, Patty's alarm clock suddenly starts beeping, corroborating what she said about the snooze alarm. Schwaemle was delighted with this find and others that Feagles had already made. But she cautioned Patty that the case could go either way. "Hope for the best," she said. "Expect the worst."

On Monday, March 8, 165 citizens answered the call for jury duty at the Dane County courthouse. They were parked in a large room and shown an instructional film explaining the process in terms of civic duty: "With the right to trial by jury comes the responsibility to serve on one." Then they waited to be dispatched in groups to various courtrooms in need of juries. Most would eventually be sent home without being picked. An especially large group—forty-four prospective jurors—was marched off to Judge Nichol's courtroom around 11 a.m.

In the courtroom beforehand, Nichol ruled that the police witnesses could testify about their statements, not their beliefs. He also agreed to let the prosecution add a witness, Patty's friend Cheryll, who had spoken with her on the day after she recanted. At this, Eisenberg renewed his push for what he said was similar evidence, regarding how Patty was "laughing and joking" after the sexual assault. The judge seemed disinclined to change his mind, but then Schwaemle, bizarrely, dropped her objections to this testimony if it was clear that alcohol was involved.

Bong, now twenty-eight, sat at the defense table, looking like a college student, with wire-rimmed glasses, gray plaid shirt, and crisply pressed pants. He would wear sharp new outfits on each day of the trial: a clean, white dress shirt, a bone-colored pullover, a gray shirt and black vest, a tan shirt and darker vest. The idea was to keep the jury from knowing he was a convict. Attached to his leg under his pants was a "stun pack" that one of the bailiffs in court could activate with the push of a button, delivering a 50,000-volt, low-amperage jolt, should he try to make a break for it. This device and other restraints made him walk with a slight but perceptible limp.

By prior agreement, prospective jurors were presented with a one-page questionnaire on a clipboard. The questions ranged from "Where do you work?" and "Have you ever served as a juror?" to "Have you ever smoked marijuana?" and "Have you or anyone you know ever had a bad experience with a person of another race?" It also asked whether they could be "a fair and impartial juror in a case in which an African-American (black) man is accused of sexual assault of a white woman." (All forty-four prospective jurors were white; slightly more than half were female.)

Then began the process of sifting and winnowing, which took several hours. Additional questions were put to juror pool members collectively in open court and, individually, in the judge's chambers. Did they know the defendant, his attorney, the prosecutor, any of the likely witnesses, or each other? A few had extraneous connections, like a friend in the district attorney's office, but felt they could still be fair. Had they read about this case, which Schwaemle said was sometimes referred to as "the Patty case," in *Isthmus* or other media? Most hadn't.

Both sides used this opportunity to plant ideas in jurors' minds. Schwaemle asked whether there was anyone in the pool who could not recall ever having told a lie. No hands went up. She then asked, "Would any of you automatically dismiss a witness who admits that he or she didn't tell the truth?" This drew the same number of hands. Eisenberg, in turn, asked whether any jurors believed an alleged victim of sexual assault "could never make it up." None did, of course.

Two women jurors were excused due to child-care duties. One young man in a leather jacket touting the NASCAR Winston Cup got the boot when he "couldn't guarantee" his bad experiences with cops, including his own police-officer father, wouldn't skew his judgment. A woman who felt she would have a hard time with what Eisenberg promised would be "very graphic and very nasty" sexual assault details was also let go.

A pool of twenty-four jurors was maintained and replenished from the courtroom reserve. After all of the questions were asked, Eisenberg and Schwaemle each struck five jurors from the bunch. They excluded a deputy sheriff who had interviewed rape victims and knew a thing or two about evidence collection and a lab technician who admitted knowing something about the science behind DNA.

The resulting panel of twelve regular and two alternate jurors consisted of nine women and five men. It included a retired registered nurse, two active health-care workers, a self-employed real estate broker, a computer technician, an insurance company executive, a day-care provider, a homemaker, and a student still in high school. Nichol's clerk had them collectively swear to "well and truly try the issues in this case . . . and a true verdict give." Then the judge ran through some rules.

Jurors were not to let their personal feelings or biases or prejudices affect them. They were not to talk about the case with anyone, including each other, until deliberations began. They were admonished not to read press accounts, including a trial preview piece on the front page of that day's *Capital Times*. They could not use the Internet or other sources to independently investigate the case. They must presume the defendant's innocence and not draw any inferences if he declined to testify on his own behalf. They must find guilt beyond a reasonable doubt, which was, said Nichol, "a doubt based on reason and common sense, a doubt for which a reason can be given."

It was now 4:15 p.m. The judge turned the floor over to Schwaemle and Eisenberg for their opening statements. The trial in the case of *State of Wisconsin vs. Joseph J. Bong* was about to begin.

30

Patty Takes the Stand

In an early episode of the television crime drama *NYPD Blue,* a defense attorney prepping a police witness declares, "The truth and a trial have about as much to do [with each other] as a hot dog and a warm puppy." Trials are about strategy. They are about marshaling evidence and arguments. They are about who can present the stronger case or make the other side's case seem weaker. But in terms of getting at the truth, trials may be, to paraphrase Winston Churchill on democracy, the worst possible approach, except for all the others that have been tried.

Schwaemle, who throughout the trial had special agent Feagles at her side, used her opening remarks to lay out what happened, from Patty's point of view: the assault, the terror, the knife at her throat in the middle of the night, the inability to see her attacker. Tellingly, she spent as much time describing the events of October 2, when Patty recanted under pressure from the police. She was told that nobody believed her—not the SANE nurse, not her daughter, not her boyfriend. "They persuaded her that she was all alone in this." The police even lied about an imaginary test for latex residue. And so, "in despair," she told the detectives what they wanted to hear. But, the very next day, she returned to her original account, which was substantiated with the discovery of semen that was ultimately traced to Joseph Bong. The path to this trial, said Schwaemle, "has had some twists and turns in it, but it's about to come to an end." That would happen when the jury found Joseph Bong guilty as charged.

Eisenberg began with a point-blank declaration of his client's innocence: "Joseph Bong did not sexually assault [Patty]. He did not break into her house, and he did not take anything from her." Like Schwaemle, he intended to make Patty the centerpiece of his case—except his goal was not to empathize with her but discredit her. This alleged victim, he said, had changed her story again and again "to suit her needs." The details of the alleged assault were all wrong. She had this crazy idea it would be good to help the man ejaculate, thinking, who knows why, that he would then leave. The condom appeared "out of nowhere" and disappeared into the same place. There was blood on the pillow but not in the closet or on her clothes. She implicated another suspect and became "more and more convinced" it was him. Bong "does not even come close to the physical description" she gave of the perpetrator. The police version of the recantation was "100 percent the opposite of what [Patty] says." There was a good reason his client's DNA was found in Patty's bed, which Eisenberg would explain in time. And then, he told the jury, "You will find Joseph Bong not guilty of these charges."

The jury was excused for the night. The following day was Patty's turn to testify and Eisenberg's chance to destroy her credibility. Beforehand, in a conference room across the hall, Mark Kerman warned Patty's mother and other family members and friends that the defense attorney would say things so "offensive" they'd want to jump up and object, which of course they shouldn't do. When Patty joined the gathering, he said the verdict could go either way but "whatever happens, Judy and I believe you. We won't stop believing in you." He also warned that some Madison detectives were so reluctant to admit they were wrong "they may even try to help the defense."

Patty actually testified twice, the first time for a few minutes before the jury was brought in. Eisenberg wanted to keep out that she offered to take a lie detector test when police confronted her on October 2, so Patty was sworn in to relate the circumstances under which she made this offer. Eisenberg asked if she thought a lie detector test would be "admissible" in court; she had no idea, saying only that she considered them reliable. Eisenberg said the standard set by case law required a belief in the test's admissibility. Nichol, after recessing to his chambers to review the law, decided to allow this in, over Eisenberg's continued objections. Requiring a belief in admissibility, the judge ruled, was "too much to expect of a lay witness." Indeed, he cracked, "I don't think most lawyers know."

Throughout the trial, a group of between six and nine members of Bong's family, including his mother, sat somberly on the wooden courtroom benches behind him. He scarcely acknowledged their presence, which seemed as obligatory as his. On the opposite side gathered members of the media and a fluctuating cast of characters who were there principally to support the victim or the prosecution. These included Patty's mother and sisters Betsy and Sue, Mark Kerman, Brian Blanchard, Mike Short, Hal Harlowe, Connie Kilmark, Cheri Maples, and Diane Nicks. As witnesses, Patty and Misty had to keep out of the courtroom except when they testified, until the closing arguments. They could not read press accounts or get information from those allowed inside.

Judge Nichol excused one of the female jurors due to a family medical emergency. That left eight women and five men. The bailiff called out "all rise for the jury," as he would whenever they filed into or out of the jury box, and they plodded to their assigned places. Patty was called back to the witness stand and sworn in.

Schwaemle began with nearly three hours of direct examination, beginning with questions about Patty's visual disability. "Can you see what I'm wearing?" the prosecutor asked from a distance of about fifteen feet. "I could tell that it's black," replied Patty. Schwaemle was wearing a dark brown suit.

Then Schwaemle coaxed forth relevant details about the assault. Patty kept money from her business and a separate phone line in her room, which for this reason was always kept locked when she was not there. She had had a fitted bottom bedsheet as well as a flat top sheet on her bed. She washed her sheets about two weeks before the assault.

Patty was mostly calm and confident in her replies, delivered after several seconds of reflection. But when she recalled the things her assailant had said about Misty, Patty's voice quaked and she began to cry. "He asked where my daughter was," she told the jury. "And he asked if I thought my daughter would be a good fuck." Schwaemle helped Patty locate the box of tissues on the witness stand.

Patty cried again when the tape of her 911 call was played for the jury. Several jurors seemed to squirm to hear Patty's distress and Misty's squeals and wails. Afterward, Schwaemle called their attention to the sudden beeping of an alarm clock about halfway through.

Next Schwaemle turned to the events of October 2. Patty recalled the optimism she felt when she arrived at this meeting, alone, thinking that the police had made a break in the case. When Woodmansee confronted her with his conclusion that she had made it up, Patty was flabbergasted. "I just couldn't believe it," she told the jury. "I really thought he was kidding."

Patty went on to recount the various representations Woodmansee had made and her offer to take a lie detector test or be hypnotized: "I just kept pleading for him to believe me." But eventually, she buckled under. "It was obvious I was just going nowhere with him so I said, 'Fine, whatever you want to hear, I'll tell you.'" When she tried going back to her original account, Woodmansee got "real mad" and threw down his notebook. So she stuck to her story about having lied, even when he hauled her off to the mental health center.

Schwaemle asked about Dominic, and how she had originally been tentative in identifying him as a suspect even though some things seemed to fit. But after police stopped investigating, she gathered more information and became "almost certain" it was him. "Basically," she explained, "I had no one else to blame."

During a break before his cross-examination, Eisenberg mused loudly outside the courtroom, "I'm going to be *so* nice to her." He even shared with Short his thoughts about the approach of attorney Brad Armstrong, calling him "a real prick." But when court resumed, he went after Patty in much the same manner.

"You're not a real truthful person, are you?" Eisenberg asked Patty early on. She disputed this. But hadn't she, by her own admission, lied to the police when she recanted? "I lied to them but told them I was lying," she said. On the stand, as on other occasions, Patty proved her truthfulness by making admissions against her interest, such as that she and others were indeed laughing and joking at what Eisenberg called her "little get-together or party" after the alleged rape, or that she wrote her angry, accusatory note to Dominic with the intention of sending it, even though she never did.

Eisenberg picked away at inconsistencies in the various accounts Patty gave to the police, wrote in her "diary," or testified to at her deposition and the preliminary hearing. Here she said her assailant's pants were off; there they were just down to his ankles. Which was it? Sometimes she said he ejaculated, other times she wasn't positive. What's up with that? During her deposition, she claimed the assailant pulled her hair. Why didn't she tell this to the police? (Deposition testimony was cited throughout the trial but the jury was never told that Patty had sued the police.)

Was she crying during the assault? Actually, said Patty, "I stayed pretty calm throughout." Then why did she say in her "diary" that she cried when she told the rapist that she couldn't see?

Like Armstrong, Eisenberg zeroed in on the most painful passages of this no-longer private writing. The one about deciding to "sensually" move her tongue around the tip of her assailant's penis and caress his testicles. Eisenberg even followed it up the same way: "And you were hoping that he would ejaculate in your mouth?" Patty answered in the affirmative but that wasn't enough. Eisenberg read from her deposition: "Question: 'It was your plan that he would have an orgasm and he would ejaculate in your mouth?' Answer: 'Right.'"

And what about this possibly apocryphal assailant's penis? Hadn't it just come from her anus? Wasn't it covered with fecal matter? Didn't it smell? How did it taste? "It was pretty disgusting," said Patty. Oh, really? Then how come she never told any of the police officers she talked to how disgusting it was?

After about two hours of this, Patty was emotionally frayed. "No, I didn't!" she shouted at Eisenberg when he asked if she had said something earlier the same way she was saying it now. "What do you want me to . . . ?" Nichol called a break. Patty collected herself. Then she got back on the witness stand and kept going.

Eisenberg dug into his Dominic Theory—that if this crazy woman didn't fabricate the rape then maybe she was right. Didn't everything seem to point to Dominic? Didn't she tell *Isthmus* she was sure it was him? Yes, she admitted. Didn't she write her accusatory note? Yes. Didn't she tell Detective Schwartz she was close to having Dominic arrested? No, she insisted. (This was a complete falsehood that Eisenberg tried to get in under the wire; Patty and Schwartz had never spoken, as Schwartz herself would later testify.)

Eisenberg attacked, and Patty held her ground. How tall was the man who raped her? Patty wasn't sure: "I'm visually impaired," she reminded him. Why would being threatened with being taken to jail on suicide watch bother her so? Hadn't she had a lot of prior contact with police? Patty shot back: "I have never had a cop tell me I was going to jail because I was raped, no."

Why, Eisenberg wanted to know, did Patty agree to make corroborating statements regarding how and why she fabricated the rape, like where she got the knife? "They were offering and I was saying 'Yeah.'" But didn't Woodmansee say he wanted her to tell the truth? "He wanted me to tell his truth." Did he put it that way: *his truth?* "He said so many times that it didn't happen, it didn't happen, it didn't happen, so I knew what his truth was, and I knew what he wanted to hear."

Did Patty ever call Tom Woodmansee a liar? "I know he's a liar," she said. Why had she canceled a follow-up meeting with the detective "to go to a tavern" with a friend? She hadn't, she said. She offered to skip the concert for which she and Mark had tickets but he told her not to: "Basically, *he* canceled." Why had she "guessed a lot," as she put it in her diary, in her answers to Woodmansee? Because he wouldn't accept that she didn't know or couldn't remember. Still, she did the best she could.

Schwaemle, on redirect, asked just a few questions. Why did Patty feel Woodmansee was annoyed by her inability to provide precise answers? Patty told the jury what he said about maybe having to go into the bedroom where the rape occurred and "role-play this thing," if necessary. Why did she write her never-sent letter to Dominic? "I was all out of hope."

How did Patty feel to learn, as the result of DNA testing, that the semen on her sheets did not belong to Dominic, the man she accused? A wave of shame washed over her, and she began to cry on the stand, as she choked out her reply: "I. Just. Felt. Really. Just. Horrible." And afterward, she never again sought to implicate Dominic: "I knew nobody else was in that bed except the rapist." So if the semen didn't belong to Dominic, he was not the one. Schwaemle followed with a masterstroke: if Patty had known the semen belonged to Joseph Bong, would she have ever accused Dominic?

"Objection," exclaimed Eisenberg. "Sustained," said Nichol. Patty wasn't allowed to answer. But, for once, there was no need to.

31

Burden of Proof

Schwaemle was not sure what to think. As well as Patty did on the stand, and as credible as she seemed, Eisenberg had done some damage. It still was possible for someone—maybe just a single juror—to doubt her account. Or the jury might consider her truthful but not be sure Joseph Bong was to blame. Patty, after all, was never able to identify him. And as Judge Nichol told the jurors repeatedly, the defense did not have to prove a thing. The burden of proof was entirely on the prosecution.

The trial resumed Wednesday at 8:30 a.m. First up was Dr. Thomas Stevens, Patty's ophthalmologist, who explained the nature and severity of her visual disability, based on his own examinations and his review of records from other doctors. He explained how macular degeneration had destroyed Patty's central vision, leaving her below the threshold of legal blindness. In one test, she had to be within five feet of an eye chart to make out the largest letter. She would have a very hard time discerning detail, especially in dim light.

Eisenberg, on cross, asked whether Patty could make out whether someone wore glasses or had facial hair if he was "right on top of her." Stevens agreed this was possible, in good lighting. Eisenberg then listed some details from Woodmansee's report, including that her assailant did not wear glasses. At just this moment, Bong absentmindedly removed his wire-rimmed glasses and set them on the table.

The next witness was crime scene investigator William Kaddatz, who explained how he collected evidence at Patty's duplex early on the morning of September 4, 1997. Schwaemle, using a device that displayed images on a television monitor that faced the jury box, had the veteran cop describe his diagrams and reports, as well as the two dozen color photographs he took at the time. She called particular attention to his photos of the bottle of Body Splash found in Patty's clothes hamper, initially covered in part by a white sock. Schwaemle also asked whether, in collecting the bedding, Kaddatz had found a fitted bottom sheet. He had not.

Kaddatz, fielding questions from Eisenberg, said he examined the phone in the kitchen and even tested it for fingerprints, along with other items. He also searched the apartment for blood but found none except on Patty's pillow.

Nichol had instructed the jurors that they could ask questions of witnesses. These had to be put in writing for prior review by the judge and opposing counsel. Kaddatz's testimony prompted one juror to ask whether he found fingerprints from Patty and Misty on the items tested. Kaddatz said there were none and that this was unusual: typically, household items would have prints on top of prints on top of prints.

Next up was Patty's old friend Cheryll, who had spoken with her at the coffee shop on October 3, 1997, the day after Patty recanted. "She was visibly upset," Cheryll told the jury. "She said that she had been raped. And she said that she wished she had never called the police." They didn't believe she was raped, Patty had said. They didn't believe she was blind. She asked for a lawyer and they refused. So, eventually, "she just outright told them what they wanted to hear . . . to get out of there." Eisenberg established that Patty had in recent weeks let Cheryll and her husband stay at her place, after they had fallen on hard times.

The prosecution called Jill Poarch. Now head of her hospital's Sexual Assault Nurse Examiner program, Poarch had by this time conducted hundreds of sexual assault exams and reviewed thousands more. She explained her examination of Patty on September 4, the tools and procedures she used, the injuries and other findings she documented. Asked about Patty's demeanor, she reviewed a behavioral checklist and read the items she'd checked: "controlled, cooperative, quiet, trembling, and tearful."

Poarch said Patty's exam was "consistent" with her account of what happened. Injuries were typically found in about 40 to 50 percent of anal assaults and would be less likely if the victim did not resist or the rapist used lubrication. In this case, there was an abrasion just next to the anus. No visual inspection was ever done of the inside of the anus, so there may have been injury that was not observed.

Eisenberg, in turn, zeroed in on the anal assault and the suspicious lack of more serious injury. Hadn't Poarch told the detective the abrasion was "like a fingernail scratch"? Hadn't she inserted a gloved finger to check for bleeding and found none? Hadn't the victim indicated that no lubricant was used? Hadn't she told Feagles she did not feel there had been significant anal penetration? Poarch confirmed all of these things. But she also answered yes when asked by Schwaemle on redirect whether full anal penetration could have occurred.

After a break for lunch, Alonzo "Lonnie" Elvord Jr., twenty-five, took the stand wearing a brown leather jacket. He identified himself as Joseph Bong's cousin. He admitted he had once been convicted of a crime, but the jury was not allowed to know this was the hotel robbery and abduction he perpetrated with Bong just days after Patty's rape. Elvord testified that he had been to Misty's place at least several times and had even helped her and Patty make the vending machine run. He knew she was blind and that she kept money from her business in zippered bags at her duplex, the door to which "was hardly ever kept locked." In September 1997 he and Bong were both living with Elvord's mother on Madison's east side, and both worked for the same employer; they sometimes went drinking together. But Elvord denied ever telling Bong details about Misty's mother or her business.

Elvord, under questioning by Eisenberg, made other statements that undercut the prosecution's case. He claimed to have picked up Bong at Misty's apartment "once or twice." He said he saw Misty enter her mother's bedroom when she was not there. He confirmed the authenticity of photos, circa 1997, showing Bong to be muscular with a tattoo on his chest. These photos were projected on the monitor for the jury to see.

The next prosecution witness was Cindy Thiesenhusen, the first officer on the scene. She recalled how Patty had been shaking and crying and gave an initial statement in which she remembered, among other things, that her assailant had "asked how old her daughter was" and if she "would be a good fuck." Was Patty freely bleeding anywhere? asked Schwaemle. "No," answered Thiesenhusen. She also attested to the chain of evidence, telling what was taken where. Lauri Schwartz, who had switched roles from detective to sergeant, would give similar just-the-facts testimony later that day.

Misty, now twenty-five and living in Sheboygan, where she worked for a security company, was called to the stand. From Schwaemle's point of view, this was a huge risk. Misty could help her case a little or hurt it a lot. Her memory was not impressive, and she could be incautious in the things she said. It was important that jurors hear from her, but more important that they believed her. And Misty might not come across as credible.

During her direct examination, Misty confirmed having dated Lonnie Elvord before she dated Dominic. She said when her mother was away, "she kept the door [to her bedroom] shut and locked." Misty was a "pretty heavy sleeper" and could never recall a time when her mother's alarm clock woke her up. She put Dominic's name on a list she produced for Woodmansee because he, like other people she named, had been to her place. She knew Joseph Bong and had "just met him once, before the second time I met him." Both times, she was still in high school, from which she graduated in June 1997. Was Bong "ever at your house on Fairmont?" asked Schwaemle. Replied Misty, "Not to my knowledge."

This threw Eisenberg for a loop. He had understood, incorrectly, that Bong was one of the names on the list of people who had been to her place. Eisenberg thought this because of Misty's later claim that she had named Bong as a suspect. He spent much of his cross-examination delving into this point of confusion, with Misty insisting that she had passed Bong's name to police much later, after John Quamme had showed up at her house and suggested him as a suspect. (This was just as my article in *Isthmus* reported, prompting a minor side issue, raised outside of the jury's presence, during the rest of the trial. At one point, Eisenberg tried to have me barred from the courtroom as a potential witness; the judge denied his request and I was never called.)

Eisenberg got Misty to admit her mother was "kind of joking and having a good time" and didn't appear too upset on the night following the assault. He asked Misty if she smoked marijuana and she said yes, sometimes she did, but hardly ever while she was pregnant. Did she ever have sex with Bong in her mother's bedroom? "No."

On the following day, before the jury filed in, Eisenberg again urged the judge to allow in evidence of prior sexual contact between Misty and

Bong. He said his witness, Ben Donahue, would testify that he went to Misty's place with Bong and happened to walk in on them while they were having sex in a back bedroom. In light of this, he said it was even more important that testimony regarding Misty's past sexual contact with the defendant be allowed into evidence. Schwaemle argued that this would be "highly prejudicial." Nichol agreed, and reaffirmed his original ruling.

There was more haggling over Eisenberg's wish to let Woodmansee and Draeger testify as to what they believed, not just what they said. Nichol, who had already ruled on this, expressed his annoyance. The detectives' beliefs, he said again, were not relevant, although the jury could and likely would infer from how they described their interaction with Patty that they "had some problems with her credibility."

The first witness of the day was Dominic's sister Dora. She testified that he was with her at their mother's apartment when the alleged rape took place. He had come there drunk after a fight with another sister; she took away his car keys and had him sleep on her sofa. She knew that's where he remained because she got up "every hour on the hour" to drink juice, per her doctor's orders, and could see him there. Eisenberg, on cross, pressed her on this point. But Dora had "no doubt about it."

Feagles testified briefly as to her role in the case, before and after Bong was identified as a suspect through DNA. The jury was not allowed to hear how this critical event happened—that Bong's DNA was in the system because he was a convicted sex offender. When Feagles obtained a DNA sample from Bong on June 28, 2001, he initially denied knowing Patty. She mentioned Lonnie's former girlfriend, and he replied, "Oh, Misty's mom."

Patty's brother-in-law Paul, a twenty-nine-year-veteran police officer, attested to her credibility, calling her a "very honest, respectful citizen and person." Then Karen Doerfer Daily was called to the stand.

Daily had never met Patty. She knew little about the circumstances of the crime or the many twists and turns it had taken. She didn't even know the back story to her own involvement—how Hal Harlowe, in his defense of a woman being charged with the crime of lying to the police, had asked why evidence collected from the scene of an alleged rape had not been examined, more than six months after the fact. But what Daily did know was critical.

Daily had worked as a forensic scientist with the Wisconsin State Crime Laboratory for more than a quarter of a century, including the last eight years as a DNA analyst. In April 1998 she had examined items including a blue bedsheet that had been retrieved from police storage. On her initial visual inspection, Daily observed what appeared to be two spots with semen stains, in close proximity to each other. These she cut out and examined under a microscope to find a total of seven sperm heads. During Daily's testimony, Schwaemle put on rubber gloves and opened the evidence bag, laying the sheet out on the courtroom floor so the jury could see the two holes.

Under further questioning by Eisenberg, Daily announced another finding whose significance she could not have known. The sheet, she related, contained a "copious quantity of dark brown hair." This undercut Eisenberg's efforts to discredit Patty's claim that the assailant pulled her hair.

The stains had what Daily determined to be a mixture of male and female DNA. The sperm was in the same place as a larger amount of female material; there was no way to know if this other material was saliva, vaginal fluid, mucus, nasal excretion, or tears. Eisenberg posited that if the mixed DNA sample were made at the same time, there should be roughly equal amounts of material from the male and female source. "Not necessarily," she said. He had better luck getting Daily to admit she could "not exclude" the possibility that the male ejaculate on the sheet was deposited "at some other time than the female portion."

Several of the jurors had questions, two of which boiled down to this: Could the mixed male-female sample have come from the oral sex? Daily thought that was possible. Whose DNA was it, anyway? Daily couldn't answer that question, but said her former colleague, Curtis Knox, was prepared to do so. Schwaemle called him as the prosecution's final witness.

A specialist in DNA analysis, Knox had interned at an FBI laboratory in Virginia and worked at a crime lab in Louisiana, before a seven-year stint at the Wisconsin State Crime Laboratory. That ended two months earlier, when he took a job with a Madison-area company that developed technologies for analyzing DNA. Knox had been involved at several stages of Patty's case. Back in July 1998 he had used the older, less efficient method of DNA analysis to exclude Dominic and two of

Patty's male friends. In early 2000 he used the newer, improved method, which required less genetic material but was even more accurate, to exclude other suspects. And in July 2001 he compared DNA from the bedsheet with that from Joseph Bong's buccal sample. The DNA profiles, he said, "match exactly."

But there was more. In June 2003 Knox analyzed the "nonsperm" portion of the bedsheet sample. "It was a mixture of DNA," he said, and it came from two contributors: Bong and Patty. The largest share of the sample was from Patty. Eisenberg again tried to argue that ratio should be about the same, but Knox said that there was no reason for this to be so. "No, I disagree with you," the expert told the defense attorney. The prosecution rested.

32

Star Witness

Of all of the strange and arguably objectionable things that happened during Patty's long ordeal, perhaps the strangest and most objectionable happened that Thursday, March 11, when Detective Tom Woodmansee came to testify. Suddenly, about a dozen Madison police officers showed up in court, badges visible, and sat on the benches behind Bong and his family. Captain Maples and two or three other officers conspicuously dissented from this show of police support for a repeat felony offender whose most recent conviction was for terrorizing two people with a sawed-off shotgun, taking their places on the opposite side.

Woodmansee was actually the fourth defense witness of the day, but clearly the most important. The first three contributed little to the defense's case.

Christopher Delp, an emergency physician, testified that he would expect to find more "evidence of trauma" in a person who was anally assaulted for up to a minute with no lubricant. But he also said the most common injuries were abrasions, and that even the use of saliva as a lubricant would reduce their likelihood.

David Exline, a privately employed forensic scientist whom the defense brought in from Pennsylvania, told the jury there was actually a test for traces of condom lubricant—rubber residue!—when condoms are used in sexual assaults. He said more rapists than ever wore rubbers, to avoid leaving DNA behind. He didn't claim to have tested for condom lubricant in Patty's case.

John Quamme, Bong's cousin, was called to say he had been at Misty's place on five to ten occasions and had noticed that the door to her mother's bedroom was open. He denied ever suggesting that Bong should be considered a suspect, saying he didn't even know Patty was raped until "a few years after it allegedly had happened." As was agreed beforehand, Quamme, then twenty-seven, admitted to having two criminal convictions. The jury didn't get to hear these were for battery and disorderly conduct, or that he was facing fresh criminal charges for allegedly pointing a firearm at someone while intoxicated.

Woodmansee was called to the stand at about 2:45 p.m. and testified for more than two hours; his contingent of police supporters remained in the courtroom behind Bong throughout. He was the defense's star witness, the person who might single-handedly convince the jury there was no need to convict Patty's rapist because there was never any rape.

Under questioning by Eisenberg, the detective reconstructed his investigation into the alleged assault. Patty, he said, was calm and open during their early discussions and able to provide details. She said "it wasn't the rape that bothered her so much [as] the fact that she woke up with a knife to her throat." She laughed when she described her assailant's penis. She described the man as almost sympathetic, which Woodmansee said he found "unusual." (It was one of several instances in which he casually strayed from the judge's instruction, restated beforehand outside the jury's presence, that he should refrain from expressing his opinions.) He noticed blood on the kitchen phone but couldn't find any in the closet where she hid.

Eisenberg quizzed his witness about the events of October 2. Woodmansee confirmed getting Patty to come to this meeting under false pretenses by saying he needed to collect some samples. He led her to the interview room, where Detective Draeger joined them. Right off the bat, "I confronted her with my belief that she wasn't telling the truth." Patty seemed taken aback and disputed this assessment. Her offer to take a polygraph test or to be hypnotized was rebuffed.

Woodmansee denied telling Patty the SANE nurse did not believe her. He testified that he didn't say she did not act like a rape victim. He didn't recall saying he might jail her on "suicide watch," and she never said, "I want to leave." In time, she admitted making the whole thing up. In this statement and when she elaborated on particulars, Patty appeared sincere. Woodmansee took her to the mental health center because he was worried she might harm herself.

After more than an hour, Schwaemle got her chance to cross-examine the detective. One of her first questions, regarding his initial meeting with Patty, was this: "She's *blind*, and you asked her for a *description?*" "Yes," answered Woodmansee. What phone had Patty used to call 911? Woodmansee thought she had said it was the kitchen phone. Retorted Schwaemle, "She didn't tell you that because you didn't ask her, did you?" The detective thumbed through his forty-eight-page report, to refresh his memory, and eventually admitted that he couldn't find he had.

Regarding the events of October 2, Schwaemle pressed Woodmansee on the difference between an interview and an interrogation. As she put it, "You interview witnesses, and you interrogate suspects." He said the goal of both was to get at the truth, but agreed his meeting with Patty was an interrogation, since his purpose was to confront her. "I told her about the inconsistencies and asked if she could explain them."

Schwaemle was angered by this sophistry. Woodmansee, she charged, hadn't asked Patty open-ended questions; he made statements designed to overwhelm her. Schwaemle went through some of them. "You told her there was no evidence that she had been assaulted at all, didn't you?" Responded Woodmansee, "I told her the SANE kit . . . showed there was no sign of sexual assault." He said he put aside three or four child abuse cases to work on Patty's case, didn't he? "It's possible, yes." In like fashion, Schwaemle got the detective to admit telling Patty that there was no blood where blood should be. That the alarm clock times did not add up. That Patty seemed to be able to see some things well. That her boyfriend and Misty had raised doubts about her.

Had Woodmansee threatened to put Patty in jail? "No," he answered firmly. Schwaemle asked if he recalled testifying before Judge Aulik in July 1998 that a supervisor had given him two options, which he then discussed with Patty. His memory thus refreshed, Woodmansee admitted, "I told her we had options of Dane County Mental Health or she could be arrested and put in jail." For once, the suppression hearing worked in Patty's favor.

Finally, Schwaemle made Woodmansee admit to his ruse about rubber residue, and then demanded, "If you are not trying to overwhelm her with how much evidence is stacked against her, why are you making stuff up?" Replied Woodmansee, "It was a bad ruse." Schwaemle wasn't done with him. When Patty finally did confess and gave the answers the detectives wanted, "what you interpreted as sincere could well have been resignation." Woodmansee: "It's possible." Eisenberg, on redirect, got Woodmansee to say his comment about putting Patty in jail was made *after* her confession, when police were deciding what to do.

Woodmansee was excused and the jury was sent home for the night, with the usual instruction that they were not to read the local papers, both of which carried daily stories on the trial. (*The Capital Times* would note that "Woodmansee's account of the interrogation of Patty on the day she recanted was strikingly similar to Patty's account.") Nichol and the lawyers stayed to hammer out jury instructions.

The following day, Friday, March 12, was the final day of trial. It began with a number of "housekeeping" tasks, performed outside of the jury's presence. Eisenberg made what he called "one last-ditch effort" to bring in Misty and Bong's known past sexual contact; Nichol again refused. Eisenberg also got turned down when he asked for dismissal of the charges on grounds that the description Patty gave of her assailant fit Dominic better than Bong. Then Judge Nichol ascertained, through a series of yes or no questions, that Bong was "freely and intelligently" waiving his right to testify. It was the only time Bong spoke at his trial.

The jury was brought back in and the defense called Captain William Housley of the Madison Police Department. He averred that Woodmansee, whom he had known for years, was "a truthful person." He also said that if a detective had gotten a tip on a suspect in an aggravated sexual assault and failed to look into it, as Misty's testimony suggested, this would be investigated internally as a serious infraction and most likely lead to discipline. It was that tight a ship. Not mentioned was that Lonnie Elvord was clearly named as a suspect but this was never looked into, even after his arrest for the hotel robbery and abduction with his cousin Joseph Bong.

Schwaemle asked Housley if he was aware of cases where people confessed to crimes, even murders, they did not commit. "That has happened, yes," agreed Housley. She also asked whether Woodmansee was "incapable of making a mistake." Shrugged Housley, "I suppose not."

Linda Draeger had waited outside the courtroom the previous afternoon, prepared to testify for the defense. Eisenberg evidently changed his mind, because he never called her. His final witness, the deus ex machina of his defense, was Ben Donahue.

Donahue, then twenty-nine, told the jury he had been good friends with Joseph Bong for fourteen years. But he also said they hadn't spoken since Bong "moved" in late summer 1997. The summer before this, he said, he and Bong ran into Misty. She wanted to buy some marijuana and Bong had some to sell. But Misty didn't have money on her so the three of them drove to her place. She went into a back bedroom, and Bong followed. After a while, Donahue got "sick of waiting and went back to find them." He peeked into the room and saw Bong lying back on the bed with his pants to his knees and Misty's head by his crotch.

Schwaemle hardly went after Donahue at all. She focused on the fact that when Feagles tried to talk with him in December 2003, he had refused. She also got Donahue to admit that he and Bong had spoken in November 2003, quite a bit more recently than he had just testified. In fact, Donahue had visited Bong in prison, which the jury couldn't be told. Donahue said he had four criminal convictions. The jury didn't get to hear they were for theft, disorderly conduct, and intimidation of a victim to dissuade reporting.

The defense rested. Schwaemle called no rebuttal witnesses, even though Patty and Misty were outside the courtroom in case they were needed. Misty had maintained all along that she didn't even know Donahue, but the prosecution considered it too risky to put her back on the stand. It would only increase the weight of this testimony in the jury's eyes. Besides, the jury could decide on its own how implausible it was that Bong would be lucky enough to have an eyewitness to a sex act that could explain away the otherwise incriminating DNA. As Mike Short remarked after Donahue's testimony, "I wouldn't believe him if he told me today is Friday."

After a short break, Judge Nichol spent a half hour explaining the "principles of law" jurors were to use in reaching their verdict. They could consider only the evidence presented at trial, but in assessing it they could draw upon their common sense and life experience. Questions and comments from opposing counsel, even opening and closing statements, were not evidence. They must give no weight to objections and disregard any question the judge did not allow answered. Specific tests, which Nichol went over, had to be met for each charge. Jurors must establish guilt beyond a reasonable doubt. While it was their duty to give the defendant the benefit of any doubt, they were to search not for doubt but for the truth. There was also a special instruction, which the two lawyers had hammered out that morning: the jury was not to pay any mind to Woodmansee's opinion of Patty's credibility, since the jury was supposed to be the "sole judge" of such things.

And with that, it was time for closing arguments.

33

Closing Arguments

Judy Schwaemle kept it as simple as she could. The jury, she said, had just two issues to decide: were the crimes in this case committed, and did Joseph Bong commit them? The evidence, she assured, led to only one answer.

As to the first issue, Schwaemle staked her case on the credibility of a single witness. Patty, she said, had come to court and told the same story she had told before to the 911 operator, to Jill Poarch, to the police, to her friends and family, in depositions, and at the preliminary hearing. For six and a half years, she had stuck to this story, with only one exception: October 2. She stuck to it despite all of the hardship it entailed.

"If these crimes hadn't happened to her," Schwaemle told the jury, "she could have given it up a long time ago. And frankly, who could have blamed her?" Patty sat in the courtroom's front row, with Misty and other family members, throughout these closing arguments.

Yes, there were "trivial inconsistencies" in Patty's account, admitted Schwaemle. But this was to be expected for a story told so many times to so many listeners, each of whom interpreted things differently. All these perceived inconsistencies were then used against her. Still, the hardest thing for Patty to bear were the words she had "uttered in a moment of hopelessness, isolation, and despair." Of course she knew, as well as anyone, that her recantation had undermined her credibility. And still, said Schwaemle, she continued to seek justice, enduring the humiliation, "because she wants you to find the truth."

Consider how Patty had cried spontaneously on the witness stand, recalling what the rapist had said about her daughter. Consider the 911 call. How could that have been an act? And then there was the crime scene itself. "Let's look at the physical evidence," said Schwaemle. "Let's do what Tom Woodmansee should have done, but didn't."

First, there was the empty bottle of Body Splash, which in the photo shown to jurors was partially covered by a sock. "Who left that there?" The rapist, she speculated, had used this sock to wipe fingerprints off the items he touched — the alarm clock, the phone, the money bag, and, finally, this bottle. But Woodmansee could not have considered this possibility because the crime scene photos were not even developed until 1998, long after he abandoned work on the case.

If Woodmansee had done his job, argued Schwaemle, he would have realized that the bottom fitted sheet that had been on Patty's bed was not among the items collected from the crime scene, nor was it left behind. Didn't it make sense, she said, that a rapist who pulled the sheets off the bed may have taken this with him to avoid leaving evidence? Maybe he used it to wrap up the knife, condom, and condom wrapper. Maybe this is why there was not more blood found from the cut on Patty's hand.

This was a rapist who knew what he was doing. He wore a condom. He wore sweatpants that could easily be pulled down with one hand while the other held a knife. He took the fitted sheet with him when he left. Said Schwaemle, "This is a smart, calculating, careful predator."

But instead of realizing this, Woodmansee botched the investigation and leapt to the wrong conclusion. He decided there "should be blood everywhere" because there was blood on the pillow and on the phone, but he never even asked what phone Patty used. And he never had the top bedsheet collected from the crime scene examined. When this was finally done, the following April, a crime lab analyst spotted visible semen stains the first time she looked at it. Even the fact that it was a tiny amount of semen corroborated Patty's account.

If Woodmansee had considered the physical evidence, he would have realized that Patty was telling the truth. "Instead," said Schwaemle, "his disregard of that evidence led him to a false conclusion [and] led him to create bad evidence" — Patty's recantation. He brought all of his mistaken beliefs and false assumptions and dumped them on her during his interrogation. It was no surprise that Patty gave in.

"People have confessed to a lot worse than lying," said Schwaemle.

"People have confessed to murders they didn't commit." And here was a woman who was especially vulnerable. Here was someone who, on account of being blind, "has to rely day in, day out, on what other people tell her is reality." She needed to trust other people even to cross the street. Said Schwaemle, pointing to herself, "She's not going to be able to contradict you if you say . . . my suit is brown." Schwaemle, on this day, was wearing a black suit. It was her way of subtly reminding jurors that Patty had earlier been mistaken about the color of her clothes.

Woodmansee, Schwaemle noted, was not "the bad cop on TV." He was, as they had seen, soft-spoken and apparently thoughtful and considerate. And here he was telling Patty in as many ways as he could think of that it didn't happen. He knew she was lying. There wasn't any evidence. He succeeded in overwhelming Patty "with what was stacked against her." What did he mean, she was free to leave? "She doesn't even know where she is!"

Schwaemle's closing, laid out in her efficient, almost methodical way yet tinged with anger, offered as distinct an assessment as could be imagined from what her former colleague Karofsky had previously said in another courtroom about the same events: "The police officers in this case ought to be proud of what they did."

In fact, Schwaemle continued, there was plenty of evidence, but Woodmansee's "tunnel vision" kept him from seeing it. The SANE nurse documented injuries, including a scratch that could have been caused by a fingernail. "Whose fingernail?" asked Schwaemle. Maybe Patty's injuries were not more severe because she offered no resistance. Maybe the rapist used his own saliva to lubricate his penis.

Schwaemle talked about the side issue of Dominic. If Patty had really set out to frame her daughter's boyfriend, wouldn't she have just come out and said it was him? She probably could have found a used condom in Misty's room and planted that. It's true Patty did come to believe Dominic was to blame, but this was the result of her own flawed investigation, after the police had dropped the case. She did, said Schwaemle, exactly the same thing as Woodmansee — "drew false conclusions based on an incomplete understanding of the evidence."

What was the evidence that Joseph Bong committed the crime? Patty was able to provide some description. He was young. He had short hair. He was mixed race or Hispanic. He seemed to know that she was blind, had a daughter, and kept money in the house. Perhaps he knew the front door was often left unlocked. And Joseph Bong had a source of knowledge—his cousin Lonnie—for all these things. The information could have even been conveyed innocently, in idle talk about Misty, whom both men knew.

And then there was the DNA evidence. Bong was the source of the only semen in Patty's bed, the sheets of which had been washed two weeks before the rape. And his seminal fluid just happened to hit the same place on a queen-size bedsheet as an excretion from Patty. The amount—"seven little sperm"—was not a full ejaculation. It was more like an accidental spill, where the rapist may have momentarily set the condom down. Joseph Bong had tried his best to get away with it. "But for his little tiny mistake, he would have," said Schwaemle. "Hold him responsible for what he did."

Nichol called a break, during which one of the jurors learned that his mother just had a stroke. The juror was excused and the last alternate was tapped. Eisenberg began his closing argument around 1 p.m. In his gruff, nasal voice, he asked jurors to use their common sense in deciding whether there was reasonable doubt. He said he would focus their attention on three elements: Misty, the DNA, and Patty.

Taking up the first element, Eisenberg apologized to jurors for having misunderstood the matter about Misty naming his client as a suspect. He thought this meant she had included Bong on her list of people who had been to her home. But he learned during trial that she actually claimed to have given Bong's name to Woodmansee later on. This, he insisted, was simply incredible. The jurors saw Woodmansee testify. Was he the sort of person who would ignore such a tip? Eisenberg recalled Captain Housley's testimony about how seriously this would be taken. "Why would [Woodmansee] want to risk his career?"

Eisenberg poked at other aspects of Misty's testimony. Her lack of recollection about certain things. How Elvord and Quamme both said they saw her mother's bedroom door left unlocked. Misty glared at Eisenberg from the courtroom's front row, her mother's arm around her.

As for the DNA evidence, what did it tell the jury, really? Patty said the "sex," as Eisenberg referred to it, occurred in the middle of the bed. But the semen stains were up at the top of the sheet. The experts couldn't tell when the semen got there. They didn't know when the material from

Patty was deposited, or even what it was: saliva, mucus, vaginal fluid, or tears.

Maybe Bong's semen was on the bed because he and Misty had sex there. Ben Donahue even saw them in the act. What's more, Donahue said he'd been there while Misty bought marijuana. That's why Eisenberg had asked Misty about marijuana use. How else would he have known this? It was not in any of the police reports, not in any depositions. "I knew to ask her about it because of what Ben said."

Patty said she changed her sheets two weeks earlier. But Kaddatz, Eisenberg claimed, had called Patty's place "a pigsty." (Actually, Kaddatz had agreed "generally" with Eisenberg's characterization that it was "pretty messy and unkempt.") Maybe she hadn't changed her sheets in a month. "There is reasonable doubt even to that piece of evidence, the DNA, and you know without the DNA, we're not even here [in court]," said Eisenberg. If there was reasonable doubt on this issue, the jury "must" find his client not guilty.

Eisenberg then got to element three: Patty. For starters, there was the issue of her recantation. Detective Woodmansee confronted her for very good reasons, after consulting with other cops, and she admitted that she made it up. "I don't have any idea whether [Patty] was assaulted or not," Eisenberg told the jury. "I'm not going to sit up here and call her a liar. But to dump all this on Tom Woodmansee and paint him as the bad guy is really unfair."

And what about Patty's reaction to the case's two main events? She was supposedly devastated by what happened on October 2. Yet after the rape itself she was "laughing and having a good time." During the rape, she was thinking pretty clearly, trying to get her pants off so she could maybe run and suggesting that she go in the closet. Yet this "big, old, bad-guy policeman" gets her "so upset."

Then Eisenberg took up the anal evidence. Having a penis stuck into her rectum should have been a "major problem." Now the prosecution was suggesting the rapist used his own saliva, but Patty never reported that. The tiny scratch that was found "could have come from her wiping herself down there." And then he took his penis from her anus and put it in her mouth? Wouldn't that cause a gag reaction? Yet never in Patty's accounts over "the last seven years" was this mentioned.

If the rapist was so worried about leaving behind spilled seed,

Eisenberg continued, why didn't he put the condom on earlier, and not just for the vaginal sex? There was no semen found on Patty, no foreign pubic hairs, no blood anywhere except on the pillow. There were no fingerprints. Patty once claimed the snooze alarm went off five times, later that it was once or twice.

Some reported rapes, Eisenberg noted, are unfounded. "Why do people make this up?" he asked. For a variety of reasons, including mental health issues, which it "was clear from the questions that Tom Woodmansee asked her" Patty had. After the alleged assault, she got to move in with Mark and "certainly got a lot of attention."

Eisenberg shifted to his other defense strategy, that if Patty wasn't completely lying maybe she was, in her initial suspicions, completely right. He pulled out a large chart listing the many ways Dominic fit what was known about the alleged rapist better than Bong. Patty told people she was sure it was Dominic. She even wrote her angry note. The jury, said Eisenberg, should not hesitate to feel sorry for Patty. "I do," he shared. "She's had a difficult and tough life. But sympathy for her is not a reason to convict Joseph Bong."

When jurors looked at all the evidence, Eisenberg said in conclusion, "you will find there is significant doubt, reasonable doubt, and you will find Joseph Bong not guilty of all the charges."

Eisenberg had done a great deal of damage. His closing was masterful. He had clearly met his much lower burden of establishing a basis for reasonable doubt. Schwaemle had one last chance to convince the jury of the strength of her case. Her rebuttal was crucial.

First off, the business about the tip. Maybe Misty had provided Bong's name to police. Maybe she hadn't. "What does it matter?" asked Schwaemle. She scoffed at the claim that Woodmansee's failure to follow through would have been a career-endangering oversight. He had by this time concluded there was never any sexual assault. Why would he continue to chase after possible suspects?

Did Dominic do it? Dora testified he was at home. No evidence put him at the scene of the crime. Why did Patty accuse him? Because after the police stopped investigating, her sister convinced her. And then Misty, "trying to stick up for her boyfriend," turned against her mother. Said Schwaemle, "Look at the damage that was done to this family by the bad investigation of the Madison Police Department."

What about the testimony of Ben Donahue? When Feagles asked to talk to him, he refused: "Why is he unwilling to tell the truth, if it is the truth, to Liz Feagles?" Maybe he wasn't sure he'd gotten his story straight yet. Even if the jurors didn't discount his testimony altogether, what did it say? Donahue said he saw his friend Bong with Misty in a back bedroom. Which bedroom?

Schwaemle talked again about Tom Woodmansee, saying she was not trying to tear him down: "He's not a bad police officer. He made a bad mistake. It wouldn't be the first time somebody had made a bad mistake." Patty also made a mistake in having recanted, but she had paid a price for hers. Maybe that accounted for the differences in tone between their two accounts of Patty's recantation, how hers seemed so much harsher than his. Why would she dwell on his "suicide watch" threat if this was not made until after she confessed? Didn't it make sense that, on reflection, the stark choice with which she was presented—go to the mental health center or go to jail—would color the whole meeting for her?

The prosecutor addressed Eisenberg's other points. There was no reason the semen stain should be in the middle of the top bedsheet, which could have been anywhere on the bed. There was nothing unusual about not finding semen or foreign pubic hair on Patty. She said the rapist pulled her hair and the crime lab found "copious amounts" of hair in the bed. Maybe he wiped off his penis before putting it in Patty's mouth. Maybe he didn't put the condom on until he knew he was about to ejaculate.

"Let's think about the rapist here," said Schwaemle. This was someone who, for whatever reason, "kind of liked to normalize what he was doing." He engaged her in sex talk: "Tell me how big I am." He asked that she wrap her legs around him. This while he's holding a knife to his victim and raping her.

Schwaemle saved one thing for nearly last. Was there, as claimed, a problem with the number of times the alarm clock went off? Patty said she set the alarm for 4 a.m. but the clock was twenty minutes fast. The snooze alarm went off every nine minutes. The jurors could hear it go off halfway through the six-minute 911 call, which began at 4:13. How many times did it go off? "You do the math," she told the jury.

Finally, there was the issue of Patty's credibility. Here was someone who admitted she intended to send her note to Dominic when she could have just denied it. Here was someone who cried on the witness stand when she recalled how she felt to learn that Dominic was not the one. Here was someone who had fought all these years to be believed.

"There's finally got to be justice for Patty," Schwaemle said in conclusion. "We have to straighten this path out, from September 4th to the present. It goes right back in a straight line to Joseph Bong."

Judge Nichol gave some final instructions to jurors, warning them not to be swayed by sympathy or prejudice. At 2:25 p.m. they trudged out of the courtroom, past Patty and her family, to begin their deliberations. None of them looked at her.

The jurors were led into a small, undecorated room with twelve chairs arranged around a large table, two bathrooms, and a blackboard. Lunch was provided just as they began; it was the only meal they'd get. Just past 4 p.m. they asked to hear the 911 tape. Nichol told the bailiff he could play it as often as the jurors wanted. Patty and her family waited in the courthouse hallways, along with members of Bong's family, until about 6 p.m. Then they left a phone number with the clerk and went to the home of Patty's mother, about a ten-minute drive away. Around 9 p.m. the jury asked to see the DNA analysts' reports, which were not among the exhibits they had been given; the judge okayed this.

At about 10:45 p.m. the calls went out—to the attorneys, to family members who had left, to members of the press. It took about twenty minutes for everyone to return. Eisenberg, in the hallway, jokingly thanked Mike Short for his lawsuit, which had generated the depositions he used to prepare for trial. Without these, he said, all he would have had was "Draeger and Woodmansee."

Four brown-shirted sheriff's deputies were stationed in the courtroom. Judge Nichol came back in at 11:08 p.m. As usual, Bong was brought in wearing cuffs with a stun belt, which were removed before the jury returned. A cliché on television crime dramas is that a jury that votes to convict will not look at the defendant. As the jurors filed back in, more than half trained their gaze directly on Joseph Bong.

"We're back on the record," said Judge Nichol. He addressed the man the jury had, at the start of its deliberations, picked to be foreperson. "Have you reached a verdict?"

The foreperson replied, "We have, your honor."

34

The Verdict

Thomas Jefferson praised the wisdom of letting juries decide questions of fact, rather than referring these "to a judge whose mind is warped by any motive whatsoever." He felt "the common sense of twelve honest [citizens] gives a better chance of just decision."

The jurors in the trial of Joseph Bong were faced with a massive amount of often-conflicting evidence. There was a victim who at one point said the crime never happened and police officers who apparently believed this was the only truthful statement she ever made. There was a defendant about whom they knew next to nothing, but this, they were told, could not influence their decision in any way. There was a second suspect, a person whom the victim and the defense attorney both implicated. There was a purported eyewitness to a sex act that could account for the incriminating DNA.

In the days after the verdict, several jurors spoke with me about the case, as the judge had told them they were free to do. At the start of their deliberations, they said, there was strong division. The first vote, taken after about an hour, was split right down the middle: six to six. People were dug in on both sides. They listened to the 911 tape and talked some more. Some jurors changed positions. They reviewed the DNA analysts' reports. Eventually, the last holdouts were persuaded, and a unanimous verdict was reached.

Bong and his attorney stood as Judge Nichol read from the pieces of paper the foreperson had produced. On the first count, burglary while armed with a dangerous weapon: guilty. On the second count, anal sexual assault while armed: guilty. On the third count, oral sexual assault

256

while armed: guilty. On the fourth count, vaginal sexual assault while armed: guilty. On the fifth count, armed robbery: guilty.

The defendant remained impassive, as he had throughout the trial. In the back of the courtroom, one of his family members began weeping loudly. Patty also began to cry. Eisenberg asked to have the jury polled, so each member had to answer "yes, your honor," when asked if he or she concurred with these verdicts. Judge Nichol thanked the jurors for their service.

Patty got hugs from her family and questions from reporters. "I'm just so happy and relieved," she said. "It's like a big exhale." She thanked Schwaemle and Feagles for their work on the case, Mike Short and Hal Harlowe for their advocacy, and her family and friends for having stood by her side. She also expressed how sorry she felt for Bong's family.

The jurors I spoke with were uniform in their assessment that the deciding factor was the DNA. They considered it overwhelmingly improbable that the mixed Bong-Patty sample could have come from two different occasions. At the start of their deliberations, some jurors were certain Patty was telling the truth—"I just couldn't imagine her making all that up," said one—and others weren't. She seemed a bit too calm. And then there was the business about her having such a good time on the night after the rape. The inconsistencies in Patty's story were not deemed significant. Many of these, the jurors noted, had to do with her inability to see.

There was deliberation over the recantation, but it was less about the veracity of Patty's account than the culpability of the police. Woodmansee, one juror told me, was seen as an "inexperienced detective who jumped to a conclusion that wasn't there." Another said the real question on jurors' minds was, "How did the police department allow this to happen?" They wondered why the interrogation had not been taped. They wondered if there were repercussions for the department or the officers involved.

Judy Schwaemle was considered competent and persuasive, but the jurors were more impressed with Mark Eisenberg. They thought he was an excellent attorney who, said one, "did a very good job of trying to confuse the jury." But in the end, "he simply didn't have enough to work with." (Eisenberg seemed to agree; after the jury left to begin its deliberations he mumbled, to no one in particular, "You can't change the facts.") The jurors kept going back to the DNA and the critical testimony of Daily and Knox. They didn't necessarily buy Schwaemle's theory that the semen on the bed was from where the rapist set the condom down. They thought it was more likely pre-ejaculate from the oral assault.

Eisenberg's Dominic Theory had little resonance among jury members. They thought it typified his cleverness in trying to throw them off track. Ben Donahue's testimony was largely dismissed, with one juror dubbing him "Mr. Four-Time Loser." To the extent that his story was given any credence, it strengthened the prosecution's case, because it meant Bong was familiar with the layout of the apartment. None of the jurors I spoke with thought it mattered that Misty had prior sexual contact with the defendant, as they learned later when they finally read the newspaper accounts; in fact, they had suspected as much. They noticed the looks that passed between Bong and Misty when she testified. They even wondered if Bong was the never-named father of her six-year-old son.

The bigger surprise ("none of us had any idea") was that Bong was already in prison and had multiple felonies on his record. He had looked so clean-cut and respectable. After the verdict, the jurors were emotional and several were crying. The bailiff told them about Bong's criminal past, which made them feel more at ease with their decision.

It was, in many ways, a decision that proved Jefferson's point. A judge might say the police are legally allowed to do this. A prosecutor might say my job is to back up the police. A regulatory board might say our hands are tied. But a group of twelve ordinary citizens could look at the same situation and say something is wrong here, and find its way to the truth.

The jury's verdicts proved decisive, and not just for Joseph Bong. Patty was transformed from victim to hero. The Madison Police Department had done nothing to keep her assailant from victimizing others. Patty had done everything she could.

On March 15, 2004, the Monday after trial, District Attorney Brian Blanchard sent Patty a letter. His first purpose, he said, was to apologize for "errors" made by his office "that caused you unnecessary anguish over a number of years." He said evidence that emerged due to the prosecution of Joseph Bong "reveals that this office should not have charged you with the crime of obstruction in 1998." He called it "now obvious

[this] was a mistake that had grave consequences for you and your family, and also potentially for the safety of others. If it is of any consolation to you, the errors of this office have resulted in a great deal of introspection here about how we handle cases of this type, reflection that should translate into better responses to victims in the future."

Blanchard's second purpose was to thank Patty for her "gracious and courageous cooperation" in bringing Bong to justice. "One of the most moving parts of a prosecutor's job," he wrote, "is working with victims and witnesses who respond to abuse with dignity and to lies with honesty. We do not judge victims for their level of heroism; a crime victim or a witness is not responsible for having to be a hero under miserable circumstances that he or she did not create. But you have done what many people would be afraid to do, and in so doing have won the genuine admiration of the staff of this office."

Chief Williams, to whom Blanchard sent a copy of this letter, took a different view. In his last days on the job, he issued a department-wide memo defending his department's handling of the case. He said the sexual assault against Patty, whom he identified by last name, had been "vigorously investigated." He even minted a fresh lie, saying allegations that Bong was identified as a suspect early on "were investigated by [special agent] Feagles and determined to be untrue." He also told the *Wisconsin State Journal,* which after the trial ran a long article on the case, that the mythical state review of his department's actions showed "we had done nothing wrong." Having fabricated this finding, who was he to argue with it?

Detective Schwartz, who once boasted of her department's commitment to "owning our mistakes," told the paper how Patty (whom she still had never met or spoken to) had not seemed credible: "We can't make cases better than they are. If we're not absolutely certain, we're supposed to err on the side of letting the guilty go free. Patty was inconsistent in what she reported." Draeger, who would retire from the police department in 2005, issued a statement saying she had accepted "responsibility for my actions," which she refused to discuss: "I feel it's time to move on and pray that we can all heal." Woodmansee declined to comment.

After Bong's trial, I reported that Woodmansee had sent his case file to the district attorney's office the day after he was presented with

Patty's letters of complaint to his boss and that he then apparently lied under oath about this in his testimony to the Madison Police and Fire Commission. Neither the police department nor the PFC did anything about it.

The outcome of Patty's case did have one immediate and arguably inappropriate consequence. Two weeks after the verdict, a twenty-year-old UW–Madison student disappeared from her apartment, sparking a massive police manhunt and drawing a horde of national media reporters. Four days later, she was found alive and unharmed. The young woman's story had multiple problems, and police obtained videotape of her buying a knife, duct tape, and other items she used to stage her own abduction. Even still, they continued to search for and even put out a sketch of her alleged assailant, ringing up tens of thousands of dollars in overtime costs. Police officials lied to the public and the press, saying they had "no reason to believe [the student's] story is made up." She eventually confessed to fabricating her ordeal to win sympathy from her boyfriend. Asked to defend their actions, the police pointed to Patty's case, with one law enforcement source telling the press, "They just can't expose themselves, considering what they've just gone through."

Joseph Bong's sentencing was originally set for mid-August, but there was, fittingly enough, another delay, this one caused when Bong went into a diabetic coma in the Dane County jail the day before. He was taken to the hospital and nearly died; he remained comatose for more than a week. There was suspicion his health crisis was self-induced, in part because Bong that day wrote his young daughter a note that had the ring of finality: "Hey, little girl. Your dad just wants you to know he love you. I'll all ways be with you. . . . I'm not saying good by . . . because Ill never really be gone."

Bong recovered, and his sentencing took place on October 11, 2004, more than seven years after Patty's sexual assault. A few days earlier, he ended up back in the hospital, and Patty was initially told the sentencing would be postponed again. But on the prescribed day, Bong was well enough to be brought back to Dane County, and Patty got a call just hours before the hearing. She headed down with her mother and sister Sue, who happened to be visiting. Bong did not wish to be present and resisted efforts to bring him back, aggressively enough that he was accompanied by five deputies. His head was again shaved nearly bald.

Schwaemle, citing Bong's history of "very brutal sexual assaults that have a unique aspect of victimization," asked for one hundred years. Eisenberg, claiming this sentence would be longer than if Bong had "walked into [Patty's] house, put a gun to her head, and shot her," asked for thirty years. He noted that his client had major problems with depression, anxiety, and substance abuse for which he never received adequate treatment. He said the three separate charges for sexual contact with different body parts ought to be treated as one offense, since they happened in rapid succession, "bang bang bang." Bong, given a chance to speak, told the court: "There are things I would like to say, but after talking to Mr. Eisenberg, he has advised me that I should probably just pipe down and deal with the appealable issues that come through. So I'm sorry I don't have more for you to go on from my side, but [it's] due to my lawyer's advice."

Nichol reflected on Bong's extensive criminal record, which he called "terrible . . . about as bad as I have seen." He told Bong that while "you weren't responsible for what the police put [Patty] through, but that too was a terrible miscarriage," Bong was clearly someone from whom the public needed protection. Nichol, less than three weeks from retirement, sentenced Bong to fifty years. When added to his existing sentence and against time served, it meant Bong would not be eligible for parole until 2014 and, more likely, would serve the rest of his life in prison, with a mandatory release date of 2048. That is, unless his appeals process were to win him a new trial and a different result.

Patty was never compensated by the city for any of the time or money she spent defending herself against criminal charges or pursuing her own path to justice. At one point, her lawyers met to discuss making overtures in this direction but decided it would be futile. For Patty, a bond was broken between her and the city where she had lived for most of her life. In late 2004 she accepted a vending route well outside of Madison and a year later moved to a small Wisconsin town, closer to her new responsibilities, finally giving up her Madison apartment in 2006. Her ordeal had made her less trusting of people in power, but it had also made her stronger, more confident in herself. She had been the perfect victim, but managed, through her own passionate commitment to the truth, to triumph over the outrageous adversity she was made to endure.

A charitable observer of Patty's tale might argue that the system is self-correcting. Mayor Bauman was drummed out of office; other players who seemed ill-suited for their roles, including Chief Williams, Deputy District Attorney Karofsky, and Detective Draeger, faded away. And, in the end, the same office that had charged Patty with a crime for having reported being raped became her avenging angel, working mightily to set the balance right.

On the other hand, the Madison Police Department never admitted error or offered Patty any apology. The only "I'm sorry" she got from the cops was in 2001, from Captain Maples, who was consequently investigated for possible disciplinary action. (She was later passed over by the PFC for the vacant chief's job and soon after resigned from the force.) The only apparent change within the Madison Police Department happened in 2003, when its policies and procedures manual was revised to specifically allow officers to engage in untruthfulness "as part of legitimate investigative activity."

The message of Patty's case, beyond the example of her remarkable courage, is that the justice system is not necessarily just. A judge who says police have the legal authority to trick a suspect into confessing may be upholding case law, but he or she is not making reasonable judgments about what is right and what is wrong. Lawyers who brutalize a blind rape victim may be looking out for their clients' financial interests, or their own, but they are not behaving decently. Cops who come to court in support of the defense of a violent rapist may be showing solidarity with a fellow officer, but they are also showing disrespect for what they are supposed to represent.

Maybe the mistakes made by Tom Woodmansee (who has remained a detective in good standing in the Madison Police Department) were understandable, given the circumstances with which he was presented. But his refusal to admit having made them, no matter how obvious it became, put his conduct in a different category. He could have proved, on any number of occasions, what he once called his "sense of values and integrity" simply by saying, "Look, guys, I think I screwed up." His failure to do so is not all his fault; in this, he was aided and abetted by others in the department and by a city that despite its air of superiority is prone to bouts of moral narcolepsy. Everyone seemed to care more about protecting his honor than doing the honorable thing. And thus he became less of a protector of the public than a danger to it.

The same can be said for the entire justice system. The truest mark of its corruption is not that it makes mistakes but that it is so reluctant to admit them. And it is not enough for the system to admit it made one here, after a jury reached this finding beyond a reasonable doubt. It is a lesson it must take to heart. The use of police interrogation techniques so effective at getting people to confess that they work even on the innocent must be reconsidered, perhaps prohibited. The unholy harmony of purpose that has developed between police and prosecutors needs to be broken, so each can serve as a check on the other. Victims of police misconduct must have access to independent oversight boards equipped with genuine power and the will to use it. And players throughout the system must find the courage to revisit cases where the exercise of their power may have produced an unjust result, like convicting the innocent.

To admit the justice system's capacity for error and abuse is not weakness but strength. To say "I'm sorry" is not just an admission of wrongdoing but also an affirmation of the desire to do what's right. For the system to work, it needs to pay attention to those times when it doesn't. After all, the people who run it are only human.

Acknowledgments

Thanks to Patty, for her courage and decency and willingness to share her often painful story; to all the members of her family, for the support they've given her and the kindness they've shown me; to attorneys Hal Harlowe and Mike Short, for allowing me access to their files and insights; to the law enforcement officers who produced such thorough reports and revealing testimony; and to the legal reporters who scrupulously recorded every word. Special thanks to Raphael Kadushin of the University of Wisconsin Press, for his passionate commitment to bringing important books into being; to my capable and conscientious editor, Sheila Moermond; and to copyeditor Diana Cook. I am also indebted to the many people who reviewed the manuscript in progress and made helpful suggestions, including Scott Russell, Bill Christofferson, Kurt Chandler, Phyllis Rose, Jeremy Solomon, Kent Williams, Dean Robbins, Ellen Meany, and Deborah Blum. Finally, and most of all, I thank my wife and best friend, Linda Falkenstein, for seeing me through this project, and through my days of darkest doubt.

Chronology

Note: The tale told in this book includes a number of surprising developments, which this chronology necessarily reveals. Readers may prefer to let the story unfold without looking ahead to these developments as they are set forth here.

SEPTEMBER 4, 1997   Patty is raped by an armed intruder in her east-side Madison home. Police are called and collect evidence.

SEPTEMBER 8, 1997   Tom Woodmansee, a Madison police detective, begins work on the case. He becomes skeptical of Patty's account and soon focuses his investigation on her.

OCTOBER 2, 1997   Woodmansee summons Patty to a meeting at police headquarters under false pretenses, where he and another detective, Linda Draeger, confront her with their conclusion that she lied about being raped. They use pressure and deception to get her to recant. Afterward, Patty immediately renounces this recantation and returns to her original account.

OCTOBER 22, 1997   The *Wisconsin State Journal* runs an article based on a police department press release, saying that a woman who reported being raped had admitted lying. Thus prompted, Patty writes two letters that she has delivered to Woodmansee's supervisor, Lieutenant Dennis George Riley, complaining that she was compelled to recant. Riley gives these letters to Woodmansee.

OCTOBER 24, 1997   Woodmansee forwards his case file to the Dane County District Attorney's Office, recommending that Patty be prosecuted for obstructing an officer.

JANUARY 15, 1998   A criminal complaint against Patty is signed by Jill Karofsky, a Dane County deputy district attorney.

JANUARY AND EARLY FEBRUARY 1998   Patty, unaware of these impending charges, is interviewed by *Isthmus* newspaper after an acquaintance convinces her to go public with her story. *Isthmus* begins to investigate. Riley tells the paper he has no recollection of Patty's letters.

FEBRUARY 9, 1998   Patty is formally charged with obstruction, a misdemeanor.

APRIL 1, 1998   *Isthmus,* through News Editor Bill Lueders, files a complaint against Riley with the Madison Police and Fire Commission (PFC), alleging that Riley violated department policy in failing to forward Patty's letters to others in the department for investigation, as well as its rules regarding truthfulness.

MAY 1998   The PFC delays action, pending resolution of the criminal case against Patty.

JUNE 29, 1998   The Wisconsin State Crime Laboratory reports finding semen on Patty's bedsheet, after her defense attorney, former District Attorney Hal Harlowe, asks why this evidence was never analyzed. Police subsequently obtain DNA samples from the man Patty identified as a chief suspect, as well as her current and former boyfriends.

JULY 9, 1998   Dane County Circuit Court Judge Jack Aulik holds a hearing on Harlowe's motion to suppress Patty's confession. Within a week, Aulik issues a ruling denying this motion.

JULY 29, 1998   DNA tests conclusively exclude the three individuals from whom samples were obtained.

AUGUST 21, 1998   The charges against Patty are dismissed. The district attorney's office admits it can't prove its case "beyond a reasonable doubt" but continues to suggest that Patty was lying about being raped.

SEPTEMBER 30, 1998   The PFC dismisses the major part of *Isthmus*'s complaint against Riley, which alleged that he violated department rules regarding complaint acceptance and investigation.

OCTOBER 15 AND 22, 1998   A PFC hearing is held on the remaining part of *Isthmus*'s complaint against Riley, alleging untruthfulness.

NOVEMBER 2, 1998   Patty formally asks the Madison Police Department to have the state Division of Criminal Investigation reopen her rape complaint. She also asks that it investigate the conduct of Madison police but is told that this will not be done.

DECEMBER 3, 1998   The PFC rules against *Isthmus.*

DECEMBER 14, 1998   Patty files her own PFC complaints against Riley and Woodmansee, alleging violations of department rules. The complaint against Riley is dismissed due to his retirement.

MARCH 5, 1999   Special agent Elizabeth Feagles of the state Division of Criminal Investigation finally contacts Patty with regard to her sexual assault case. Over the next year, Feagles pursues numerous leads and obtains DNA samples from several suspects; none match.

MAY 18, 1999   The PFC dismisses Patty's complaint.

NOVEMBER 17, 1999   Attorney Mike Short, representing Patty, files a lawsuit in federal court against three Madison detectives: Woodmansee, Draeger, and Lauri Schwartz, who did follow-up work on the case.

MARCH–MAY 2000   Extensive depositions and other discovery are conducted in the civil case, by both sides. Patty is deposed three times, for a total of more than nineteen hours.

MAY 18, 2000   Federal Judge John Shabaz throws out Patty's lawsuit.

MAY 29, 2001   A profile obtained five years earlier from a convicted sex offender is entered into a federal DNA data bank.

JUNE 11, 2001   Wisconsin State Crime Laboratory contacts Feagles to report that DNA from this sex offender matches that found on Patty's bedsheet.

AUGUST 2001   Judy Schwaemle of the Dane County District Attorney's Office obtains transcripts of Patty's deposition testimony from the federal lawsuit.

OCTOBER 25, 2001   A meeting is held involving Patty, Harlowe, Schwaemle, District Attorney Brian Blanchard, and victim/witness advocate Mark Kerman.

DECEMBER 5, 2001   Another meeting is held, this one with Schwaemle, Kerman, Harlowe, and Patty. Patty is told that the state will prosecute if she desires. She does.

MAY 19, 2002   After additional delays, the district attorney's office drafts a criminal complaint. The suspect makes his initial appearance in Dane County court, where he is charged with five felony offenses.

JULY 22, 2002   Patty testifies at a preliminary hearing; the judge decides there is enough evidence to make the suspect stand trial.

AUGUST 2002   The suspect is arraigned and enters a plea of not guilty.

DECEMBER 2003   A pretrial hearing is held in Dane County court.

FEBRUARY 2003   A status conference is held; Judge Gerald Nichol denies a defense motion to dismiss the charges.

JULY 2003   The trial is delayed due to newly discovered additional DNA evidence.

SEPTEMBER 2003   A motion hearing is held; Judge Nichol subsequently orders all of Patty's psychological records turned over to the defense.

NOVEMBER 2003   The trial is postponed again, this time because the defendant is ill.

FEBRUARY 27, 2004   A motion hearing is held regarding Patty's "prior untruthful allegations of sexual assault."

MARCH 8, 2004   A jury is selected and the trial begins.

MARCH 12, 2004   The trial concludes and a jury verdict is rendered.

Recurring Characters

PATTY: Resident of Madison, Wisconsin; employed by Business Enterprise, a state-run program providing franchise businesses to the visually impaired.

ALBERT, JOHN: Dane County circuit court judge.

"ALICIA": Pseudonym for the thirteen-month-old girl whom Susan Pankow was accused of injuring.

ARMSTRONG, BRADLEY: Senior partner with Axley Brynelson, a Madison law firm.

AULIK, JACK: Dane County circuit court judge; assigned to Patty's criminal case.

BALISTRERI, TED: Assistant chief for the Madison Police Department.

BARTELL, NINA: Clinical psychologist whom Patty saw several times after the rape.

BAUMAN, SUE: Mayor of Madison from 1997 to 2003.

BETSY: Patty's sister, who worked at a local charity.

BLANCHARD, BRIAN: District attorney for Dane County; elected in 2000, defeating Brian Brophy.

BOBBY: Patty's brother.

BONG, JOSEPH: Cousin of Alonzo Elvord, whom Misty had dated.

BRENDA: Patty's younger sister, who previously had dated Dominic.

BROPHY, BRIAN: Assistant district attorney for Dane County; appointed district attorney in 2000, replacing Diane Nicks.

CAMI: Madison woman who took an active interest in Patty's case.

CAROL: Dominic's mother.

"CATHY": Pseudonym for a local high school student whose sexual assault complaint was investigated by Detective Tom Woodmansee.

CHERYLL: Friend of Patty's; worked in the agriculture building, where Patty ran her coffee shop.

DAILY, KAREN DOERFER: Forensic scientist with the Wisconsin State Crime Laboratory.

DOMINIC: Misty's boyfriend at the time of the rape; worked for his mother's housecleaning service.

DONAHUE, BEN: Friend of the defendant.

DORA: Dominic's sister.

DOUG: A man Patty had dated briefly in 1997.

DRAEGER, LINDA: Madison police detective who helped Woodmansee interrogate Dominic and Patty.

EISEN, MARC: Editor of *Isthmus* newspaper.

EISENBERG, MARK: Local criminal defense attorney.

ELVORD, ALONZO "LONNIE": Misty's former boyfriend.

FEAGLES, ELIZABETH "LIZ": Special agent with the Wisconsin Justice Department's Division of Criminal Investigation; reopened the investigation into Patty's rape.

FRIEDMAN, JAMES: Madison attorney; played role in Madison Police and Fire Commission case.

HARLOWE, HAL: Madison criminal defense attorney; former district attorney for Dane County; represented Patty in the criminal case.

HERRICK, SCOTT: Attorney for the Madison Police and Fire Commission.

HOUSLEY, WILLIAM: Lieutenant with the Madison Police Department; headed the Dane County Narcotics and Gang Task Force.

KADDATZ, WILLIAM: Crime scene investigator for the Madison Police Department; gathered evidence from Patty's home.

KAROFSKY, JILL: Deputy district attorney for Dane County; prosecuted Patty in the criminal case.

KENNETH: Dominic's friend and running buddy.

KERMAN, MARK: Victim/witness specialist for the Dane County District Attorney's Office.

KILMARK, CONNIE: Madison financial counselor brought in by Business Enterprise to help Patty.

KNOLL, DAVID: Patty's initial attorney.

KNOX, CURTIS: DNA specialist; formerly with the state crime lab.

KUYKENDALL, DEBRA: Supervisor at the Rape Crisis Center.

LAMAR, JEFFREY: Madison police captain; one of Woodmansee's supervisors.

MALLOY, PATRICK: Madison police lieutenant; head of the department's Professional Standards Unit.

MAPLES, CHERI: Madison police lieutenant; promoted to captain in 1999.

MARK: Patty's longtime friend and boyfriend at the time of the rape.

MCGUIRE, DANIELLE: Madison student and purported sexual assault victim.

MISTY: Patty's second child. (Her first daughter was raised by her family.)

MODL, MICHAEL: Attorney for Axley Brynelson, a Madison law firm.

MOSTON, LINDA: Madison psychologist; had counseled Patty and other members of her family.

NICHOL, GERALD: Dane County circuit court judge; named Judge of the Year by the State Bar of Wisconsin in 2003.

NICKS, DIANE: Dane County district attorney from 1997 to 2000.

O BRIEN, COLLEEN: Supervisor at Meriter Hospital.

PANKOW, SUSAN: Local child-care provider charged with child abuse after a Madison Police Department investigation.

PEGGY: Patty's sister-in-law.

POARCH, JILL: Sexual assault nurse employed by Meriter Hospital; examined Patty and later spoke with Madison police.

QUAMME, JOHN: Acquaintance of Misty.

RIESELMAN, MIKE: Attorney who had practiced in California; expressed interest in filing a lawsuit on Patty's behalf.

RILEY, DENNIS GEORGE: Madison police lieutenant; Woodmansee's direct supervisor.

SCHWARZENBART, PAUL: Madison attorney hired by the city to represent Lieutenant Riley.

RUSS: Patty's former boyfriend.

SCHWAEMLE, JUDY: Deputy district attorney for Dane County.

SCHWARTZ, LAURI: Madison police detective who worked with Woodmansee on the Pankow case and later took over as lead detective on Patty's case.

SHABAZ, JOHN: Federal judge for the Western District of Wisconsin; presided over Patty's civil suit.

SHORT, MIKE: Madison attorney who represented Patty in her civil lawsuit.

SNYDER, TOM: Officer and spokesperson for the Madison police department.

STEVENS, DR. THOMAS: Patty's ophthalmologist.

SUE: Patty's sister; lived in La Crosse, Wisconsin, and was married to a police officer.

THIESENHUSEN, CINDY: The first police officer to interview Patty following the rape.

THORNLEY, ERIN: Executive director of the Wisconsin Coalition Against Sexual Assault.

WESTERFELT, BECKY: Executive director of the local Rape Crisis Center.

WILLIAMS, RICHARD K.: Chief of police for the Madison Police Department from 1993 to 2004.

WOODMANSEE, TOM: Madison police officer since 1990; promoted to detective in January 1997; assigned that September to be the lead detective on Patty's case.

About the Author

Bill Lueders, born in Milwaukee in 1959, is the news editor of *Isthmus,* a popular weekly newspaper in Madison, Wisconsin, and the elected president of the Wisconsin Freedom of Information Council, a statewide group devoted to protecting public access to meetings and records. He is the editor of an anthology of Milwaukee poets and a cofounder of *The Crazy Shepherd,* now the successful Milwaukee weekly, *Shepherd Express.* Lueders (pronounced "Leaders") has worked at *Isthmus* since 1986, receiving national awards for editorial writing and state awards for investigative reporting, civil liberties reporting, interpretative reporting, business reporting, and column writing. He is the author of *An Enemy of the State: The Life of Erwin Knoll,* published in 1996 by Common Courage Press. He lives on Madison's north side with his wife, Linda, son, Jesse, and two much-loved dogs.

For articles and primary documents, see www.cryrapebook.com